FOAL

PARANOID SCIENCE

Paranoid Science

The Christian Right's War on Reality

Antony Alumkal

NEW YORK UNIVERSITY PRESS

New York

NEW YORK UNIVERSITY PRESS
New York
www.nyupress.org

References to Internet websites (URLs) were accurate at the time of writing.
Neither the author nor New York University Press is responsible for URLs that may have
expired or changed since the manuscript was prepared.

ISBN: 978-1-4798-2713-8

For Library of Congress Cataloging-in-Publication data, please contact the
Library of Congress.

New York University Press books are printed on acid-free paper, and their binding materials
are chosen for strength and durability.
We strive to use environmentally responsible suppliers and materials to the greatest extent
possible in publishing our books.

Manufactured in the United States of America

10 9 8 7 6 5 4 3 2 1

Also available as an ebook

For Elizabeth and Isabel

CONTENTS

My book's basic premise is that science is under attack by the Christian Right, whose leaders appeal to paranoid conspiracy theories by claiming that many scientists peddle misinformation and conceal their actions from the public. Supposedly these scientists threaten to undermine the moral foundation of American society. The four most significant offensives in this attack come from proponents of intelligent design, the ex-gay movement, conservative bioethics, and climate change denial. The combined effect of these four "paranoid science" movements is to create an alternative reality where Christian Right leaders' religious beliefs are safe from disconfirmation.

I write as a sociologist trained in the study of religion. Science is the terrain on which these four movements fight, but ultimately they're driven by religious and political dynamics. These dynamics are what I analyze in the pages ahead.[1] I also write as a "critical" sociologist. I believe that sociology is called to a careful study of the facts about human societies, but there's room in the discipline for discussing what kind of society we should be.

My writing is clearly influenced by my social location. I've spent a decade and a half as a faculty member at the Iliff School of Theology, a United Methodist seminary with historic ties to the liberal or progressive wing of American Christianity, which holds that Christians should constantly revise their beliefs in light of new knowledge.[2] I want to analyze and critique the Christian Right because I believe that Christianity should have a much different expression in American society; it should support the scientific enterprise and counter social oppression rather than reinforce it. That being said, I'm also writing for a broad audience, including people of all religious persuasions as well as those who don't consider themselves religious (or even "spiritual") at all. I'm writing for anyone who wants to understand more about how the Christian Right attacks science.[3]

I'm sure that someone, somewhere who identifies with the Christian Right will say that in writing this book, *I'm* being paranoid. So let's set the record straight. In order for this book to fit Richard Hofstadter's definition of the paranoid style, I would have to put forth a *grand* conspiracy theory—claiming that the secret actions of the Christian Right's evil leaders threaten to destroy American society. I argue no such thing. First of all, the Christian Right's anti-science agenda is very public, as it needs to be if it wants to mobilize grassroots support. I found all of the data for this book in publicly accessible documents. If these leaders have any secrets, I failed to uncover them. Second, I don't personally know any of the Christian Right leaders whom I write about, and I can't judge their motives. I assume that, however misguided they may be, most of them believe that they're doing the right thing. What about cases in which they blatantly distort the truth, which are numerous? It's likely that they're engaging in *self-deception*, believing what they want to believe. Essentially, they're inviting others to join the alternative reality that they inhabit.[4] Finally, I don't claim that the Christian Right is the only group (or even the worst group) that negatively impacts society. There's a lot of blame to go around for this country's shortcomings.[5]

I've been working on this book for a long time, so I have many people to thank. First mention goes to the fine research assistants with whom I had the pleasure of working: Kevin Hall, Kyle Talley, Andy Boesenecker, Amy Hanson, Tucker Plumlee, and Dan Lillie. A number of scholars gave me valuable feedback on early drafts of this material, especially Laurel Kearns, Dawne Moon, Jerry Park, and Nancy Wadsworth, along with my faculty colleagues at Iliff. Iliff and University of Denver students too numerous to name have also helped me to think through this material. Members and clergy in several Denver churches were willing to respond to presentations about this material, including Messiah Lutheran Church, Christ Church United Methodist, Park Hill Congregational United Church of Christ, and my own congregation, St. Thomas Episcopal Church. Special thanks to my editor at New York University Press, Jennifer Hammer, for sage guidance along the way.

The biggest thanks goes to the two lovely ladies with whom I share a home, Elizabeth and Isabel, for putting up with the many hours when I was hard at work and unavailable to them.

Introduction

In 2002 I was reading the *Christian Century*, the flagship magazine of the mainline Protestant world, when an article caught my eye. A biblical scholar named Robert A. J. Gagnon was responding to a previous issue, where his book *The Bible and Homosexual Practice: Texts and Hermeneutics* was negatively reviewed by the liberal biblical scholar Walter Wink. Gagnon offered the expected assertions about the Bible and church tradition condemning homosexuality, but he also appealed to social science data in his attempt to prove that "the negative effects attending homosexual behavior are disproportionately high, often grossly so."[1] His primary evidence was the alleged lack of long-term monogamous relationships among gay men and lesbians; biology rather than social stigma was presumably the cause. "These problems persist," Gagnon wrote, "even in homosexual-supportive areas such as San Francisco. The main culprit is probably sexual noncomplementarity, not societal 'homophobia.'"[2]

Since I'm a sociologist, my first reaction was to chuckle at his clumsy attempt at social science reasoning. This Gagnon fellow, clearly, was in over his head. But then I felt puzzled. Why on earth would a biblical scholar use social science data to support his interpretation of the Bible? As a faculty member at a school of theology, I knew that this wasn't how biblical scholarship worked, at least among academically reputable scholars. I was intrigued enough to pick up a copy of Gagnon's controversial book.

It turned out that Gagnon was a leader of a movement claiming that homosexuality was a curable illness and that the psychiatric establishment was covering up this fact because it had been taken over by gay activists motivated by "politics" rather than "science." His book recycled arguments that went back nearly two decades. I've done significant research on American evangelicalism, and I was certainly aware that evangelical leaders condemned homosexual behavior and offered "healing" to those who wished to become straight. What I hadn't known was that these practices were supported by a movement, called the ex-gay movement, with an extensive organizational infrastructure, and that for members of this movement, science was contested territory, a terrain on which to wage battle. This reminded me of another emerging movement of evangelicals battling over scientific truth—intelligent design. A foray into the intelligent design literature revealed some striking parallels with the ex-gay movement. Further research uncovered two other evangelical movements challenging the work of scientists, one promoting conservative stances on bioethical issues and a second denying the existence of anthropogenic (human-induced) climate change.

No one had yet written a comparison of these four movements, and I knew I had the subject matter for a book. After finishing up some other research projects, I dove into the materials (books, websites, and DVDs) that each movement had produced. I found lots of fascinating and disturbing details about each. However, I still struggled to articulate the underlying theme that linked the four movements. Then, while reading through the scholarly literature on evangelicalism, I came across a reference to the work of the historian Richard Hofstadter. Hofstadter's classic essay "The Paranoid Style in American Politics" had attracted renewed attention in the media when critics of the Bush/Cheney administration charged that its policies were rooted in paranoid thought rather than reality. Something told me I needed to read that essay for myself.

Did I ever. I was stunned by how much Hofstadter's description of paranoid political movements matched the behavior of the four evangelical movements I had been studying. I soon realized that they weren't simply advancing pseudoscience, they were advancing *paranoid science*.

Paranoid-Style Politics

To understand the four paranoid science movements that I focus on in this book, we need to look at Hofstadter's classic essay. Hofstadter first presented "The Paranoid Style in American Politics" as the Herbert Spencer Lecture at Oxford University in November 1963. He included an expanded and revised version in his 1965 book *The Paranoid Style in American Politics and Other Essays*, which is the version I'll discuss here. The essay described a recurring style in American political life that

Hofstadter referred to as paranoid "because no other word adequately evokes the heated exaggerations, suspiciousness, and conspiratorial fantasy that I have in mind."[3] Hofstadter made clear that he wasn't referring to people who were clinically paranoid; movements led by such people would have a limited impact. Rather, "it is the use of paranoid modes of expression by more or less normal people that makes the phenomenon significant."[4] His examples of paranoid-style political movements in American history included the panic over the Bavarian Illuminati at the end of the eighteenth century, the anti-Mason movement of the 1820s and 1830s, the anti-Catholic movement, the anti-Mormon movement, McCarthyism, and the Goldwater movement.

Hofstadter identified several features common to paranoid-style movements. At the center is the image of "a vast and sinister conspiracy, a gigantic and yet subtle machinery of influence set in motion to undermine and destroy a way of life."[5] He recognized that there have been conspiratorial acts in history, and there's nothing paranoid about noting them. However, the paranoid style goes beyond seeing conspiracies here and there in history. Instead, history itself is supposedly the product of a "vast" or "gigantic" conspiracy with enormous stakes: "The paranoid spokesman sees the fate of this conspiracy in apocalyptic terms—he traffics in the birth and death of whole worlds, whole political orders, whole systems of human value."[6] This is a Manichean (dualistic) mentality— that is, it sees the world in terms of black and white, absolute good versus absolute evil. This kind of mentality doesn't tolerate compromise with political opponents. Only complete victory will do. Furthermore, those operating in the paranoid style believe that their enemy is not only evil but immensely powerful. Different paranoid movements imagine this power in different ways: "[The enemy] controls the press; he directs the public mind through 'managed news'; he has unlimited funds; he has a secret for influencing the mind (brainwashing); he has a special technique for seduction (the Catholic confessional); he is gaining a stranglehold on the educational system."[7]

In the foreword to the 2008 edition of *The Paranoid Style in American Politics and Other Essays*, the Princeton University historian Sean Wilentz described the continued relevance of Hofstadter's signature essay, noting the many organizations and spokespeople over the previous three decades that had followed the paranoid-style tradition. Christian

Right leaders such as Phyllis Schlafly and Pat Robertson continued to argue that conspiracies involving communists and liberals threatened the United States. With the growth of right-wing talk radio, "the radio airwaves became conduits for every variety of right-wing conspiracy theory, along with character assassination of all liberals and of Democrats in particular."[8] Wilentz's essay is dated December 18, 2007. Had he written it a year later, he could have commented on the flood of racist paranoia during the 2008 presidential race as Barack Obama became the first person of African descent to be nominated by a major political party. The paranoid conspiracy theories of "birthers" and others were unrelenting during Obama's two terms as president. It doesn't look as if the paranoid style is leaving American culture anytime soon.

Updating Hofstadter's Theory

Hofstadter noted that even though the paranoid style retained basic elements, it evolved over time. The paranoid spokespeople of the nineteenth century considered themselves to be part of the establishment that controlled the country, even as they fended off threats to that establishment. In contrast, Hofstadter observed, the paranoid right wing of the mid-twentieth century "feels dispossessed: America has been largely taken away from them and their kind, though they are determined to try to repossess it and to prevent the final destructive act of subversion."[9] He also noted how the birth of the mass media had affected paranoid rhetoric:

> The villains of the modern right are much more vivid than those of their paranoid predecessors, much better known to the public; the contemporary literature of the paranoid style is by the same token richer and more circumstantial in personal description and personal invective. For the vaguely delineated villains of the anti-Masons, for the obscure and disguised Jesuit agents, the little-known papal delegates of the anti-Catholics, for the shadowy international bankers of the monetary conspiracies, we may now substitute eminent public figures like Presidents Roosevelt, Truman, and Eisenhower, Secretaries of State like Marshall, Acheson, and Dulles, justices of the Supreme Court like Frankfurter and Warren, and the whole battery of lesser but still famous and vivid conspirators headed by Alger Hiss.[10]

What about the paranoid right of the late twentieth and early twenty-first centuries? The sense of dispossession is still very clear in both religious and secular right leaders who want to "take back the country" from liberals, secularists, and (in some cases) racial minorities. Of course, mass media have grown even more massive, as well as ideologically segregated. News and commentary are now available twenty-four hours a day from cable channels like CNN or Fox News, from talk radio or public radio stations around the country, and from the Internet. Individuals can choose the news sources that reinforce their political views, whether conservative, moderate, or liberal.[11] It's hard to overstate the influence of the development of social media on contemporary paranoid thought. Paranoid ideas can quickly spread to massive numbers of people on Facebook and Twitter.[12] And social media accelerate the trend that began with the earlier Internet technology (chat rooms, discussion boards) that made paranoia interactive in nature.

In this new environment, facts now play a different role in paranoid rhetoric. Hofstadter wrote that "what distinguishes the paranoid style is not, then, the absence of verifiable facts (though it is occasionally true that in his extravagant passion for facts the paranoid occasionally manufactures them), but rather the curious leap in imagination that is always made at some critical point in the recital of events."[13] But contemporary peddlers of paranoia constantly manufacture facts. Lies that are repeated often enough are accepted as facts, at least by a segment of the population.

As Hofstadter noted, the paranoid style is marked by an apocalypticism that "runs dangerously near to hopeless pessimism, but usually stops short of it."[14] And the demand for unqualified victories leads to unrealistic goals, so "failure constantly heightens the paranoid frustration."[15] This pessimistic type of paranoia certainly exists today, but Hofstadter overlooked the possibility that paranoia could fuel an arrogant optimism. A perfect example is the so-called New Christian Right, which first emerged in the late 1970s to mobilize evangelicals in the political sphere. Consider the name of one of the seminal New Christian Right organizations: the Moral Majority. These organizations believe that they operate "with God on our side," to use William Martin's phrase.[16] The short-term challenges may be immense, but God will guarantee a victory in the end.

In his essay, Hofstadter referred briefly to a "curious leap in imagination," or the use of illogic in the paranoid style. With even a quick glance at paranoid thought, you'll see a frequent use of fallacies—errors in reasoning that lead to logically unsound conclusions. There are many types of fallacies, and three of them are particularly common in paranoid thought. Each of those three fallacies figures prominently in the paranoid science movements featured in this book.

The first is the false choice (or false dichotomy) fallacy, which insists that you have to select *only* between choices 1 and 2. There are no additional choices. Since only one choice is desirable, that's the one you should select. For example, many commercials for laundry detergent have a simple message: buy our brand or suffer with poorly washed clothes. No other brand (choice) will get the job done. Obviously, these claims portray the competition unfairly. A variation on this fallacy involves two desirable choices. For example, "Do you want the mayor to prevent terror attacks or make sure that potholes get filled?" Since preventing terror attacks is presumably more important, you're asked to excuse the potholes. Of course, any competent mayor would attend to both tasks. The false choice fallacy is popular in paranoid thought because it can express a dualistic worldview that divides the world into absolute good and absolute evil, with no compromise possible. It appeals to those who like to see the world in simplistic terms and are loath to acknowledge nuance and complexity.

A second common fallacy in paranoid thought is the slippery slope fallacy. Here, you're deciding between choice number 1, at the top of the slope, and choice number 2, at the bottom of the slope. Don't bother trying to find a middle ground between them; you'll only slide down the slope to choice 2. Since choice 1 (the top) is clearly preferable to choice 2 (the bottom), you should go with choice 1. Any step that takes you away from choice 1 means you're crossing a threshold onto the slope, inevitably landing you in choice 2. For example, gun rights activists claim that legal restrictions on firearm ownership, such as assault weapon bans, place us on a slippery slope that will lead to a repeal of the Second Amendment. In other words, our only two choices are unrestricted access to firearms or no right to bear arms. Obviously the slippery slope fallacy has the same basic structure as the false choice fallacy, but adds the concept of motion over time. Besides being dualistic in nature, the slippery slope fallacy also plays to fears of uncontrollable change. It's better to stick with the safe status quo (the top of the slope) than to risk disaster. Fear is one of the basic elements of the paranoid style, so it's not surprising to see this fallacy embraced by paranoid movements.

A third common fallacy in paranoid thought is the straw person (or straw man) fallacy. When you knock down a straw person, you're attacking a fabricated version of your opponent's assertions. Paranoid thought involves demonizing enemies, often to the point where paranoid movement leaders are unable to distinguish the real claims made by their opponents from the ones they created in their imaginations. Ironically, paranoid leaders often portray their opponents as too deceptive to represent themselves accurately, which means they have no right to contest the fabrications.

The Paranoid Style in American Evangelicalism

Evangelicalism doesn't require formal membership like Roman Catholicism. It's a religious subculture with ambiguous and shifting boundaries. In his book *American Evangelical Christianity: An Introduction*, the historian Mark Noll provides a succinct description of this subculture:

> "Evangelical" refers to the heirs of [eighteenth-century] Anglo-American revivals, but it also designates a consistent pattern of convictions and attitudes. In one of the most useful summaries of that pattern, the British historian David Bebbington has identified the key ingredients of evangelicalism as conversionism (an emphasis on the "new birth" as a life-changing experience of God), Biblicism (a reliance on the Bible as ultimate religious authority), activism (a concern for sharing the faith), and crucicentrism (a focus on Christ's redeeming work on the cross, usually pictured as the only way to salvation). These evangelical traits have never by themselves yielded cohesive, institutionally compact, or clearly demarcated groups of Christians. But they do serve to identify a large family of churches and religious enterprises.[17]

Other scholars of American religion point out that evangelicalism's influence cuts across other religious boundaries, so that some members of the so-called mainline denominations like the United Methodist

Church or the Presbyterian Church (U.S.A.) share the beliefs and practices of evangelicalism, and others don't.[18]

Even a casual observer of American evangelicalism can detect the presence of the paranoid style, especially in the subculture's obsession with the End Times, as seen in the best-selling *Left Behind* novel series by Tim LaHaye and Jerry B. Jenkins.[19] The formal name for the End Times doctrine that most evangelicals affirm is premillennial dispensationalism. According to this doctrine, society will continually grow worse (especially morally) until God removes all true Christian believers from the Earth in an event called the Rapture. After this, the Anti-Christ will assume power over the Earth until he and his followers are defeated by God in an epic battle. Christ will then return and reign over the Earth for a millennium.

This doctrine was first brought to the United States in the mid-nineteenth century by an Englishman named John Nelson Darby.[20] Elements of the paranoid style are very evident in more recent versions of the doctrine offered by Hal Lindsey, Pat Robertson, and Tim LaHaye and Jerry B. Jenkins, who perceive threats to American power from rival nations and institutions like the Soviet Union, the United Nations, and the European Union. Here we see the grand conspiracy theory and Manichean mentality (perceiving a battle between absolute good and absolute evil) described by Hofstadter.

Beyond these apocalyptic beliefs, we can see the paranoid style in the basic evangelical cultural orientation described by the sociologist Christian Smith in his book *American Evangelicalism: Embattled and Thriving*:

> Distinction, engagement, and conflict vis-à-vis outsiders constitutes a crucial element of what we might call the "cultural DNA" of American evangelicalism. The evangelical tradition's entire history, theology, and self-identity presupposes and reflects strong cultural boundaries with nonevangelicals; a zealous burden to convert and transform the world outside of itself; and a keen perception of external threats and crises seen as menacing what it views to be true, good, and valuable.[21]

That perception of "threats and crises," supposedly endangering the Christian foundation of American society and/or the evangelical way of life, is an important part of the paranoid style.

Smith found that evangelical laypeople shared the same sense of embattlement articulated by generations of evangelical leaders. Most of the evangelicals that Smith and his research team interviewed believe that the broader American culture has abandoned God's ways in pursuit of narcissistic, licentious, and self-destructive values and lifestyles: "On television, in schools, on the news, and at work, evangelicals see and hear a set of values and lifestyle commitments that feel to them fundamentally alien and inhospitable."[22] They believe that this state of affairs is a departure from some previous (and preferable) time when evangelical Christian values were the mainstream: "Widespread among evangelicals is the belief that America was founded as a Christian nation, that America is now turning its back on its Judeo-Christian roots, that mainstream institutions are becoming increasingly anti-Christian, and that as a consequence America is in a state of moral and social degeneration."[23] At the very least, they think this shift has turned evangelicals into a marginalized group of "second-class citizens." But some see an even more serious situation emerging. According to Smith,

> More than a few evangelicals are concerned by what they believe are increasingly powerful, organized groups in America with clearly anti-Christian agendas. To be sure, some evangelicals express tremendous self-confidence and see no particular conspiracy set on undermining Christianity. However, other evangelicals do discern rumblings of what they fear could become a frightful future. And yet others, a definite minority, are convinced that the barbarians are already now battering down the gates.[24]

It's true that evangelicals are a religious minority group. But so are Catholics, liberal Protestants, Unitarians, Jews, Muslims, and Buddhists (not to mention atheists, if we count them as a "religious" group). Yet, as Protestant Christians, evangelicals enjoy a degree of social privilege not shared by groups outside the American religious mainstream.[25] And evangelicals wield considerable political power. A Republican presidential candidate would have little chance of winning their party's nomination without strong support from evangelical voters, and candidates' stump speeches clearly show this. The evangelical sense of embattlement also reflects feelings of entitlement based on the inaccurate belief that the Founding Fathers were a group of mostly evangelical Christians. As the sociologists Andrew Greeley and Michael Hout observe, "The Conservative Protestant leadership talks like people who feel they are outside by mistake. They are certain of their place at the heart of America just as they are certain of their faith in God. . . . To evangelical leaders, Conservative Protestants deserve more say, and the [other outsider groups] can wait to speak."[26] In sum, evangelical embattlement is rooted more in imagination than reality, the result of unrealistic expectations for dominance in a pluralistic culture.

There's a lot of diversity in evangelical thought at both the elite and popular levels, and I don't want to make a sweeping claim that all evangelicals are hard-core practitioners of Hofstadter's paranoid style. Yet the paranoid style is undoubtedly a significant feature of American evangelical culture. And even those who aren't worried by grand conspiracies often share with the paranoid a false sense of marginalization.

The Christian Right within the American Evangelical Elite

Contrary to popular belief and some media portrayals, not all evangelicals are politically conservative. In his 2008 book *The Future of Faith in American Politics: The Public Witness of the Evangelical Center*, the ethicist David P. Gushee identifies three camps among American evangelical elites and organizations: right, left, and center.[27]

"Evangelical right" organizations include the Christian Coalition, the Family Research Council, Focus on the Family, and the Southern Baptist Convention Ethics and Religious Liberty Commission. According to Gushee, the evangelical right is guided by a narrative of "decline, defense, and combat" that goes something like this:

> The United States of America was once the greatest nation on earth, because it was founded on Judeo-Christian principles, and these governed both the private and public lives of its citizenry. . . . However, America went into decline when its commitment to this faith and way of life was shaken by the introduction of an alien faith and vision of life. This alien ideology is secularist, morally relativist, and profoundly corrosive to the well-being of families and the society as a whole. . . . Thoughtful Christians must join together, mobilize for action, and take back their society.[28]

Then there's the "evangelical left," including the Sojourners (headed by Jim Wallis), the sociology professor Tony Campolo, and the author Brian McLaren. As Gushee describes it, "The evangelical left is *left* because it reads scripture and interprets the demands of Christian discipleship to require what in our contemporary American and Christian contexts are considered left-leaning moral commitments."[29] Its main goals are reducing poverty, war, racism, and sexism and protecting the environment. It tends to downplay the issues of abortion and homosexuality.

This leaves the "evangelical center," which includes most major evangelical institutions not associated with the other two camps. Among these Gushee mentions *Christianity Today* magazine, the National Association of Evangelicals (NAE), and InterVarsity Press. He also includes prominent megachurch pastors Rick Warren (of Saddleback Church), Joel Hunter (of Northland Church), and Rich Nathan (of Vineyard Church). According to Gushee, the evangelical center shares several key characteristics with the evangelical right, including a clearly articulated opposition to abortion and euthanasia, a rejection of the morality of sex outside heterosexual marriage, and a rejection of gay marriage. However, he maintains that the evangelical center has a "broad and holistic moral agenda," in contrast to the evangelical right's narrow focus on abortion and homosexuality.[30] This holistic agenda includes "creation care" (the evangelical term for religiously motivated environmentalism) and acceptance of the seriousness of the global warming problem.[31] He also claims that the evangelical center rejects the evangelical right's "mood of angry nostalgia and aggrieved entitlement about the Christian role in American society."[32] As Gushee sees it, the evangelical center shares several characteristics with the evangelical left, including concern for the plight of the poor, concern for racism as a moral and policy issue, and a commitment to human rights that includes opposition to the use of torture on detainees in the "war on terror." He notes numerous differences with the evangelical left, including greater sympathy with global capitalism, more willingness to support wars if they adhere to traditional just-war theory, and less focus on the needs of the urban poor.

Gushee's aim was to champion the American evangelical "emerging center," and this agenda led him to produce a somewhat distorted picture.[33] At least two corrections are in order. First, the evangelical center has much stronger ideological and institutional ties with the evangelical right than with the evangelical left. The result is that the evangelical left is marginalized within American evangelicalism, leaving the evangelical center and right as the dominant players that together form two wings of an evangelical mainstream. Second, the evangelical center is hardly politically centrist (or moderate) when mapped against the entire American political landscape. In fact, the evangelical center and right should be called the evangelical right and far right. The overall rightward orientation of evangelicalism also affects the evangelical left, which is only moderately liberal at best and avoids the more radical critiques of American society characteristic of liberation thought.[34] However, evangelical left, center, and right can be useful as *relative* terms describing the internal dynamics of the evangelical world, as well as the self-understanding of many evangelical elites.

I use the term "Christian Right" in this book for *both* the evangelical center and the evangelical right as described by Gushee. This coalition shares the belief that abortion and sexuality outside the context of heterosexual marriage are the most pressing moral issues facing American society. What's more, they believe that evangelicals are called to serve as America's moral guardians, monitoring the extent to which society strays from biblical standards and fighting for a return to them.[35] As I'll show in the following chapters, these two camps work together to support the paranoid science of intelligent design, the ex-gay movement, and conservative bioethics. The issue of climate change is where these two camps diverge: the evangelical center has formed a rare coalition with the evangelical left to argue that climate change is real, while the evangelical right still denies it.

The Christian Right's Paranoid Science Agenda

The Christian Right's battle against science is selective. Influential figures among the Christian Right accept theories on subatomic particles, but oppose evolutionary theory. They accept genetically modified food crops, but oppose human genetic engineering. They raise no objections to the American Psychiatric Association's stance on post-traumatic stress disorder, but strenuously object to the APA's stance on homosexuality. What's the pattern here? What I've found is that Christian Right leaders will attack a scientific theory or practice when they think it violates one of their strongly held beliefs.

There are three types of beliefs that are most relevant for the four movements discussed in this book. The first type of belief relates to the Christian Right's notions of morality. For the Christian Right, sexual morality (opposition to sexual activity outside heterosexual marriage) and opposition to abortion are of primary importance. The second type of belief relates to the core worldview held by most evangelicals, which is based on a fairly literal interpretation of the Bible.[36] Most evangelicals have an *anthropocentric* view of the universe, believing that the universe was created around and for humans. The Earth is not simply an insignificant "pale blue dot" in the vastness of space (as Carl Sagan famously described it in his *Cosmos* series), but God's special creation. Humans are not simply the most evolutionarily advanced species on Earth, but the only creatures created in the image of God (human exceptionalism). The division of humans into males and females is not simply an evolutionary adaptation but part of God's special design for humans known as "gender complementarity"—God created men and women with different characteristics so that they could exercise different roles in the family (with the man as the head) as part of a monogamous, heterosexual couple. A third type of belief relates to the Christian Right's political and economic views, specifically, a commitment to American exceptionalism and free market capitalism.

In each of the four paranoid science movements, the Christian Right is trying to push back against scientific advances that threaten its beliefs. Intelligent design's main foe is evolutionary biology, which, most evangelicals claim, denies God's role as creator. Intelligent design proponents also challenge modern cosmology by insisting that the Earth is a "privileged planet" specifically designed by God for the benefit of humans. The ex-gay movement challenges the decision by the American Psychiatric Association to declassify homosexuality as a curable psychiatric illness, thus helping to normalize it. This is an obvious threat to evangelical notions of sexual morality, but for the Christian Right, it's also a denial of God's intention for gender complementarity. The Christian Right's bioethics movement responds to perceived attacks on "human dignity" rooted in the denial that humans are created in God's image.

These perceived attacks include embryonic stem cell research (which involves the "murder" of embryonic human beings, making it similar to abortion), human genetic engineering (which usurps God's role as the designer of human life), and euthanasia (which usurps God's role of determining the length of human lives). Finally, the evangelical right's campaign of climate change denial responds to fears that environmentalists seek to restrain free markets, create a world government that will subvert American sovereignty, and ultimately replace Judeo-Christian morality with Paganism.

Each of the four movements proclaims that particular sectors of science are unsound and rely on incorrect data and/or flawed theories. But, as paranoid-style movements, they also make much more sweeping claims. The offending sectors of science are conspiring to mislead the public. What's more, these sectors threaten the moral foundation of American society. The appropriate response, according to the Christian Right, is to expose the deceptions, fight any further advances, and replace flawed scientific theories with more scientifically sound ones, which naturally come from the Christian Right and its allies.

The Christian Right's War on Reality

In a 2004 New York Times Magazine article, the journalist Ron Suskind revealed how George W. Bush replaced fact-based analysis with a faith-based approach to reality, one that provides easy certainty rather than encouraging deep reflection. Here is part of Suskind's conversation with an unnamed presidential aide (widely known to be Karl Rove):[37]

> The aide said that guys like me were "in what we call the reality-based community," which he defined as people who "believe that solutions emerge from your judicious study of discernible reality." I nodded and murmured something about enlightenment principles and empiricism. He cut me off. "That's not the way the world really works anymore," he continued. "We're an empire now, and when we act, we create our own reality. And while you're studying that reality—judiciously, as you will—we'll act again, creating other new realities, which you can study too, and that's how things will sort out. We're history's actors . . . and you, all of you, will be left to just study what we do."[38]

Rove intended "reality-based community" to be a derogatory term, but, not surprisingly, many critics of the Bush administration chose to wear it as a badge of honor. As Bush's declaration of "mission accomplished" in Iraq gave way to a worsening quagmire, his critics felt increasingly vindicated. Faith in the efficacy of American power combined with faith that Bush was God's instrument was no substitute for a foreign policy based on a careful analysis of the facts.

The Christian Right has been waging a war against reality in the realm of science similar to what the Bush administration tried to do in the realm of policy. When Christian Right leaders feel that scientific theories or practices are threatening their strongly held beliefs, they attack the offending sectors of science with paranoid-style conspiracy theories. But there's at least one major difference between these two wars against reality. The Bush administration was dismissive of factual analysis, but the paranoid science of the Christian Right actually claims to outdo mainstream science (that is, real science) in factual analysis. Christian Right authors don't concede scientific truth, they create an alternative science—and thus an alternative reality—where their religious beliefs are safe from threat. In this alternative reality the scientific data indicate that humans were intelligently designed by a creator, gays can be cured of their "illness," embryonic stem cell research is unnecessary for medical progress, and humans can consume all the fossil fuel they want with no harmful effects on the environment. The anthropocentric universe based on a literal reading of the Bible is not only still plausible but actually supported by scientific investigation. Those who disagree are obviously driven by some sinister political motive, but certainly not by the pursuit of scientific truth.

1

Fear of a Darwinist Culture

The Intelligent Design Movement

As Republican presidential hopefuls gathered for debates leading up to the 2012 primaries, they focused on the perennial Republican issues of the economy, foreign policy, and abortion, plus the new issue of health care reform. But former Utah governor Jon Huntsman Jr. managed to inject another issue into the debates: science. Huntsman took aim at candidates who rejected the scientific consensus regarding evolution and climate change. At a September 2011 debate at the Reagan Library he declared, "Listen, when you make comments that fly in the face of what 98 out of 100 climate scientists have said, when you call into question the science of evolution, all I'm saying is that, in order for the Republican Party to win, we can't run from science."[1] This brought sharp responses from other Republican candidates during and after the debate. Former senator Rick Santorum of Pennsylvania, Texas governor Rick Perry, and Minnesota representative Michele Bachmann all endorsed intelligent design and said that it should have a place in public school curricula.

For Santorum (the eventual winner of the Iowa Caucus) in particular, this was no election-year posturing. He was deeply involved in the intelligent design movement, having introduced an amendment in the Senate that was supportive of the movement and having written the foreword to the intelligent design anthology *Darwin's Nemesis*.[2] Intelligent design was dismissed by the vast majority of biologists and rebuffed in the courts, but it had clearly gained a foothold in the Republican Party. Why would a failed scientific movement achieve such a significant level of political success? This is a hint that the movement has always been about more than just science.[3]

The intelligent design movement emerged in the early 1990s and offered a new challenge to evolutionary biology. Earlier fundamentalist and evangelical critics of evolution insisted that the scientific evidence demonstrates the accuracy of a literal reading of the creation account recorded in the book of Genesis.[4] Some of these creationists were willing to accept that the Earth is billions of years old, while others, "young-earth creationists," insisted that the Earth is less than ten thousand years old. All of them rejected the evolutionary account of the development of life, which they dismissed as flawed science.

The intelligent design movement also argued that evolution was flawed science. But instead of focusing on how evolution diverges from the Genesis creation account, leaders of the movement attacked the belief that unguided natural processes are responsible for both the origins of life on Earth and its subsequent development. They insist that the scientific evidence points to life on Earth being the product of a designer. This designer is sometimes identified as the biblical God and at other times left unidentified. To understand the cultural underpinnings of the intelligent design movement, we need to consider the profound effects that Enlightenment science has had on Protestantism broadly and American evangelicalism in particular.

Protestantism and Enlightenment "Faith" in Science

The Enlightenment is the name given by historians to a group of interlocking intellectual movements that emerged in eighteenth-century Europe. One of the principal themes of the Enlightenment was a firm belief in the scientific method as a path to the truth. Some strains of the Enlightenment were hostile to religious belief and tried to pit science against religion, but Protestant theologians in Europe (and later in the United States) attempted to find ways to reconcile their religious beliefs with the Enlightenment commitment to science. These efforts gained momentum in the nineteenth century and continue even now.

Some Protestant theologians believed that advances by modern science required a substantial revision of Christian doctrines. Darwin's theory of evolution made it impossible to read the book of Genesis literally. Newtonian physics, which described the physical world as orderly and predictable, cast doubt on the existence of miracles.[5] Modern methods from the academic discipline of history applied to the study of the Bible, known as historical critical scholarship, cast doubt on the historical reliability of much of the Bible. Those who thought along these lines were known as liberal Protestants. They insisted that Christianity could survive in the modern world only if it abandoned or reinterpreted doctrines that contradicted science.

Predictably, more traditionally minded Protestants condemned liberal Protestantism for abandoning essential elements of the faith, including belief in the Bible as the revealed Word of God rather than a primarily human document. But conservative Protestants eventually absorbed the Enlightenment "faith" in science, which they combined with their faith in the veracity of the Bible. Nowhere was this truer than among American evangelicals. As the historian Theodore Dwight Bozeman discusses in his book *Protestants in an Age of Science: The Baconian Ideal and Antebellum American Religious Thought*, nineteenth-century American evangelicals integrated the scientific perspectives of Francis Bacon (as interpreted by the leaders of the Scottish Enlightenment) into their theology of scripture.[6] Baconian thought involved "a strenuously empiricist approach to all forms of knowledge, a declared greed for the objective *fact*, and a corresponding distrust for 'hypotheses,' of 'imagination,' and indeed, of reason itself."[7]

Reading the Bible through this Baconian lens, American evangelicals came to see the Bible as a source of objective facts (as opposed to subjective interpretations) not only about God but also about history, geography, and science. Furthermore, American evangelicals frequently used findings from scientific research to construct apologetic arguments, claiming that empirical data prove that the Bible is true. To sum up the difference between liberal and evangelical Protestants: liberal Protestants believed that knowledge generated by science "trumped" the Bible, and American evangelicals believed that science and the Bible formed one truth. If scientists offered ideas that contradicted the Bible, evangelicals saw this as a sign that those particular scientists practiced flawed science; they were certain that properly executed science would eventually come along and correct the error.[8]

Contrary to popular belief, American evangelicals weren't unanimous in rejecting evolution when the theory emerged. Some managed to reconcile the biblical account with evolution, suggesting, for example, that God's "days" described in Genesis were extremely long periods of time rather than the twenty-four-hour days of humans. However, over time anti-evolution sentiments grew. In the 1960s a prominent new movement known as creation science claimed scientific confirmation of a literal reading of Genesis. Creation science didn't originate in American evangelicalism, but evangelicals enthusiastically embraced its ideas.[9]

Supporters of creation science made repeated attempts to get their views taught in public schools alongside evolution. By the early 1990s, however, creation science was at a legal dead end, its proponents having lost in the U.S. Supreme Court. Many evangelical academics subscribed to forms of theistic evolution (the belief that God created life through evolution), but there was potential demand for a new evangelical approach. Intelligent design quickly capitalized on the demand.

Intelligent Design Takes Flight

Intelligent design proponents like to point out that the idea that life on Earth is the product of design has a long history stretching back to the ancient Greeks. As the historian Ronald L. Numbers describes, the intellectual foundation for the contemporary intelligent design movement can be found in three books published in the 1980s: *The Mystery of Life's Origin*, by Charles B. Thaxton, Walter L. Bradley, and Roger L. Olson; *Evolution: A Theory in Crisis*, by Michael Denton; and *Of Pandas and People*, by Percival Davis and Dean H. Kenyon.[10] Soon afterward, intelligent design transformed into a full-fledged social movement, thanks to Phillip E. Johnson, a law professor at University of California at Berkeley.

In an interview with *Insight* magazine, Johnson traces the personal journey that led him to spearhead intelligent design.[11] He was raised as a nominal Christian, eventually became an agnostic, and at age seventeen went off to Harvard, where he decided to adopt the thinking of people he perceived to be the leading intellectuals of American culture. He found great success in his academic pursuits: he graduated at the top of his class at the University of Chicago Law School, served as a law clerk to Supreme Court Chief Justice Earl Warren, and became a professor at Berkeley's Boalt Law School.

All of this changed for Johnson following a divorce and a personal crisis in his thirties that led to a conversion to evangelical Christianity:

> The experience of having marriage and family life crash under me, and of achieving a certain amount of academic success and seeing the meaning-

lessness of it, made me listen and give myself to Christ at the advanced age of 38. And that aroused a particular level of intellectual interest in the question of why the intellectual world is so dominated by naturalistic and agnostic thinking.[12]

About a decade later, in 1987–1988, Johnson was on sabbatical in London. He happened to come across a scientific bookstore promoting *The Blind Watchmaker* by the British evolutionary biologist and outspoken atheist Richard Dawkins. He bought the book and became fascinated with the topic of evolution—and alarmed that it threatened Christianity. Further reading convinced him that evolution was a flawed theory.

Johnson presented his critique of evolutionary biology in his 1991 book *Darwin on Trial*.[13] His main point was that the beliefs of modern "Darwinist" scientists aren't supported by empirical evidence, but rather by the philosophy of *naturalism*, which rules out the possibility of action by a divine creator. Johnson also contends that Darwinism is antagonistic to genuine religious belief and that it has corrupted the educational system.

Evangelicals had mixed reactions to the book. Young-earth creationists attacked it because it didn't endorse their view that the Earth is less than ten thousand years old. Evangelical academics who supported theistic evolution asserted that Johnson misrepresented the religious implications of evolution. Nonetheless, Johnson quickly attracted supporters, some of whom became co-leaders of the intelligent design movement. Among these was the Lehigh University biochemist Michael J. Behe. Since Johnson lacked scientific credentials, gaining the support of a respected scientist was a big boost for the movement (although Johnson insisted that his lack of scientific background was irrelevant, since Darwinism was based on philosophy rather than empirical evidence). Other emerging co-leaders included the mathematician and philosopher William A. Dembski, the philosophers of science Stephen C. Meyer and Paul A. Nelson, and the biochemist Jonathan Wells.

Most of those who became active in the intelligent design movement can be described as evangelical Protestants, but Behe is a Roman Catholic, and Wells is a member of the Unification Church. It's significant that the core leaders of the movement include both young-earth creationists and those who believe that the Earth is billions of years old. Johnson has pursued a "big tent" strategy, conceding that movement leaders can agree to disagree on the age of the Earth until after the naturalists have been defeated.

The movement gained valuable institutional structure when the Discovery Institute, a conservative think tank based in Seattle, invited intelligent design supporters to create a unit that was called the Center for the Renewal of Science and Culture (later changed to the Center for Science and Culture), which began its work in 1996. The list of fellows on the CSC website contains nearly everyone of significance in the intelligent design movement. Additional institutional support for the movement came from InterVarsity Press, which picked up *Darwin on Trial* from the smaller Regnery Gateway and subsequently became the primary publisher of books on intelligent design. Given that InterVarsity Press is the most prominent publisher associated with the evangelical center, this gave the movement considerable legitimacy in the evangelical world. Eventually, institutions associated with the evangelical right, such as Focus on the Family, also began promoting the movement. The evangelical left, however, has never warmed to it.[14] Intelligent design's primary support comes from a center-right evangelical coalition.

Phillip E. Johnson's Paranoid Vision

Michael Behe, William Dembski, and others made important contributions to intelligent design, but the central vision of the movement was crafted by Phillip E. Johnson. His decision to attack evolution is not itself an example of the paranoid style. Even if we can demonstrate that his critique of evolution is highly flawed, this merely shows that he's ignorant of scientific matters. Other factors establish that Johnson—and by extension the intelligent design movement—operates in a paranoid style: (1) the belief that Darwinism is part of a vast atheist conspiracy, (2) the belief that Darwinism has undermined the moral foundation of American society and threatens to do further damage, and (3) a Manichean mentality that rejects all attempts at compromise with the opposing camp of Darwinist scientists.

Like other "highbrow" paranoid movements, intelligent design isn't entirely devoid of verifiable facts or logical arguments. But there are enough falsehoods and flawed arguments to keep the movement's description of the world at odds with reality. At the heart of the movement's ideology is a false choice fallacy: Christianity and evolution are mutually incompatible belief systems, and only a fool would attempt to embrace both. To support this claim, intelligent design proponents draw on a straw person portrayal of biologists as nearly unanimous in their hostility toward religion. Also, intelligent design proponents' consistent use of the term "Darwinism" to describe modern evolutionary biology at least borders on a straw person portrayal, as it obscures the vast progress made since Darwin's day.[15]

Johnson's paranoid vision didn't appear fully formed. It developed over the years as he continued to contemplate the specter of naturalism, took in advice from allies, and responded to critics. So it's useful to trace how his message developed in his books. Of course, Johnson has published in other venues, especially essays and book reviews in conservative Christian journals like *First Things* and *Books & Culture*. But the principal ideas from these shorter writings always made their way into a subsequent book. Let's turn our attention now to these books.

Stage 1: Laying the Foundation

As I mentioned, Phillip E. Johnson launched his career as an intelligent design spokesperson with *Darwin on Trial*. The book's thesis is that Darwinism has no empirical data to support it. Instead, it relies on the naturalistic philosophy of scientists who simply assume that no supernatural creator was involved in the origin or development of life on Earth. According to Johnson, scientists provide evidence for microevolution (variations within a species) and then falsely conclude that this demonstrates the existence of macroevolution (the creation of new species). These same scientists offer no evidence that natural forces (for example, chemical evolution) can successfully create life from nonliving chemicals.

Recall Hofstadter's observation that operating in a paranoid style involves believing not just in a conspiracy but in a vast conspiracy that threatens the social order. In *Darwin on Trial* Johnson doesn't reveal his entire paranoid vision, but he does lay the foundation for it by claiming that Darwinist scientists are conspiring to mislead the public. For example, Johnson writes that these scientists play games with terminology to cover up the inadequacy of their empirical evidence:

If laboratory science cannot establish a mechanism [for macroevolution], and if the fossil studies cannot find the common ancestors and transitional links, then Darwinism fails as an empirical theory. But Darwinists suppress the consideration of that possibility by invoking a distinction between the "fact" of evolution and Darwin's particular theory. Objections based upon the fossil record and the inadequacy of the Darwinist mechanism go only to the theory, they argue. Evolution itself (the logical explanation for relationships) remains a fact, by which they seem to mean it is an inescapable deduction from the fact of relationship.[16]

For Johnson, there's a lot at stake in this cover-up. The economic livelihood of scientists is on the line, and so is Darwinism as a *cultural* movement:

The story of human descent from apes in not merely a scientific hypothesis; it is the secular equivalent of the story of Adam and Eve, and a matter of immense cultural importance. Propagating the story requires illustrations, museum exhibits, and television reenactments. It also requires a priesthood in the form of thousands of researchers, teachers, and artists who provide realistic and imaginative detail and carry the story out to the general public. The needs of the public and the profession ensure that confirming evidence will be found, but only an audit performed by a person not committed in advance to the hypothesis under investigation can tell us whether the evidence has any value as confirmation.[17]

Johnson presents himself as just such a disinterested auditor.

Johnson's conspiratorial view relies on the assumption that Darwinism isn't compatible with authentic religious belief. For Johnson, this follows logically from Darwinists' commitment to naturalism:

Naturalism does not explicitly deny the mere existence of God, but it does deny that a supernatural being could in any way influence natural events, such as evolution, or communicate with natural creatures like ourselves. *Scientific* naturalism makes the same point by starting with the assumption that science, which studies the natural, is our only reliable path to knowledge. A God who can never do anything that makes a difference, and of whom we can have no reliable knowledge, is of no importance to us.[18]

Consequently, "theistic evolution" (evolution guided by a divine creator) is a logical impossibility, an argument that Johnson expanded on in later writings.

Johnson is frustrated that elite scientists actively conceal the incompatibility of Darwinism and religion, rather than publicly acknowledge it. In a chapter titled "Darwinist Religion," Johnson accuses the National Academy of Sciences of acting disingenuously, particularly in its 1984 pamphlet *Science and Creationism: A View from the National Academy of Sciences*. He also condemns the Harvard paleontologist Stephen Jay Gould for falsely assuring the public that "most scientists show no hostility to religion."[19] In contrast, Johnson praises the Cornell University historian of science William Provine for honestly admitting that Darwinism and religion are in conflict. As Johnson summarizes it,

> Gould had assured [journalist Irving] Kristol that among evolutionary biologists there is "an entire spectrum of religious attitudes—from devout daily prayer and worship to resolute atheism." I have myself noticed a great deal more of the latter than the former, and Provine agrees with me. He reports that most evolutionary biologists are atheists, "and many have been driven there by their understanding of the evolutionary process and other science." The few who see no conflict between their biology and their religion "are either obtuse or compartmentalizing in their thinking, or are effective atheists without realizing it." Scientific organizations hide the conflict for fear of jeopardizing the funding for scientific research, or because they feel that religion plays a useful role in moral education.[20]

In case the reader continues to harbor any illusions that Darwinism and religion are compatible, Johnson states his point even more strongly a few pages later: "To the [Darwinist] zealots, people who say they believe in God are either harmless sentimentalists who add some vague God-talk to a basically naturalistic worldview, or they are creationists. In either case they are fools, but in the latter case they are also a menace."[21]

Darwin on Trial focuses mainly on a conspiracy among scientists, particularly elite ones, but a chapter entitled "Darwinist Education" also asserts that the educational system is being infected by naturalism. Johnson's main example is the California State Board of Education, which adopted a *Policy Statement* on the teaching of science in 1989. At first glance, Johnson says, the *Policy Statement* seems reasonable and broad-minded: "The *Policy Statement* emphasizes that neither science nor anything else should be taught dogmatically, because 'Compelling beliefs is inconsistent with the goal of education,' which is to encourage understanding."[22] He warns, though, that readers shouldn't be fooled by this, since the statement's definition of science endorses the naturalism of elite Darwinists. Thus, according to Johnson, "The purpose of the *Policy Statement* is not to protect dissent, but to establish a philosophical justification for teaching naturalistic evolution as 'fact' in an educational system that is at least nominally opposed to dogmatism."[23] That naturalism was spreading beyond the scientific establishment and infecting other areas of society was a theme Johnson expanded on in subsequent books as he revealed the full scope of his paranoid vision.

As I mentioned earlier, *Darwin on Trial* was criticized by both young-earth creationists and biologists. Johnson produced a second edition of the book, published by InterVarsity Press in 1993, that added a chapter titled "A Book and Its Critics" responding to many of these criticisms. By this time, Johnson was beginning to make the transition from mere author to leader of a fledgling social movement, and he began to reveal more of the paranoid vision that would mobilize followers. For example, Johnson argues, "My primary goal in writing *Darwin on Trial* was to legitimate the assertion of a theistic worldview in the secular universities."[24] This implies that universities as a whole, not simply departments in the biological sciences, are infected by naturalism. In an even more significant statement, Johnson reveals the scope of the Darwinist establishment's power: "Naturalistic evolution is not merely a scientific theory; it is the official story of modern culture. The scientific priesthood that has the authority to interpret the official creation story gains immense cultural influence thereby, which it might lose if the story were called into question."[25] The Darwinist conspiracy is not simply about the control of science, but also about the control of "modern culture." The stakes are now immensely higher, including the "whole systems of human value" that Hofstadter mentioned in his description of the paranoid style. In his follow-up book, Johnson aimed to clarify just how high the stakes were.

Stage 2: A Fully Paranoid Worldview

Two years later, in 1995, InterVarsity Press published Phillip E. Johnson's second book related to intelligent design, *Reason in the Balance: The Case against Naturalism in Science, Law, and Education.*[26] By this time intelligent design was gaining momentum as a social movement, and Johnson revealed the full scope of the paranoid vision that would guide the movement. He opens the book by arguing that although most Americans claim to be theists (people who believe that God created them and has a purpose for their lives), the most influential intellectuals in the nation and around the world are naturalists (people who believe that God exists only as an idea in the minds of religious believers). This can be seen first in American universities, where "naturalism—the doctrine that nature is 'all there is'—is the virtually unquestioned assumption that underlies not only natural science but intellectual work of all kinds."[27] There are religious believers and active churchgoers who hold prestigious appointments in universities, but most of these people maintain their respectability by accommodating to the university's dominant ethos of naturalism: "They explicitly or implicitly concede that their theism is a matter of 'faith' and agree to leave the realm of 'reason' to the agnostics."[28] Judges and journalists receive their training in universities, and their work also becomes infected by naturalistic assumptions.

In a chapter provocatively titled "Is God Unconstitutional?" Johnson condemns a judicial system that, he claims, is gripped by naturalism and a public education system shaped by the naturalistic courts. He begins by citing a legal dispute between an evangelical church known as Lamb's Chapel and a New York public school district. In Johnson's account of the dispute, the minister of Lamb's Chapel applied to use the school's auditorium to show a six-part film series featuring Focus on the Family leader James Dobson lecturing on parent-child relationships. The school district, backed by the state attorney general, refused to give permission for the films to be shown, citing state policy that banned religious activities from school property. State courts sided with the school district. However, the U.S. Supreme Court sided with Lamb's Chapel, on the grounds that family relationships were a legitimate subject matter for discussion in the public schools, and a viewpoint should not be excluded simply because it was religiously based. Johnson describes the lesson he drew from the dispute:

> The Lamb's Chapel case illustrates how classifying a viewpoint or theory as "religious" may have the effect of *marginalizing* it. A viewpoint or theory is marginalized when, without being refuted, it is categorized in such a way that it can be excluded from serious consideration. The technique of marginalizing a viewpoint by labeling it "religion" is particularly effective in late-twentieth-century America, because there is a general impression, reinforced by Supreme Court decisions, that religion does not belong in public institutions.[29]

According to Johnson, one effect of this marginalization of religion is that New York public schools take a relativistic approach to sexual morality in their sex education curriculum. This "progressive" approach redefines the family to include any persons who live together in a sexual relationship, whether or not they're legally married. Furthermore, progressive sex education emphasizes "safe sex" over abstinence, which is "about as rational as pouring gasoline on a raging fire."[30] This metaphor depicts sexuality as a dangerous force, and naturalistic philosophy as negligent for encouraging this force to run rampant. Clearly, gender and sexuality—and the fear of them escaping from proper bounds—are central to Johnson's paranoid vision.

In case the reader thought that the Supreme Court's decision to side with Lamb's Chapel showed that it was unaffected by naturalism, Johnson turns to the 1987 *Edwards v. Aguillard* case, in which the Supreme Court struck down a Louisiana law that required balanced treatment between "evolution-science" and "creation-science," arguing that the law was an unconstitutional establishment of religion. According to Johnson, the Supreme Court decision went beyond preventing the teaching of young-earth creationism, and in fact prevented anything other than a completely naturalistic view of biology. "What Justice Brennan described as 'a religious viewpoint' is the broad proposition that a purposeful supernatural being—God—is responsible for our existence. The leading alternative to that belief is that purposeless material processes created us and that purpose and consciousness did not exist in the cosmos until they evolved naturalistically."[31] Far from being neutral on religious matters, the Supreme Court decision marginalizes religion and gives a monopoly to naturalistic opinions.

In a chapter titled "The Established Religious Philosophy of America," Johnson writes, "The United States of America does not have an established church, but it does have (and always has had) an established religion, or at least a dominant religious philosophy, an established way of thinking about religion."[32] According to Johnson, there was nothing sinister or unconstitutional about this arrangement, since the philosophy wasn't formally enacted and dissenters weren't punished. The philosophy was "established" in the sense that it provided a basis for lawmaking and public education, preventing these from becoming incoherent or chaotic. In the nineteenth century the established religious philosophy was the Protestant version of Christianity. Protestant tolerance of Catholics and Jews "varied greatly depending on time or place," but there was little dispute on basic moral questions, since these groups "agreed upon a common tradition stemming from the Bible."[33]

Johnson sees a much different situation in the second half of the twentieth century, as the old religious philosophy has been replaced by a new one:

> When I want a long and fully descriptive name for it, I call the established religious philosophy of late-twentieth-century America "scientific naturalism and liberal rationalism." When I just want a convenient label, I shorten this cumbersome term and call the ruling philosophy simply "naturalism" or "modernism." Modernism as an intellectual condition begins when people realize that God is really dead and that humankind is therefore on its own.[34]

But Johnson isn't ready to let this new philosophy go unchallenged. He stakes out an alternative position that he labels "theistic realism," a term that "signifies that I am convinced that God is objectively real, not merely a concept or fantasy in my own mind."[35]

With the battle lines between naturalism and theistic realism drawn in appropriate Manichean fashion, Johnson laments the lack of soldiers on the theistic side:

What is missing from the contemporary intellectual world is a qualified opposition party that is willing and able to challenge the established religious philosophy itself, the metaphysical naturalism that is so successfully promoted in the name of science by such as Weinberg, Hawking, Sagan, Gould, Dawkins and Crick. The logical opposition party would consist of scientifically informed theologians, or perhaps theologically informed scientists, who respect the experimental method within its limits but who do not assume a priori that all of reality can be understood in naturalistic or materialistic terms.[36]

According to Johnson, the absence of an "opposition party" is proof of the power of naturalism in the academy, which forces theistic scientists and even Christian theologians to accommodate to its vision in order to survive.

Johnson once again makes his case for theistic realism. This time he invokes the Bible, but not the section previously associated with creationism:

The most important statement in Scripture about creation is not contained in Genesis but in the opening verses of the Gospel of John:

In the beginning was the Word, and the Word was with God, and Word was God. He was in the beginning. All things came into being through him, and without him not one thing came into being. (John 1:1–3)

This statement plainly says that creation was by a force that was (and is) intelligent and personal.

The essential, bedrock position of scientific naturalism is the direct opposite of John 1:1–3. Naturalistic evolutionary theory, as part of the grand metaphysical story of science, says that creation was by impersonal and unintelligent forces.[37]

The closing section of the book's final chapter is titled "The Choice We Face," and it reinforces Johnson's call for Christians to join the fight against naturalism rather than engage in fruitless accommodation. Theologians of the nineteenth and twentieth centuries made the tragic mistake of going along with naturalism in science, failing to understand the all-encompassing ambitions of scientists. Naturalistic science eventually claimed the authority to interpret objective reality, leaving theology with mere subjective experience. Naturalistic Christianity, Johnson writes, is "a hollow shell," and Christian institutions that accept naturalistic metaphysics inevitably go down the path of secularization that formerly Christian universities went down in the past (a clear use of the slippery slope fallacy). The alternative choice is to follow Johnson's call to fight for theistic realism, "to assert that God is real and that the evidence reflects the truth that nature was created by God."[38]

With the publication of *Reason in the Balance*, Johnson established the core ideological themes of the intelligent design movement. Subsequent books by Johnson and other leaders elaborated on these themes and defended them from critics.

Stage 3: Reaching New Audiences

Phillip E. Johnson followed *Reason in the Balance* with a pair of shorter, less weighty books. After having a conversation with staff at InterVarsity Press, Johnson decided to write a third book for them titled *Defeating Darwinism by Opening Minds*.[39] This book was aimed at high school juniors and seniors and beginning college undergraduates, along with their parents, with the goal of helping young people "to protect themselves against the indoctrination in naturalism that so often accompanies education."[40]

For the most part, this book reiterates the arguments of his previous two in simpler, less technical language. However, in a chapter commenting on the pro-evolution play *Inherit the Wind*, Johnson expands his critique of the media, essentially portraying the media as an extension of the Darwinist establishment. He also expands his critique of liberal Protestantism. It's bad enough that adopting liberal (that is, naturalistic) Christianity causes universities to secularize, but it also leads individual Christians to lose their faith. Johnson issues a warning to evangelical Christians entering universities to stand fast against the naturalistic environment:

> Young intellectuals may insist for years that they are still believers, but then one day they wake up to realize that their belief has been emptied

of its content, and they either throw away the empty shell or fill it with something else. That is why every mainstream Christian institution is beset from within these days by people who want the church to turn away from the old business of sin and salvation and devote its energies to whatever social causes are currently fashionable in the secular world.[41]

Again, we see the argument that naturalism places authentic Christian faith on a slippery slope.

A year later InterVarsity Press published *Objections Sustained: Subversive Essays on Evolution, Law and Culture.*[42] This book reprinted essays and book reviews that Johnson had written over the previous few years, most of which were published in the conservative Christian journals *First Things* and *Books & Culture* (which is affiliated with *Christianity Today*, the flagship magazine of the evangelical center). Here we see Johnson working out many of the ideas that would appear in later books.

Stage 4: Twenty-First-Century Optimism

In 2000 InterVarsity Press published Johnson's fifth book related to intelligent design, *The Wedge of Truth: Splitting the Foundations of Naturalism.*[43] This book included Johnson's critiques of Darwinism (most of them recycled from previous books) but also looked forward optimistically to what the intelligent design movement would accomplish in the twenty-first century. The "Wedge" in the title was Johnson's metaphor for the movement, which was hard at work splitting the "log" of naturalism that blocked progress for society.

The introduction to the book discussed how the movement would accomplish its goal:

> Our strategy is to drive the thin edge of our Wedge into the cracks in the log of naturalism by bringing long-neglected questions to the surface and introducing them into public debate. Of course, the initial penetration is not the whole story, because the Wedge can split the log only if it thickens as it penetrates. If we are raising the right questions after a long period in which those questions have been suppressed, then new avenues of inquiry should be suggested, and thinking will go off in new directions. A new body of research and scholarship will gradually emerge, and in time

the adherents of the old dogma will be left behind, unable to comprehend the questions that have suddenly become too important to ignore.[44]

Here we see the overconfidence that is so characteristic of the Christian Right. The assumption is that, with God on their side, success is inevitable despite the formidable power of the opposition.

Stage 5: Intelligent Design in the Post-9/11 Era

Johnson's next book, published by InterVarsity Press in 2002, was *The Right Questions: Truth, Meaning and Public Debate*.[45] The tone of this book is markedly different, the result of two major "catastrophes" that impacted Johnson's life, one personal and one public, in 2001. The personal catastrophe, which occurred in July of that year, was a stroke that threatened to end his career as a writer and speaker for intelligent design. The public catastrophe was of course the September 11 terrorist attacks on the United States. His books had always espoused politically conservative ideas, but this one was unprecedented in its blatant partisanship. Johnson praises President George W. Bush and the war in Afghanistan, while condemning former president George H. W. Bush for having left Saddam Hussein in power following the first Gulf War. Johnson condemns liberal media, clergy, and intellectuals for not backing George W. Bush's anti-terrorism agenda, and he lauds the new conservative media outlets for their "critical analysis" of liberal elites.[46]

As we've seen, Johnson embraces a Manichean vision that pits authentic Christian faith against Darwinist naturalism, with no compromise possible. It's not surprising, then, that he embraced George W. Bush's Manichean foreign policy vision. In *The Right Questions*, Johnson draws a parallel between Bush and the Russian novelist and political dissident Aleksandr Solzhenitsyn. In a 1978 speech, Solzhenitsyn had talked about the distinction between "the freedom for good deeds and the freedom for evil deeds." Johnson comments, "By 1978 drawing a sharp distinction between good and evil seemed obsolete and illiberal to fashionable opinion. Twenty-four years later a similar relativist fashion deplored President George W. Bush's reference to an 'axis of evil.'"[47]

This was clearly a straw person attack. Critics of Bush's "axis of evil" comment knew that there's a difference between good and evil actions.

What they objected to was that Bush labeled particular *nations* entirely good or entirely evil. What's more, Solzhenitsyn himself warned in *The Gulag Archipelago* that the line dividing good and evil doesn't run between people, but cuts through the heart of every human being.[48] It's a huge understatement to say that Bush lacked Solzhenitsyn's intellect, but their differences were apparently lost on Johnson. This was a disturbing indication of Johnson's own state of mind.

Yet another striking feature of *The Right Questions* was Johnson's most explicit effort yet to link the intelligent design project to conservative views on gender. A chapter titled "Genesis and Gender" opens with the story of a university professor who embraced feminist theory, a product of naturalistic thought. While the professor and his wife claimed that they would have been comfortable had their son come out as gay, they struggled when he instead came out as transgender and insisted on being accepted as a woman. Johnson comments, "My reaction to the story was not to ridicule but to pity, and to reflect on how both the father's confusion and the son's preposterous rebellion both grew logically from ideas that are so taken for granted in the academic world that it would be difficult to find a professor who could forcefully and persuasively refute them."[49] The problem, according to Johnson, was that Darwinist thinking had erased the biblical teaching that God created people male and female and that gender reflects God's purpose for our lives.[50] "People in our time," Johnson says, "are so ignorant of the order of creation that they imagine that the distinctions of feminine and masculine natures are things that man invented and that man can abolish or alter."[51]

Stage 6: Engaging the New Atheism

Phillip E. Johnson's seventh intelligent design book, cowritten with the Biola University philosophy professor John Mark Reynolds, was *Against All Gods: What's Right and Wrong about the New Atheism*, published in 2010 by InterVarsity Press's new IVP Books division.[52] The book addresses the so-called new atheist authors Richard Dawkins, Sam Harris, and Daniel Dennett. Rather than assaulting these authors, Johnson and Reynolds use a calm tone. Johnson proclaims in the book's introduction, "What I like about atheists is that although they tend to give the wrong answers, they also tend to raise the right questions."[53] The coauthors feel that the case for atheism "should be taken seriously and considered both respectfully and critically" and that discussions about it should take place in academic settings.[54]

Conclusion: Intelligent Design's Paranoid Foundation

We can sum up Phillip E. Johnson's paranoid vision as follows: An American society once dominated by Christianity has been taken over by the naturalist thinking associated with Darwinism. Christians are still numerous but have been pushed to the margins in terms of cultural influence. Meanwhile, Darwinists conceal from the public both the flaws in their scientific theory and the extent to which Darwinism is incompatible with authentic religious belief. Under these conditions, compromising with the enemy camp is foolish and self-defeating. Christians need to fight back and destroy the Darwinist establishment. Indeed, the "wedge" strategy is already bearing fruit and will achieve success before the twenty-first century is over.

A quick glance at books by other promoters of intelligent design tells us that the movement as a whole adopted Johnson's paranoid vision. We can see this dynamic in *Darwin's Nemesis: Phillip Johnson and the Intelligent Design Movement*, a collection of essays by intelligent design luminaries celebrating Johnson's leadership in the movement. The preface, by William A. Dembski, recalls a banquet at Biola University in which Johnson's colleagues in the movement heaped praise on him. This included comments by John Mark Reynolds, who "lauded his mentor as the 'Wizard of Berkeley' and likened him to Tolkien's Gandalf leading his followers to destroy the ring of Scientific Naturalism."[55] Anyone familiar with Tolkien's *Lord of the Rings* trilogy knows that it's an epic tale of good struggling to overcome powerful evil forces, and Christian interpreters of the book have viewed Gandalf as a Christ figure.[56] Reynolds was giving Johnson high praise indeed while at the same time affirming his Manichean vision. The epilogue by the Baylor engineering professor Walter L. Bradley is also very revealing:

> With the publication of *Darwin on Trial*, Phillip Johnson immediately became recognized as the intellectual leader of the group of scholars that God had raised up to address the question of biological origins and

the troubling issue of naturalism that invariably accompanies this question. . . . His ability to energize and organize all of us who had previously labored more or less independently to begin to function as a larger organic whole was the beginning of the ID movement. Phil saw himself appropriately as the intellectual architect of this movement, sketching in broad strokes the critical questions, both scientifically and philosophically, and then depending on those with various scientific and philosophical expertises to address these questions in depth.[57]

In other words, the other movement leaders built upon, but never challenged, the paranoid vision that Johnson established.

Reaching for Scientific Credibility

Phillip E. Johnson's expertise is in law, not science. He has always insisted that scientific training isn't necessary for critiquing Darwinism, since it's a belief system supported by philosophical assumptions, not empirical evidence. Nevertheless, the intelligent design movement needed input from those with scientific expertise if it stood any chance of achieving scientific credibility. Arguably, the two most important contributions along these lines came from the biochemist Michael J. Behe and the mathematician and philosopher William A. Dembski. Johnson's later books draw significantly on both men's arguments.

Behe gave the intelligent design movement a significant boost with the publication of his 1996 book *Darwin's Black Box: The Biochemical Challenge to Evolution*.[58] The book's title refers to the fact that Darwin had no knowledge of the biochemical structures inside cells. According to Behe, once we understand the complexity of these structures, we realize that Darwinism is insufficient to explain their origins. The signature idea that Behe introduces in the book is *irreducible complexity*. According to Darwin's theory of evolution, biological organisms undergo incremental change through natural selection fueled by random mutation. However, according to Behe, some biological systems cannot evolve piecemeal because they offer no survival advantage to organisms unless all the pieces are in place. He uses the analogy of a mousetrap, which won't catch any mice unless all the parts are present and assembled correctly. A mousetrap is irreducibly complex, as are many of the structures in cells. From this we have to conclude that the design of an intelligent agent, not random mutation, is the correct explanation for the origin of these structures.

Dembski offers ideas that are complementary to Behe's in his 1998 book *The Design Inference*.[59] Here the signature concept is *specified complexity*. According to Dembski, we can recognize design in nature when we come across highly improbable (complex) events that fit an independently identifiable pattern (in other words, they have specification). He expands on this concept in his next monograph, *Intelligent Design: The Bridge between Science and Theology*, in which he presents intelligent design as a theory of information.[60] He argues that life requires vast amounts of information encoded in DNA, and only intelligence can provide it. "Neither algorithms nor natural laws, however, are capable of producing information. The great myth of modern evolutionary biology is that information can be gotten on the cheap without recourse to intelligence."[61]

Intelligent Design on a Cosmic Scale

Not content with arguing for the intelligent design of new species and cell structures, the intelligent design movement eventually expanded its scope to argue for the intelligent design of Earth's location in the cosmos and the physical properties of the universe that make life possible. This new agenda was the work of the astronomer Guillermo Gonzalez and the philosopher (and Discovery Institute vice president) Jay W. Richards, which they presented in their 2004 book *The Privileged Planet: How Our Place in the Cosmos Is Designed for Discovery*.[62] Gonzalez and Richards begin by challenging the notion that the vastness of the universe guarantees an abundance of life, including intelligent life: "Mounting evidence suggests that the conditions necessary for complex life are exceedingly rare, and that the probability of them all converging at the same place and time is minute."[63] Furthermore, there's reason to believe that Earth's rare combination of conditions is more than a fluke. Not only does Earth's location make it ideal for developing complex life, contend the authors, but it also makes it ideal for scientific discovery: "Our claim is that Earth's conditions allow for a stunning diversity of measurements, from cosmology and galactic astronomy to stellar astrophysics and geophysics."[64] For example, the moon is correctly placed to create perfect solar eclipses, which "are optimal for measuring a range of important phenomena, such as solar flash spectrum, [solar] prominences, starlight deflection, and the Earth's rotation."[65] The authors suggest that the convergence on Earth of "habitability and measurability" point to the work of an intelligent designer:

> Even more mysterious than the fact that our location is so congenial to diverse measurement and discovery is that these same conditions appear to correlate with habitability. This is strange, because there's no obvious reason to assume that the very same rare properties that allow for our existence would also provide the best overall setting to make discoveries about the world around us. We don't think this is merely coincidental. It cries out for another explanation, an explanation that suggests there's more to the cosmos than we have been willing to entertain or even imagine.[66]

The authors go on to discuss the physical laws and constants of the universe: mass density, weak nuclear force, strong nuclear force, proton-to-electron mass ratio, gravitational force, cosmological constant, and electromagnetic force. They conclude that these appear to be fine-tuned to just the right values that would allow the existence of life. Again, they see compelling evidence for the work of an intelligent designer.

The authors insist that all of this refutes the Copernican Principle, also known as the Principle of Mediocrity or Principle of Indifference, adhered to by the scientific establishment. The "modest" version states that "we should assume that there's nothing special or exceptional about the time or place of Earth in the cosmos."[67] The authors express particular concern about the "more expansive" version: "We're not here for a purpose, and the cosmos isn't arranged with us in mind. Our metaphysical status is as insignificant as our astronomical location."[68] The authors associate the expansive version with naturalism, "the view that the (impersonal) material world is all there is and that it exists for no purpose," a view that enjoys "official majority status among the cultural elite."[69] In language echoing Johnson's, Gonzalez and Richards repeatedly condemn the Copernican Principle as "dogma" unsupported by the scientific evidence. Also echoing Johnson, Gonzalez and Richards claim that the dreaded philosophy of naturalism infects not only the "Darwinist establishment" of biology, but also scientists working in fields such as physics and astronomy.

Intelligent Design and Its Critics

Not surprisingly, the combined efforts of Johnson, Behe, Dembski, and other champions of intelligent design have not been enough to gain the movement acceptance as genuine science. Most advocates of evolution simply dismiss intelligent design as a repackaged form of creation science unworthy of formal response. Those who have taken the time to respond have found numerous flaws with the movement. Among the most articulate critics of intelligent design is the philosopher of science Robert Pennock. After writing several articles criticizing intelligent design, he published his 1999 book *Tower of Babel: The Evidence against the New Creationism.*[70] Other books have contained criticisms of intelligent design as part of a larger discussion of science and religion, including Kenneth R. Miller's *Finding Darwin's God: A Scientist's Search for Common Ground between God and Evolution* and Francis S. Collins's *The Language of God: A Scientist Presents Evidence for Belief.*[71]

In most cases, a social movement will want to respond effectively to its critics. Criticism makes it more difficult for a movement to secure resources and attract followers. But a paranoid social movement will often respond to critics by depicting them as part of the "vast conspiracy" that the movement is fighting. Outside criticism, then, isn't evidence of flaws in the movement, it shows the determination of evil or ignorant enemies to stop the movement. We can see this pattern in intelligent design supporters' responses to criticism from evolutionists.

Chapter 6 of Johnson's book *The Wedge of Truth* is titled "The Empire Strikes Back: What Are the Arguments against Intelligent Design?" The *Star Wars* reference immediately transports us to a Manichean world where intelligent design partisans are the heroes of the Rebel Alliance, while critics are the evil Imperial Stormtroopers, or perhaps even Darth Vader. If you're expecting Johnson to grab his rhetorical light saber, you won't be disappointed. The chapter begins with Johnson describing Pennock's *Tower of Babel* and Miller's *Finding Darwin's God* as "the best that Darwinists have been able to do in meeting the arguments for intelligent design."[72] He then quickly dismisses them: "Both books simply refuse to take seriously any arguments against Darwinism or materialism, relying heavily on caricatures, ridicule and the strong negative implications of the term *creationism*. The basic line of attack is that any dissent from evolutionary naturalism is founded not on scientific evidence but on religious prejudice."[73] After responding to some of the authors' specific criticisms of intelligent design, Johnson argues that "the barrage of rhetorical missiles is an offensive in a culture war rather than a serious attempt to grapple with scientific issues."[74] He then extends his condemnation to Darwinists more broadly:

> Seeing themselves as embattled in a culture war against barbarians who want to return society to something like the Dark Ages, the defenders of scientific naturalism are extraordinarily undiscriminating about the arguments they employ. The strategy is to throw everything that comes to hand at the enemy in the hope that something will destroy this baffling, irrational menace.[75]

William A. Dembski offers a similar if less dramatic defense of the intelligent design movement. The appendix to Dembski's book *Intelligent Design* responds to some of the objections to the movement's arguments, but not before he offers a conspiratorial interpretation of why these objections exist in the first place:

> The objections considered here are better called "gatekeeper" objections. They find fault with design because of the threat that design is said to pose to science and not because the theoretical or empirical case for design is scientifically substandard. The impulse behind these objections is to keep the world safe for science and science safe from the world; the impulse is not to expand the boundaries of science and thereby enhance our knowledge of the world.[76]

In other words, these critiques of the intelligent design movement are simply further evidence of the determination of Darwinists to maintain their power.

It's beyond the scope of this chapter to review all the back-and-forth arguments between intelligent design proponents and their critics. What I'll do instead is focus on one significant criticism of intelligent design and the response to it, so you can see how a paranoid science movement defends itself.

After Johnson published *Darwin on Trial*, Robert Pennock wrote a review of the book entitled "Naturalism, Evidence, and Creationism: The Case of Phillip Johnson," which appeared in the journal *Biology and Philosophy* in 1996.[77] Pennock pointed out that Johnson's critique of naturalism failed to account for the different varieties of naturalism. In particular, Johnson failed to differentiate between methodological naturalism, a mode of scientific inquiry that seeks explanations in the natural world, and ontological naturalism, which "makes a commitment to substantive claims about what exists in nature, and then adds a closure clause stating 'and that is all there is.'"[78] According to Pennock, by conflating these two forms of naturalism, Johnson was falsely accusing scientists of ontological naturalism. Pennock's critique framed Johnson as someone unschooled in even the basics of the philosophy of science and thus unqualified to stand in judgment of evolutionary biology. In other words, Pennock declared a "mistrial" of Darwin.

The journal's editors let Johnson know about Pennock's impending article and gave him the opportunity to write a reply for the same issue. In "Response to Pennock," Johnson insisted that the distinction between methodological and ontological naturalism was illusory:

> We who know how this game of bait-and-switch is played just look for the "switch" that turns innocent "methodological" naturalism into the real thing. In Pennock's version, the switch is the argument that naturalism and rationality are virtually identical—because he thinks that attributing the design of organisms to an intelligence would imply that all events occur at the whim of capricious gods, so that there would be no regularities for scientists to observe.[79]

The insistence that methodological naturalism and ontological naturalism are virtually equivalent has become a standard feature of intelligent design writings. In his book *Intelligent Design*, Dembski follows Johnson's lead:

> We need to realize that methodological naturalism is the functional equivalent of a full-blown metaphysical naturalism. Metaphysical natu-

ralism asserts that nature is self-sufficient. Methodological naturalism asks us for the sake of science to pretend that nature is self-sufficient. But once science is taken as the only universally valid form of knowledge within a culture, it follows that methodological and metaphysical naturalism become functionally equivalent.[80]

In their responses to Pennock, Johnson and Dembski try to reinforce a conspiratorial view of scientists. Johnson accuses Pennock of acting disingenuously to hide the real agenda of naturalists. In Dembski's phrase "once science is taken as the only universally valid form of knowledge within a culture," he's suggesting that Darwinist scientists have the status of cultural overlords. We can see a second dynamic at work in these responses as well. Intelligent design supporters respond to calls to add nuance to their dualistic picture of the world by vigorously reasserting the original dualism. Essentially, Pennock and other critics were insisting, "It's not that simple," and intelligent design proponents were responding, "Yes it is!"

Intelligent Design's Atheist "Frenemies"

Phillip E. Johnson has nothing but scorn for Christians who accept evolution. He places both Robert Pennock and Kenneth Miller in this category (what he calls "theistic modernists"), and we've seen the rhetorical assaults he unleashes on both. You might think that Johnson and his colleagues would have even harsher words for openly atheist evolution advocates, but that's not the case. Intelligent design defenders approach their atheist opponents with a combination of criticism and praise, and even maintain friendly personal relationships with some of them.

This dynamic first surfaced in the epilogue to the 1993 second edition of Johnson's *Darwin on Trial*. Johnson mentions the Cornell University historian of science William Provine, an evolutionist and atheist, whose first interaction with Johnson was to write a scathing critique of one of Johnson's articles. However, Provine came to see the common ground that they shared. As Johnson describes their unfolding relationship,

In his words, we both think that "prominent evolutionists have joined with equally prominent theologians and religious leaders to sweep under the rug the incompatibilities of evolution and [theistic] religion, and we both deplore this strategy." A year after *Darwin on Trial* appeared, and after Provine and I had met in a friendly debate, the area of agreement seemed to expand. Provine teaches a course in evolutionary biology at Cornell University with over 400 students, and he assigned all of them to read my book and write a term paper on it. He sought me out in Berkeley for a memorable breakfast discussion and invited me to Cornell that fall to guest-lecture in his course and to spend a full day discussing the issue with the students and graduate teaching assistants. . . . Provine and I have become very friendly adversaries, because our agreement about how to define the question is more important than our disagreement about how to answer it.[81]

We see a similar congenial attitude in Johnson and Reynolds's 2010 book *Against All Gods: What's Right and Wrong about the New Atheism.* As Johnson and Reynolds state in the introduction,

Our attitude toward the surge in atheism is that it opens up an opportunity for university discussions in and out of the classroom that can make teaching more exciting for the instructor and for the students. With that in mind, our intention is not to attack the atheists but to explore the case they are making, in the hope of encouraging classroom instructors to put the arguments for atheism on the table for academic consideration.[82]

This is quite a contrast with Johnson's rhetorical approach to "theistic modernists" such as Pennock and Miller. The authors go on to say that they agree with "our atheist friends" that all views should be subject to critical analysis. What stands out in this statement is not the agreement, but that they would use "friends" to describe atheists. Given intelligent design leaders' Manichean worldview that equates Darwinism with the forces of darkness, this is a startling choice of words.

How do we explain intelligent design proponents' paradoxical attitude toward atheists, particularly the so-called new atheists? It's helpful to understand that new atheists occupy a paranoid world of their own that is the mirror image of the intelligent design world. For the defenders of intelligent design, naturalism is the most significant negative force in society. The new atheists view religion the same way. Johnson and

Reynolds recognize the parallels between themselves and new atheists even if they fail to recognize the shared paranoia:

> Dawkins and Dennett seem to think that the American and British people live in an age of theocratic oppression, from which they will want to escape if they are shown that escape is possible. I argue that the true oppressor in our time is scientific naturalism, a philosophy that has become dominant in culture and government because eloquent representatives of the scientific establishment have taught us to believe that the success of science in providing technology is tied to the worldview of naturalism, so that any questioning of the worldview endangers the continuance of the technology.[83]

As inhabitants of Manichean worlds that mirror each other, intelligent design proponents and new atheists share a common enemy—those nonparanoid moderates who seek harmony rather than warfare between religion and evolution.

Yet the new atheists don't reciprocate the friendly treatment they receive from the intelligent design movement. (Provine, who had friendly relations with Johnson, was not considered part of the new atheism.) This is because the intelligent design movement depends on the new atheists for credibility, but the converse isn't true. As I've noted, one significant element of Johnson's paranoid worldview is the claim that leading Darwinists are hiding from the public the fact that their theory is incompatible with authentic religious belief. As evidence for this claim, Johnson and other intelligent design authors point to the pronouncements of the new atheists, whom they claim are publicly saying what other Darwinists say in private. This conspiratorial view is summed up nicely in Johnson and Reynolds's *Against All Gods*:

> Up to the present time, scientific authorities have thought that the only way to persuade the American public to accept the Darwinian theory of evolution is to reassure them that a fully naturalistic account of the history of life poses no threat to a religious belief in the existence of God. Only fundamentalist varieties of religion that ought to be discarded anyway are threatened by evolutionary science, these authorities say.

The new breed of scientific atheists dismisses these reassurances as dishonest, reflecting a cowardly spirit of appeasement. Instead of appeasing the forces of unreason, why not go to the root of the problem and show that the very concept of a supernatural being or force is delusional, and leads only to harm.[84]

In the continuing trial of Darwinism, new atheists provide essential testimony for the prosecution without which their case crumbles. That the witnesses are making false statements is a reality that the prosecution would just as soon ignore.

The Dover Trial

The intelligent design movement reached the peak of its notoriety in 2005 as a result of a court case from Dover, Pennsylvania, entitled *Tammy Kitzmiller et al. v. Dover Area School District et al.* Parents of students enrolled in the Dover public schools had sued the school district for its inclusion of intelligent design in the school curriculum, arguing that this was an unconstitutional establishment of religion. The Dover policy was not created in consultation with the Discovery Institute, yet the writings of intelligent design proponents were very much part of the trial, and Michael Behe appeared as a witness for the defense. Given intelligent design's extensive use of religious language, it's hardly surprising that Judge John E. Jones III concluded in his ruling that intelligent design is an inherently religious project. However, it was the religious motives of members of the district's school board that ultimately led Jones to side with the plaintiffs.[85]

Judge Jones rendered his decision just as the previously mentioned book *Darwin's Nemesis* was going to press. However, editor William A. Dembski was able to add a section titled "Life after Dover" to the preface. Dembski warns against viewing the ruling as a Waterloo for the intelligent design movement. Since the Supreme Court has not ruled on the legality of teaching intelligent design in public schools, he reasons, we can expect continued grassroots pressure to promote this alternative to Darwinism. Moreover, the courts are powerless to censor intelligent design on college and university campuses where an increasing number of students are showing interest. He even goes so far as to suggest that it was better that Judge Jones ruled against intelligent design, since a favorable ruling "would have encouraged complacency."[86] He concludes by insisting that Darwinism, not intelligent design, is in trouble:

> Just as a tree that has been "ringed" (i.e., had its bark completely cut through on all sides) is effectively dead even if it retains its leaves and appears alive, so Darwinism has met its match with the movement initiated by Phillip Johnson. Expect Darwinism's death throes, like Judge Jones's decision, to continue for some time. But don't mistake death throes for true vitality. Ironically, Judge Jones's decision is likely to prove a blessing for the intelligent design movement, spurring its proponents to greater heights and thereby fostering its intellectual vitality and ultimate success.[87]

Judge Jones's decision does appear to have spurred Dembski to greater heights—of imagination. Framing the humiliating loss at the Dover trial as a positive event for the intelligent design movement was no easy feat. However, given the movement leaders' confidence that God will bring them victory, Dembski had no choice but to insert a message like this into the book before it went to press.

Intelligent Design Goes Hollywood

No discussion of the intelligent design movement's paranoia would be complete without including the 2008 pro–intelligent design movie *Expelled: No Intelligence Allowed*, starring the actor, comedian, and conservative political activist Ben Stein. The early scenes in the movie show Stein investigating intelligent design by meeting with various people associated with the movement, skeptically asking whether intelligent design is a legitimate scientific movement or just about religion. Driving to a coffee shop to meet Stephen Meyer, director of the Discovery Institute's Center for Science and Culture, Stein proclaims, "I'll pin him down like a butterfly on a butterfly board—a butterfly killing board." These displays of skepticism are contrived, of course. The pseudo-documentary was planned from the beginning to make a case for intelligent design. Any skepticism Stein had about the intelligent design movement was over long before the cameras started rolling.

Also deceptive are the scenes of Stein's first visit to the Discovery Institute's headquarters in Seattle, Washington. Stein asks people on the streets of Seattle to point him in the direction of the Discovery Institute, and none of them knows the location. When he does find the office, he makes a big deal about the fact that it occupies only one floor of the office building. Discovery Institute director Bruce Chapman responds, "We're like the little boy who said the emperor has no clothes, and he didn't have a big organization, either." All of this is meant to portray the Discovery Institute as a small and marginal organization, as opposed to a right-wing think tank backed by wealthy donors. The fact that people on the street are unaware of its location is hardly surprising, given that political elites largely operate out of the public eye. And one floor of a large office building is plenty of space, considering that most Discovery Institute fellows are employed elsewhere and have their own offices.

For the most part, *Expelled* repeats the arguments for intelligent design found in the writings of movement leaders but takes advantage of the extra capacity for drama allowed by an audiovisual medium. We see the faces and hear the voices of supposed victims of the dreaded "Darwinist establishment" employed in academia, journalism, and the Smithsonian National Museum of Natural History. Archival footage of the Berlin Wall being constructed makes the not-so-subtle point that the Darwinist oppression of science resembles the oppression by Communist regimes. The outrage is punctuated by a comic element, as you would expect from Ben Stein, mostly snippets of old movies to create humorous juxtapositions and to poke fun at advocates of evolution. Also significant is Stein's school uniform with sneakers, a nod to AC/DC guitarist and bad boy Angus Young.

The movie takes intelligent design paranoia to the next level by suggesting that Darwinism bears significant responsibility for the creation of Nazism. After touring the Dachau memorial to victims of the Holocaust, Stein further ponders the connection between Darwinism and Nazism: "I know that Darwinism does not automatically equate to Nazism, but if Darwinism inspired and justified such horrific events in the past, could it be used to rationalize similar initiatives today?" His answer is yes, it can. As evidence he cites societal tolerance for abortion, which he implicitly equates with the Holocaust, a common rhetorical move among anti-abortion activists. He also cites the growing tolerance for euthanasia, which he allows Discovery Institute fellow David Berlinski to define as "getting rid of useless people," as opposed to giving suffering individuals the freedom to end their own lives. Both trends, according to Stein, follow from a Darwin-inspired devaluing of the human.

Expelled was embraced by much of the evangelical world. The back of the DVD displays the endorsement of the right-wing paranoid icon Glenn Beck, who declared, "You will cheer!" However, the movie was ridiculed by almost everyone else reviewing it. The *New York Times* review called it "one of the sleaziest documentaries to arrive in a very long time, . . . a conspiracy-theory rant masquerading as investigative inquiry."[88] A review in the mainline Protestant magazine the *Christian Century* wryly noted, "Stein violates Godwin's Law about fighting on blogs: the first person to mention the Nazis loses. And does Stein ever mention the Nazis!"[89] The National Center for Science Education created a website titled "Expelled Exposed: Why Expelled Flunks" (expelledexposed.com), copying the graffiti font styles used in the movie and effectively debunking many of the movie's arguments.

The Continued Battle over Public School Curricula

Expelled demonstrates clearly that intelligent design advocates have no intention of giving up the fight in the wake of their defeat in Dover. Even though they make no new arguments, they continue to churn out books promoting the movement. But the most significant work being done to advance intelligent design is taking place in state legislatures, particularly where Republicans dominate. These activities are carefully tracked and publicized by the National Center for Science Education, a long-time creationism foe (NCSE.com). The pro–intelligent design actions in Dover were a grassroots effort, but legislative attempts to promote intelligent design in public schools have usually featured close involvement by the Discovery Institute, sometimes supported by Focus on the Family affiliates.

These efforts have succeeded in Louisiana and Tennessee. The Louisiana state legislature passed the 2008 Science Education Act, which interferes with the teaching of evolution (along with climate change and human cloning) by using the familiar "teach the controversy" approach pioneered by the creation science movement. The stated goal of the Louisiana legislation is "to create and foster an environment within public elementary and secondary schools that promotes critical thinking skills, logical analysis, and open and objective discussion of scientific theories being studied including, but not limited to, evolution, the origins of life, global warming, and human cloning."[90] To discourage court challenges on First Amendment grounds, the legislation adds the disingenuous qualification, "This Section shall not be construed to promote any religious doctrine, promote discrimination for or against a particular set of religious beliefs, or promote discrimination for or against religion or nonreligion."[91] The Tennessee state legislature passed similar legislation, derided in the media as the "Tennessee Monkey Bill," in 2012.[92] Until such laws are declared unconstitutional, we can expect the Discovery Institute and its allies to continue to push for similar laws wherever the political climate is favorable.

Intelligent Design's Identity Crisis

Many critics say that intelligent design supporters publicly misrepresent the true nature of the movement. The reality is actually worse—the movement doesn't even have a coherent representation of itself. Instead, it simultaneously presents two diametrically opposed messages about its identity. To understand this contradiction, we need to consider a branch of sociology known as social movement theory. According to this theory, social movements employ *collective action frames*, which the sociologists Robert Benford and David Snow define as "action-oriented sets of beliefs and meanings that inspire and legitimate the activities and campaigns of a social movement organization."[93] It's the task of a movement's leaders to articulate a frame for the movement that clearly defines who they are and why others should support them.[94]

For intelligent design, however, this task is nearly impossible, because the movement is situated at the intersection of science, religion, and politics. To be accepted as a legitimate scientific movement in the contemporary world, the intelligent design movement needs to come up with a frame suggesting that intelligent design is disconnected from religion and politics.[95] I call this the "pure science" frame. At stake is not only entrance into public school curricula but acceptance by universities and organizations that fund scientific research.

At the same time, intelligent design is a religious and political movement with clear ties to the American Christian Right. To be successful, leaders must persuade evangelicals and other religious conservatives to support their cause. They try to do this with what I call the "religious crusade" frame. Since intelligent design faces competition from both its "right" (creation science) and its "left" (theistic evolution), support from religious conservatives has never been guaranteed.[96] Moreover, the intelligent design movement needs individuals who will actively support it (for example, run for local school boards in order to influence science curricula) as opposed to merely accepting its ideas. Intelligent design proponents use the "religious crusade" frame to persuade religious conservatives that supporting the movement is a moral imperative.

The intelligent design movement employs three different strategies for managing the contradiction between these two frames. These strategies are division of labor, discursive tacking, and distinguishing between supposed primary and secondary missions.

Division of Labor

The division of labor strategy means that certain authors emphasize one frame while others emphasize the other frame. Phillip E. Johnson is clearly the main proponent responsible for articulating the "religious crusade" frame, and we've already seen significant religious and political elements in his paranoid vision. Particularly important is his call for "theistic realism" based on his reading of John 1:1–3.

We can also find the "religious crusade" frame in the work of the evangelical writer Lee Strobel. Strobel has worked as a teaching pastor at two of the largest evangelical megachurches in the United States, Saddleback and Willow Creek. He has also written several popular apologetic books. He reveals his connection to intelligent design in *The Case for a Creator: A Journalist Investigates Scientific Evidence That Points toward God*.[97] The book tells the story of how Darwinism caused Strobel to abandon his Christian faith as a teenager. However, after recommitting to Christianity as an adult, he eventually learned about prominent scientists who argued that Darwinism is flawed. This led him, in good journalistic fashion, to investigate the evidence. The heart of the book consists of chapters devoted to interviews with these scientific "experts," who, of course, are none other than prominent intelligent design advocates such as Stephen Meyer, Michael Behe, and Guillermo Gonzalez. The book ends with Strobel's conclusion that the cumulative evidence points decisively to the existence of a creator, not the random process of natural selection. As the title of the book makes clear and the content makes clearer, the "creator" is not some anonymous designer but the God of the Bible. *The Case for a Creator* isn't as overtly political as Johnson's writings, but it does argue that Darwinism is a threat to Christian faith and that Christians should throw their support behind the courageous work of intelligent design scientists.

We find quite a different atmosphere when we turn to Michael Behe's book *Darwin's Black Box*, which is firmly rooted in the "pure science" frame. As I discussed earlier, Behe's thesis is that natural selection can't explain the development of "irreducibly complex" cell structures, suggesting that they are the product of an intelligent designer. However, Behe is careful to sidestep theological issues by refusing to speculate on the identity of the designer:

> The conclusion that something was designed can be made quite independently of knowledge of the designer. As a matter of procedure, the design must first be apprehended before there can be any further question about the designer. The inference to design can be held with all the firmness that is possible in this world, without knowing anything about the designer.[98]

Unlike Johnson, Behe's book never identifies the designer with the God of the Bible. Behe even argues that the designer need not be a supernatural agent, citing Francis Crick's belief that "life on earth may have begun when aliens from another planet sent a rocket ship containing spores to seed the earth."[99] Behe's follow-up book, *The Edge of Evolution*, again offers a critique of Darwinism without advocating religious beliefs, Christian or otherwise.[100]

The "pure science" frame can also be found in an essay titled "The Origin of Intelligent Design: A Brief History of the Scientific Theory of Intelligent Design," written by Jonathan Witt, a senior fellow at the Discovery Institute, and posted on the Discovery Institute's website. According to Witt,

The theory of intelligent design isn't based on religious presuppositions but simply argues that an intelligent cause is the best explanation for certain features of the natural world. Unlike [creationism or creation science], the theory of intelligent design does not consider the identity of the designer nor does it defend the Genesis account (or any other sacred text for that matter). . . . The fact that intelligent design does not identify the source of design is not political calculation but precise thinking, refusing to go beyond what the scientific evidence tells us.[101]

Notice the denial that intelligent design scientists engage in political calculation. This is a clear case of "boundary work" to emphasize the purity of intelligent design's scientific agenda.

Discursive Tacking

Intelligent design proponents also use a second strategy to manage their contradictory frames, a rhetorical technique that the sociologist John Bartkowski calls "discursive tacking." In his study of the Promise Keepers, Bartkowski found that its leaders embrace two contrasting views of godly manhood in their books and lectures: a traditionalist view celebrating the "rational patriarch" and a view more consistent with men's liberation celebrating "expressive egalitarianism."[102] Promise Keepers manage the ideological contradiction by shifting between the two views in a manner analogous to a boater tacking left and right while sailing against the wind. The result is that these views "seem to overlap rather than overtly contradict one another."[103]

The intelligent design movement, which is sailing against the "headwind" of science, employs this strategy in some of its publications. For example, in the preface to *Darwin's Nemesis*, William A. Dembski refers to an early intelligent design symposium to support the view that intelligent design is pure science disconnected from religion:

Here, for the first time, a radical non-materialist critique of Darwinism and naturalistic evolutionary theories was put on the table for high-level, reasoned, academic discussion without anyone promoting a religious or sectarian agenda. In particular, this symposium was not about reconciling science with the Bible or about showing that evolution is inconsistent with traditional views about religion or morality.[104]

Dembski goes on to say that the intelligent design movement is about following evidence wherever it leads. Consequently, the movement is a "big tent," and "agnostics and atheists are not in principle excluded, provided they can adopt this open attitude of mind."[105]

Later in the same essay Dembski tacks back to a religious—and more specifically evangelical—critique of Darwinism:

> The trouble with Darwinian naturalism is that it turns nature into an idol, making brute material forces rather than the all-wise God the source of creativity in nature. Moreover, it tries to justify this idolatry in the name of science. . . . Like [evangelical leader] Francis Schaeffer a generation before him, Phillip Johnson has put his finger on the key place where our generation has forgotten God. For this generation it is the place of our origin. To a generation that regards God as increasingly distant, with nature as all there is and humans as mere appendages of nature, Johnson the prophet points us to the true God, the one in whose image we are made and to whom we must ultimately render an account.[106]

Still later in the essay, Dembski boasts of the growth of the intelligent design movement and tacks in the opposite direction, discursively detaching the movement from specific religious commitments: "Moreover, I've seen intelligent design embraced by Jews, Muslims, Hindus, Buddhists, agnostics and even atheists. The idea that intelligent design is purely an 'American thing' or an 'evangelical Christian thing' can therefore no longer be maintained."[107] Thus, we see in the preface to a major intelligent design movement book the type of discursive tacking that Bartkowski found among Promise Keepers. More examples can be found in the writings of other intelligent design advocates.

Distinguishing between Supposed Primary and Secondary Missions

There is yet a third strategy for managing the contradiction between the "pure science" and "religious crusade" frames. We can see it in publications by the Discovery Institute's Center for Science and Culture, which claims that there's a distinction between its supposed primary mission of producing and disseminating scientific research and its supposed secondary mission of supporting religious organizations and reshaping the broader culture. The strategy emerged as the center engaged in damage control after an internal fundraising document known as the "Wedge Document" was leaked to the Internet. Critics claimed that the "Wedge Document" was proof that intelligent design is fundamentally driven by religion rather than science.[108]

The document states that "design theory promises to reverse the stifling dominance of the materialistic worldview, and to replace it with a science consonant with Christian and theistic convictions."[109] The document also expresses the center's particular concern with reaching Christians: "Alongside a focus on influential opinion-makers, we also seek to build up a popular base of support among our natural constituency, namely, Christians. We will do this primarily through apologetics seminars. We intend these to encourage and equip believers with new scientific evidences that support the faith, as well as to 'popularize' our ideas in the broader culture."[110]

As the "Wedge Document" proved useful to intelligent design's critics, the center was forced to respond with a defense of the document, posting an article on its website titled "The 'Wedge Document': 'So What?'" This reiterates the scientific nature of the center's mission, but acknowledges that the center makes its research available to those who find that intelligent design supports their religious beliefs:

> For many the scandal of the "Wedge Document" is nothing more and nothing less than its mention of "Christian and theistic convictions" and our stated intention to support scientific research that is "consonant" with such convictions.
>
> But why should this be upsetting?
>
> Please note first, that "consonant with" means "in harmony with" or "consistent with." It does not mean the "same as." Recent developments in physics, cosmology, biochemistry, and related sciences may lead to a new harmony between science and religion. Many of us happen to think that they will, and we are not alone in that. But that doesn't mean we think

religion and science are the same thing. We don't. Nor do we want to impose a religious agenda on the practice of science.

This passage instead was referring to our conviction that science, rather than supporting a materialistic philosophy, is at least consistent with theistic belief, including Christian belief.[111]

Of course, the center was very selective in which portions of the "Wedge Document" it chose to quote. The text as a whole is dominated by the "religious crusade" frame, as we would expect from a document designed to help raise funds from its conservative Christian base. But in the face of withering criticism that called into question its "pure science" frame, the center chose to present the document as being primarily about pursuing scientific truth and only secondarily about supporting religious groups.

Conclusion: Even Worse Than a Trojan Horse

Among the best-known books criticizing the intelligent design movement is *Creationism's Trojan Horse: The Wedge of Intelligent Design* by Barbara Forrest and Paul R. Gross.[112] The book's thesis is that intelligent design is a religious movement masquerading as science in order to gain entry into public schools, with the eventual goal of creating a theocratic state. The book was the result of painstaking detective work, and the authors managed to uncover numerous instances of deception by intelligent design advocates. Nevertheless, their Trojan horse metaphor doesn't fully capture the messy reality that I've described.[113] Essentially, Forrest and Gross give their opponents too much credit. The Trojan horse metaphor implies a well-disciplined movement that effectively controls its public image. In contrast, the threefold strategy described here is an inevitably haphazard affair, even if it's the best that the intelligent design movement can manage, given its incompatible goals of mobilizing religious conservatives and gaining scientific respectability.[114] It's not clear that there's a single metaphor that can capture this reality. Perhaps "two-headed ogre" would be more accurate.

Reality Check: How Secular Is the Academy?

A foundational element of Phillip E. Johnson's paranoid vision is the claim that American colleges and universities are hostile to religious faith. But is this claim true? Fortunately, a considerable amount of social science data is available to help us gauge the level of secularism in the academic world. Let's examine Johnson's specific arguments and then subject them to a reality check by reviewing the empirical evidence.

In the second edition of *Darwin on Trial*, Johnson states that his primary goal for writing the book was to "legitimate the assertion of a theistic worldview in the secular universities."[115] He elaborated on his understanding of universities in his next book, *Reason in the Balance*. According to Johnson, the vast majority of Americans are theists, people who believe that they were created by a God who provides purpose for their lives. In contrast, most leading intellectuals are naturalists who assume that God exists only as an idea in the minds of religious believers: "In our greatest universities, naturalism—the doctrine that nature is 'all there is'—is the virtually unquestioned assumption that underlies not only natural science but intellectual work of all kinds."[116] Johnson admits that there are religious believers in universities, including some holding prestigious academic appointments. However, he portrays these individuals as a marginalized group that must accommodate to the dominant naturalism of the academy: "With very few exceptions, these believers maintain their respectability by tacitly accepting the naturalistic rules that define rationality in the universities. They explicitly or implicitly concede that their theism is a matter of 'faith' and agree to leave the realm of 'reason' to the agnostics."[117] As I discussed earlier, Johnson refuses to acknowledge the distinction between methodological naturalism and ontological naturalism. Consequently, he portrays those religious academics who assent to the former as being dominated by the latter worldview.

Is the American academy as starkly secular as Johnson asserts? Recent studies suggest a more complicated picture. Sociologists and historians do describe American colleges and universities as having undergone a "secularization" process over the last two centuries.[118] At one time, most American colleges and universities were connected to religious (usually Protestant) bodies. Today an ever smaller minority of schools have such ties. Religious instruction was once interwoven through the curricula of colleges and universities, but now classroom instruction is largely detached from religious concerns. This type of institutional separation from the religious sphere, however, does *not* necessarily mean that colleges and universities are hostile to religious belief. Several recent studies suggest that religious believers find a much more hospitable climate than Johnson is willing to recognize.

One such study is *Religion on Campus*, by the religious historians Conrad Cherry, Betty A. Deberg, and Amanda Porterfield.[119] The book examines four schools in the United States representing diverse geographical settings and different perceived relationship to religion (public non-affiliated, private non-affiliated, Catholic, and Lutheran). Their observations are in sharp contrast to Johnson's perceptions of campus life:

> We discovered little resistance or hostility at any school to either the practice or the teaching of religion. Only at the Catholic university, where the most strenuous and concerted efforts were made to bring campus life into conformity with religious ideals, did we hear anyone complain about campus religion being oppressive. On all four campuses, lively differences of opinion on religious matters were aired, and in the vast majority of cases, religion was respected and widely viewed as a salutary dimension of human life.[120]

Their observations at the public university are particularly significant. The absence of religious affiliation didn't diminish religion; instead, it fostered religious pluralism by creating a neutral space in which non-Christian groups could operate on equal footing with Christian ones.[121]

We should also consider an excellent study by Neil Gross and Solon Simmons titled "The Religiosity of American College and University Professors."[122] The authors utilize a nationally representative survey of American college and university professors to examine how religious these individuals are in their personal lives. Like the previous study, this one presents findings that directly contradict Johnson's perceptions of academic life: "While atheism and agnosticism are more common among professors than within the U.S. population as a whole, religious skepticism represents a minority position, even among professors teaching at elite research universities."[123] The authors also note that institutional secularization (severing of ties to religious bodies) has no implications for the religious lives of faculty members: "But the hypothesis that the university is a secular *institution* because of the irreligious tendencies of the faculty does not withstand empirical scrutiny: *it is a secular institution despite the fact that most of its key personnel are themselves religious believers*."[124]

Since Gross and Simmons break down their survey results by academic discipline, let's consider the responses for professors of biology, the supposed leaders of the "Darwinist establishment" at the heart of the intelligent design conspiracy theory. It's true that atheists and agnostics together make up the majority of the biology sample at 60.8 percent (compared to only 22.9 percent of the entire professoriate). But we don't find the overwhelming secularism described by intelligent design proponents. Theists, those claiming to believe in a God, make up more than a third (35.3 percent) of the total.[125] This is in sharp contrast to Johnson's depictions of theists in biology departments as a small and beleaguered minority.[126]

In sum, Johnson's crusade to defend theism on college and university campuses is a solution to a nonexistent problem.[127] If Johnson's colleagues really want to compare him to a great literary figure, perhaps Don Quixote is more appropriate than Gandalf.

Unmasking "Theistic Realism"

If defenders of intelligent design hold the illusory view that universities are hostile to religious belief, they hold the equally illusory view that scientists are cultural overlords who have the power to define what is and is not accepted as reality. In fact, strong cultural tendencies toward populism and individualism have meant that Americans have long been suspicious of elites and experts of all kinds, including scientists. Around 40 percent of Americans continue to espouse creationism,[128] an indication of evolutionary biologists' limited hold on popular sentiment, and Johnson is well aware of this statistic.[129] Widespread skepticism of anthropogenic global warming also tells us how mistrustful Americans are of scientists. And in the academic world, various forms of post-enlightenment and postmodern thought have sought to knock science off its pedestal as the sole arbiter of truth.

A segment of the evangelical world has sought to embrace a "soft" version of postmodernism and to cut evangelical theology loose from its moorings in Enlightenment thought. In particular, they want to replace the doctrine of biblical inerrancy, which treats the Bible as a book of facts and holds that every verse in the Bible is without error, with a more holistic reading that emphasizes the Bible's overall message. The academic version of the movement is known as postconservative theology.[130] Outside academia, Emerging/Emergent Church leaders such as Brian McLaren engage in a similar enterprise.[131]

However, the mainstream of American evangelicalism still reads the Bible through an Enlightenment (in particular, Baconian) lens. This means that the Bible is viewed as a source of objective facts, including facts about science. In this context we can understand that Johnson's project of "theistic realism"—the argument that God can be accepted as objectively real and that the empirical evidence indicates that God created the universe—is simply a reiteration of mainstream evangelical biblical hermeneutics. A more accurate description of Johnson's project would be "theistic positivism," as his goal is for evangelical beliefs about God to be accepted as scientific facts.

This project has multiple problems. Conservative evangelicals believe that the doctrine of biblical inerrancy represents ancient Christian orthodoxy, but in fact the doctrine is a product of modern, Western cultural assumptions that emerged out of the Enlightenment.[132] And while science is surely a means for learning truths, it is quite another thing to treat science as Truth with a capital *T* and to ignore its limitations. Science can't answer normative questions of right and wrong. Nor can science comment on realities beyond what can be observed by humans. Forcing Christian faith into the framework of science ultimately degrades both.

What could motivate intelligent design authors to advocate theistic positivism? Johnson and others in the intelligent design movement make it clear that their goal is to replace Darwinists as the dominant force in American culture. This is consistent with the Christian Right's perception of themselves as outsiders who are entitled to be the insiders (as I discussed in the introduction). If scientists rule culture, then evangelical Christianity must be accepted as science for this regime change to take place.[133]

Fair-Weather Postmodernists

If the "pure science" versus "religious crusade" framing were the only inconsistency in the intelligent design movement, that would be more than enough to disqualify it from being a serious intellectual project. But we can find yet another major inconsistency in its public rhetoric. As discussed above, intelligent design proponents' basic worldview, like that of other conservative evangelicals, is a blend of biblicism and cultural assumptions based in Enlightenment (modern) thought. However, this hasn't stopped intelligent design authors, especially Johnson, from appropriating postmodernist rhetoric in a strategic manner.

Why would postmodernism, with its tendency toward cultural relativism (at least in its extreme form), appeal to a group of religious conservatives who view the Bible as objective truth? The reason is that postmodern philosophy challenges scientists' claim that they uncover objective truths about the world. Postmodernists attempt to reduce science to just one of many arbitrary viewpoints. What's more, they claim that the authority of science is rooted in power politics rather than superior insight into reality.[134] Intelligent design proponents aim to challenge the power of scientists by persuading the public that Darwinism has no empirical evidence to support it but is rooted in atheistic philosophy. It makes sense that the postmodern-style "hermeneutics of suspicion" appeals so strongly to them.

In his book *Tower of Babel*, the philosopher of science Robert Pennock gives readers an extensive analysis of postmodernist rhetoric in the intelligent design movement. He points out that Johnson's original title for *Darwin on Trial* was *Darwin Deconstructed* and then elaborates on Johnson's strategy:

> Once one is sensitized to this, one finds postmodernist language throughout Johnson's work. When he claims, for example, that scientists are attracted to naturalism because "It gives science a virtual monopoly on the production of knowledge," he is echoing the deconstructionist charge that knowledge is not discovered but rather fabricated by the intellectual capitalists who own the factories of the knowledge business. When he equates scientific naturalism with "scientism" he is repeating the name-calling led by antiscientific cultural relativists. When he says Darwinism is science's

"creation story" he is echoing the social constructionist charge that science simply delivers narratives that are epistemically on a par with other myths and stories. . . . When he describes the scientific community as a "priesthood" that "guards the door" of knowledge, he is making the central postmodern point that knowledge is simply the story whose authors have the power to suppress other stories.[135]

Pennock also discusses the intelligent design "affair" with postmodernism in an article titled "The Postmodern Sin of Intelligent Design Creationism."[136] But he fails to mention one very significant example of Johnson's attitude toward postmodern thought. In a 1996 issue of *Books & Culture*, Johnson published an essay titled "Pomo Science" (later reprinted in *Objections Sustained*). This essay reviewed a special issue of the postmodern journal *Social Text* titled "The Science Wars." This issue became infamous as part of what has been dubbed the "Sokal hoax." The New York University physicist Alan Sokal decided to expose the ignorance of postmodern science critics by writing a fake article (a parody of postmodern scholarship that he falsely presented as a serious piece) that he titled "Transgressing the Boundaries: Towards a Transformative Hermeneutics of Quantum Gravity." The editors of *Social Text* accepted the fake article and published it in "The Science Wars." Sokal then publicly revealed his hoax. The *Social Text* editors were greeted with a barrage of ridicule, to which Johnson added some of his own: "The editors made themselves look still worse by their response [to critics], saying among other foolish things that the article's 'status as a parody does not alter substantially our interest in the piece itself as a symptomatic document.' That confirmed Sokal's point that a parody of Pomo science-talk is hard to distinguish from the real thing."[137]

Here we see Johnson deriding the same kind of "Pomo science-talk" that he and his intelligent design colleagues use regularly in their war against Darwinism. As bad as this looks, there's more to the story. Among the non-hoax articles—the "real thing" that Johnson claims is indistinguishable from a parody—was one by the postmodern philosopher and sociologist Steve Fuller titled "Does Science Put an End to History, or History to Science?"[138] Fuller later appeared at the Dover trial as an expert witness on behalf of the Dover school board, where he testified that intelligent design was scientific in nature. Fuller also got considerable face time in the pseudo-documentary *Expelled*, in which he made a series of critical comments about Darwinism. Finally, Fuller's endorsements appear on the back covers of two books produced by intelligent design proponents, *Explore Evolution* and *Signature in the Cell*.[139] Regarding the second book, Fuller wrote, "Meyer has provided no less than a blueprint for 21st century biological science. . . . After this book, readers will wonder whether anything more than sentimentality lies behind the continued association of Darwin's name with modern biology."[140]

To sum up: intelligent design advocates are committed modernists, yet they employ postmodernist rhetoric to attack Darwinism, which doesn't change the fact that they despise "Pomo science-talk," which doesn't stop them from repeatedly calling on a postmodernist scholar whose support is useful to them. The intelligent design movement seeks not only basic intellectual respect, but the domination of American universities. It obviously deserves neither.

Conclusion

Hofstadter noted that one recurring aspect of the paranoid style was its use of "renegades" from the enemy cause. Anti-Catholic movements had runaway nuns. Anti-Mormon movements had former polygamous wives. Hofstadter used the example of ex-communists:

> In contemporary right-wing movements a particularly important part has been played by ex-Communists who have moved rapidly, though not without anguish, from the paranoid left to the paranoid right, clinging all the while to the fundamentally Manichean psychology that underlies both. Such authorities on communism remind one of those ancient converts from paganism to Christianity of whom it is told that upon their conversion they did not entirely cease to believe in their old gods but converted them into demons.[141]

With this in mind, we can understand that Phillip E. Johnson's obsession with the secular academy is really a fight with his pre-conversion self. And just as runaway nuns constructed fantastic tales of the depraved behavior secretly occurring in convents, so Johnson has constructed a fantastic tale of militantly secular professors, intoxicated by the naturalistic philosophy of Darwinism, bent on strengthening their dominance of American culture. Unfortunately, what should have remained a private fantasy produced by a midlife crisis grew into an enduring social movement.

As with any social movement, the successful launch of intelligent design was the result of multiple factors. Johnson's new approach to creationism came along at a time when creation science had hit a legal dead end. Equally important, Johnson had been profoundly shaped by the Christian Right worldview, and so crafted a message that combined the Christian Right's main concern (lack of control of American culture) with a variation on its "secular humanist" adversaries (Darwinist intellectuals) and a straightforward solution (expose Darwinism as a hoax).

Intelligent design never stood a chance of triumphing in the halls of science, because the movement was never really about interpreting scientific data. As a religio-political movement, however, it's been quite successful. As Ronald L. Numbers points out, intelligent design's popularity among rank-and-file religious conservatives is difficult to measure, partially because not everyone encountering the movement understands its radical methodological claims or is able to distinguish its arguments from those of the creation science movement. Still, Numbers writes, "there was no denying that the coterie of design theorists associated with the Discovery Institute had captured worldwide attention."[142] With supporters ranging from InterVarsity Press to Saddleback Church to Focus on the Family, intelligent design appears to be the dominant approach to human origins among the American evangelical elite. The defeat in Dover, Pennsylvania, hasn't stopped efforts in other states to get intelligent design into public schools. And given that evangelicals are a key part of the Republican Party's base, it's not surprising to see Republican politicians pushing the intelligent design project. We can expect intelligent design to remain active as a movement for the foreseeable future.

* * *

We've seen that as far as Phillip E. Johnson is concerned, conservative beliefs on sexual morality and gender have been abandoned because the culture is now dominated by Darwin-inspired naturalism. The next Christian Right movement we'll consider makes the degradation of sexual morality and gender its main focus. It's implicitly rooted in a creationist worldview, but it aims its rhetorical fire not at Darwinists but at unrepentant homosexuals and the psychiatrists who allegedly ignore scientific evidence in order to declare them healthy.

2

Sex, Sin, and Science

The Persistence of the Ex-Gay Movement

By the 1970s, there was a vast network of local evangelical ministries whose mission was to work with individuals trying to overcome same-sex attraction. Exodus International was founded in 1976 as an umbrella group providing leadership to this network. Exodus's advertisements featured pictures of smiling men and women of various races and promised "freedom" to those struggling with homosexuality. After some initial indifference, the evangelical center and right both embraced the work of Exodus, along with the larger "ex-gay" project. *Christianity Today* gave frequent coverage to Exodus leaders. Focus on the Family partnered with Exodus in launching its own ex-gay campaign.

But in 2013 signs began to emerge that Exodus leaders were starting to shift from the views on homosexuality held by the evangelical center-right coalition. First, these leaders suggested that, although homosexual activity is a sin, it's still possible for unrepentant homosexuals to go to heaven. Second, Exodus president Alan Chambers began to question publicly whether it was possible to change someone's sexual orientation. Evangelical leaders associated with the ex-gay movement reacted to these developments with strong criticism.

This shift turned out to be merely a prelude to something much bigger. In June 2013 the Exodus board of directors dropped a bombshell on the evangelical world by announcing its decision to close the ministry and start a new ministry with a radically different mission. The announcement came with a lengthy apology to the gay and lesbian community from Alan Chambers, who again disavowed efforts to change sexual orientation and acknowledged insensitivity:

> I am sorry that some of you spent years working through the shame and
> guilt you felt when your attractions didn't change. I am sorry we pro-

moted sexual orientation change efforts and reparative theories about sexual orientation that stigmatized parents. I am sorry that there were times I didn't stand up to people publicly "on my side" who called you names like sodomite—or worse. I am sorry that I, knowing some of you so well, failed to share publicly that the gay and lesbian people I know were every bit as capable of being amazing parents as the straight people that I know.[1]

Though he still believed that the Bible teaches that sexual activity is only appropriate within heterosexual marriage, Chambers promised to "exercise my beliefs with great care and respect for those who do not share them." This included a promise not to oppose efforts to legalize gay marriage. Finally, the apology indicated what he saw as the future mission for Exodus leaders' new organization, ReduceFear.org: "Moving forward, we will serve in our pluralistic culture by hosting thoughtful and safe conversations about gender and sexuality, while partnering with others to reduce fear, inspire hope, and cultivate human flourishing."[2]

Exodus's move brought swift responses from Christian leaders on both sides of the debate over gays and lesbians. Responses from pro-gay Christians ranged from skepticism to modest approval—modest because Chambers continued to believe that homosexual relations were sinful. Leaders from the evangelical center and right, including those involved in the ex-gay movement, quickly condemned Exodus leaders. In *Christianity Today*, Wheaton College provost and psychology professor Stanton L. Jones wrote that "Chambers's [apology] reflects aspects of theological drift and a capitulation to a prevailing culture that is unbecoming to an organization grounded in scriptural truths." Jones further proclaimed, "The Bible teaches that homosexual conduct is immoral, and both the testimony of Scripture itself, and empirical research and credible personal testimony suggest change is possible for some."[3] Andrew Comiskey, founder of the ex-gay Desert Stream Ministries, tweeted, "How merciful of God to shut down Exodus, which under Alan Chambers' leadership had completely veered off the course of its mission."[4]

Exodus's closing followed three other challenging episodes for the ex-gay movement. The psychiatrist Robert Spitzer was the author of a prominent study supporting the efficacy of ex-gay therapy and one of the movement's few secular leaders. In April 2012 he released a letter of apology to the gay community, stating, "I now judged the major critiques of the study as largely correct."[5] John Paulk, a former ex-gay leader who had spearheaded Focus on the Family's campaign against homosexuality, issued a similar apology to the gay and lesbian community in April 2013, in which he renounced his ex-gay writings.[6] In September 2012, California became the first state to ban licensed mental health professionals from performing ex-gay therapy on minors. New Jersey soon followed suit, and opponents began launching similar efforts throughout the United States. Clearly, the ex-gay movement was in a state of crisis.

But it was far from dead. Many ex-gay ministries that had been affiliated with Exodus chose to cut their ties and continue their work under a new umbrella group called the Restored Hope Network. The new group proclaimed on its website, "Yet we hold up the power of God to redeem individuals and families from sin's control, even in the area of homosexuality."[7] As their reactions to the Exodus closing made clear, leaders in the center and right segments of American evangelicalism had no intention of modifying their stances on homosexuality.

To understand the persistent support for the ex-gay movement, we need to appreciate that it's based on more than the belief that same-sex attraction can be reduced by psychiatric and/or spiritual means. It's also based on a conspiracy theory that depicts the psychiatric, psychological, and medical establishments as suppressing the scientific truth about homosexuality as they carry out the political agenda of gay activists. Throw in the common evangelical belief that the "traditional" (heterosexual and monogamous) family is the moral foundation of society and we have all the ingredients for the classic paranoid style, an appealing state for those who thrive on feeling embattled. The ex-gay movement also resonates with the desire of many evangelicals to have scientific data confirm their reading of the Bible (in this case, that homosexuality is contrary to God's will). Finally, it resonates with a deep-seated evangelical belief that humans are responsible for their individual destinies, and that God can deliver miracles for those with sufficient faith.

All of these advantages help to counteract a vulnerability that the other Christian Right movements aren't burdened with. Intelligent design concerns events from the distant past. Conservative bioethicists warn against a hypothetical dystopian future. Deniers of anthropogenic climate change can dispute future climate predictions and blame nature for current trends. This means that these three movements can conceal their scientific failures, at least from those who don't want to know about them. In contrast, the ex-gay movement makes a claim about the *daily experience* of gays and lesbians who chose to undergo treatment—that their attraction to members of the same sex will decrease. The failure of ex-gay therapy, and the science behind it, eventually becomes obvious to those who seek treatment. This is a problem that the movement can only manage imperfectly. Still, leaders from the evangelical center and right remain committed, so the movement goes on.

Psychiatry and Homosexuality

Beginning with Sigmund Freud, psychiatrists have been inconsistent in their views on homosexuality. According to the psychiatrist Jack Dresher, Freud's position on homosexuality can be difficult to figure out. Freud never dedicated a major work solely to the topic; he wrote about it over the course of almost twenty years (from 1905 to 1923); and his writings need to be understood in their historical context.[8] Freud proposed that homosexuality was the result of libidinal (psychosexual) development that either had failed to reach the final stage or had regressed to an earlier stage. The status of this condition was ambiguous. "Although an arrested libidinal development was not an illness," Dresher writes, "neither did Freud believe that it implied health."[9] This was a tolerant position compared to dominant Western understandings of homosexuality as an abomination and/or a criminal activity. On a number of occasions Freud attempted to alter a client's homosexual orientation, but eventually grew pessimistic about the effectiveness of such therapy.

Later understandings of homosexuality shifted as psychiatrists, especially those in the psychoanalytic tradition, increasingly saw it as a pathology and not merely an undesirable condition. In addition, changes in psychoanalytic theory led to the belief that homosexuality could potentially be cured. The theoretical foundation for what would later be called "reparative therapy" (and still later "ex-gay therapy") was laid by the Hungarian-born psychiatrist Sandor Rado. Rado was a protégé of Freud, who invited him to become executive editor of the two official journals of psychoanalysis, *Zeitschrift* and *Imago*, in 1924.[10] Rado believed that homosexuality was caused when individuals overreacted to parental pressure to abstain from premarital sex. Rado's theory rests on two major Freudian concepts, castration anxiety (a boy's fear of being castrated by his father as punishment for sexual feelings toward the boy's mother) and penis envy (a girl's feeling of incompleteness when she discovers that she does not have a penis):

> Why is the so-called homosexual forced to escape from the male-female pair? This brings us back to the familiar campaign of deterrence that parents wage to prohibit the sexual activity of the child. The campaign causes the female to view the male organ as a destructive weapon. Therefore the female partners are reassured by the absence in both of them of the male organ. The campaign causes the male to see in the mutilated female organ [the lack of the penis] a reminder of inescapable punishment [castration]. When the never-recognized fear and resentment of the opposite organ becomes insurmountable, the individual may escape into homosexuality. The male partners are reassured by the presence in both of them of the male organ.[11]

Rado added the additional explanation that the lesbian "usually harbors bitter resentment against her father or mother or both because she was denied parental affection and because a son was preferred to her."[12] Homosexuality is pathological because it represents an adaptation to unrealistic fears.

The American psychiatrist Irving Bieber's theories of male homosexuality built on Rado's understanding that "homosexual adaptation is a result of 'hidden but incapacitating fears of the opposite sex.'"[13] In his 1962 book *Homosexuality: A Psychoanalytic Study*, Bieber wrote that this fear of sexual relations with the opposite sex is brought about by disturbed parent-child relationships, which Bieber interpreted through the Freudian lens of the Oedipus complex. Regarding the fathers of the homosexual subjects in his research, he claimed that "in the majority of instances the father was explicitly detached and hostile. In only a minority of cases was paternal destructiveness effected through indifference or default."[14] For Bieber, the homosexual subjects' relationships with their mothers were equally problematic: "Most . . . mothers were explicitly seductive, and even where they were not, the closeness of the bond with the son appeared to be in itself sexually provocative. . . . These data point to maternal attempts to fulfill frustrated marital gratification with the homosexual son."[15]

The American psychiatrist Charles Socarides's writings on homosexuality, even more so than those of Rado and Bieber, were awash in Freudian terminology. His 1968 book *The Overt Homosexual* offered an explanation for the development of male homosexuality that built on familiar oedipal theory:

> It is well known that an over-intense affective relationship to the mother often with conscious incestuous desires and a father who is inaccessible to the child are standard factors in the production of overt male homosexuality. The sexual wish for the mother leads to anxiety, guilt and a conflicting urge to cling to and simultaneously to avoid intimate contact with her and later all other women.[16]

Given the resultant guilt and anxiety, the individual is forced to repress his desires through displacement and substitution, turning to desire for the same sex. "Instead of the mother's body it is the male body and instead of the mother's breast it is the penis."[17] Socarides believed that a similar displacement and substitution mechanism operated in female homosexuality:

> Often a young girl will respond to disappointment over her oedipal wishes with an identification with the father and consequently assume an active relation to women who represent mother substitutes. The attitude of these active masculine homosexual women toward their mother-equivalent objects is frequently combined with all the features of a wish-fulfillment type of female castration complex.[18]

Consequently, therapeutic treatment of homosexuality must involve addressing the anxieties that led to the repression of heterosexual desire.

While not all American psychiatrists subscribed to the views of Rado, Bieber, and Socarides, there was consensus in the 1950s and 1960s that homosexuality was a pathological condition. This was reflected in the American Psychiatric Association's first edition of the *Diagnostic and Statistical Manual, Mental Disorders* (*DSM-I*), which was published in 1952 and contained the association's official list of recognized mental disorders. It classified homosexuality and other types of sexual behavior judged to be deviant as "sociopathic personality disturbances."[19] The 1968 revised *Diagnostic and Statistical Manual of Psychiatric Disorders* (*DSM-II*) classified homosexuality among "other non-psychotic mental disorders."[20]

Only two years later, in 1970, the APA's views on homosexuality came under fire from gay and lesbian activists eager to transform major social institutions. This set off an internal debate in the APA, with the result that homosexuality was deleted from the 1973 version of the *Diagnostic and Statistical Manual of Psychiatric Disorders* (*DSM-III*). The definitive account of this transformation is provided by Ronald Bayer in his book *Homosexuality and American Psychiatry: The Politics of Diagnosis.*[21]

The opening salvo by gay and lesbian activists occurred at the 1970 APA annual meeting in San Francisco. Activists surprised those gathered by disrupting the proceedings. According to Bayer, "Guerrilla theater tactics and more straightforward shouting matches characterized their presence."[22] Irving Bieber was among those verbally attacked for advancing theories that portray homosexuality as a pathological condition.[23] It was at this time that the APA program chair agreed to allow gays and lesbians to present a panel at the following year's meeting in Washington, D.C., hoping to avoid further disruptions.[24] Despite this concession, activists decided to stage another round of disruptions at the 1971 meeting in order to keep up the pressure for change. It was toward the end of the meeting that activists first informed APA officials of their specific demand to have homosexuality deleted from the *DSM-II*.

By the 1972 meeting, pressure to change the APA's position on homosexuality was increasingly internal as well as external. According to Bayer, "The presence at the 1972 APA meeting of psychiatrists critical of their own profession's attitude toward homosexuality was indicative of a much broader process of reevaluation that had begun to take place."[25] People questioned whether the belief that homosexuality is a pathological condition was based on scientific data or whether it represented an unscientific endorsement of society's dominant sexual mores.

The issue was soon taken up by the APA's Nomenclature Committee. Henry Brill officially chaired the committee, but Robert Spitzer exercised the most influence in guiding its deliberations.[26] Based on input from this committee, the APA board of trustees voted in 1973 to remove homosexuality from the *DSM*. In its place they added the classification "sexual orientation disturbance," which applied only to those gays and lesbians who wished to change their sexual orientation. The trustees also approved a civil rights proposal crafted by Spitzer that put the APA on record as opposing discrimination against gays and lesbians and opposing laws that made homosexual activity a criminal offense.[27]

As significant as these changes were, the APA fell short of acknowledging that homosexuality is as healthy an expression of human sexuality as heterosexuality. A key component of Spitzer's argument for deleting homosexuality from the *DSM* was a higher threshold at which a condition would be classified as a disorder. In Spitzer's view, homosexuality was a "suboptimal" condition, but it didn't meet the criteria for being considered pathological. In the press release that followed the 1973 decision, APA president Alfred Freedman clarified that the board had not declared homosexuality "normal" or as desirable as heterosexuality.[28] It's also important to note that the category of "sexual orientation disturbance" left the door open for therapies designed to change a patient's sexual orientation.

Opponents of the nomenclature change, led by Charles Socarides, pushed for a vote of the APA's full membership to overturn the decision. The APA decided to allow the referendum. In the end, the APA's decision was upheld, with 58 percent voting in support, 37 percent opposing, and 3 percent abstaining.[29] Just as important as the vote itself was the rhetoric that emerged among the opposing camps. Each side claimed that it was motivated by "science" and that the other side was motivated by "politics." According to Bayer,

> Those who opposed the nomenclature change believed that the psychiatrists who voted to reverse the board's decision had rallied to the banner of science and objectivity while those who voted to affirm the [board's] action were guilty of attempting to impose their own social values under the guise of science. On the other hand, those who supported the change portrayed their own affirmative votes as indicating their commitment to the scientific tradition of psychiatry, and they excoriated those who supported the Socarides position for their value-laden attachment to an unscientific perspective on homosexuality.[30]

Bayer concluded his 1981 book by suggesting that the APA's decision to declassify homosexuality was unlikely to endure. The problem was that American society continued to condemn homosexuality, and over time the APA would be forced to conform:

> [Psychiatry] cannot hold to discordant views regarding the normal and abnormal, the desirable and undesirable, and continue to perform its socially sanctioned function. Only if American society were to change dramatically in the next years would the 1973 decision to remove homosexuality from the list of psychiatric disorders become securely rooted. There is every indication that the necessary social transformation will not occur.[31]

Bayer also suggested that if the APA decided to reclassify homosexuality as an illness, it would find the necessary psychiatric and scientific justification.

Obviously, Bayer's predictions turned out to be incorrect.[32] After the APA's decision, other professional guilds in the fields of psychology, counseling, and medicine changed to more gay-affirming stances. By the 1990s social acceptance of gays and lesbians was climbing steadily, even though it was still limited. The APA itself moved from its limited and technical acceptance of homosexuality to more genuine acceptance, a trend that coincided with increased criticism of ex-gay (reparative) therapy. In 1998 the APA issued a statement officially condemning such therapy: "The APA opposes any psychiatric treatment, such as 'reparative' or 'conversion' therapy, that is based on the assumption that homosexuality per se is a mental disorder or is based on the a priori assumption that the patient should change his or her homosexual orientation."[33]

The Formation of NARTH

As anti-gay views were increasingly marginalized in the fields of psychiatry and psychology, proponents of these views began to consider forming an alternative professional guild. In 1992 Charles Socarides, Benjamin Kaufman, and Joseph Nicolosi formed the National Association for Research and Therapy of Homosexuality (NARTH). Socarides and Kaufman seem to have been motivated primarily by their loyalty to older psychoanalytic paradigms that pathologized homosexuality. Nicolosi, a devout Roman Catholic, was founder and clinical director of the Thomas Aquinas Psychological Clinic in Encino, California. This center offers ex-gay therapy and proclaims on its website that only heterosexuality is compatible with the design of human bodies as understood in the Judeo-Christian tradition.[34] None of NARTH's founders were evangelicals, and two of them were essentially secular in their motivations, but NARTH was inevitably influenced by the fact that the ex-gay movement has always been dominated by evangelicals. The evangelical dominance has been so pronounced that NARTH, like the Discovery Institute, has had to employ the "pure science" framing in order to defend its scientific credibility. Yet anyone browsing its website over the years would also have seen the evangelical-style "religious crusade" frame in abundance.

NARTH's leaders built on the rhetoric that emerged on the losing side of the APA's battle over the classification of homosexuality. According to NARTH, the winning side has abandoned science for politics. To this basic template it has added a good dose of conspiracy theory that closely parallels that found in the intelligent design movement. Intelligent design proponents claim that the "Darwinist establishment" is hiding the lack of empirical support for evolution along with its atheist agenda. NARTH claimed that the APA is suppressing the truth about homosexuality, including that it is curable and that homosexual behavior is associated with increased psychological and physical health risks. Furthermore, NARTH argued that this pro-gay political agenda has affected other related mental health organizations. One section of the NARTH website (circa 2013) titled "NARTH and the APA—A Brief History" was devoted to criticizing the American Psychological Association (which confusingly uses the same APA acronym as the American Psychiatric Association) for abandoning science for politics:

> When NARTH was founded twenty years ago many of our clinical members were members of the American Psychological Association. As the then leading organization for mental health professionals we hoped that our continued involvement would encourage the APA to return to its science and research based tradition. Sadly, many mental health professionals have been disappointed as the drift into politics and policy making

has generally discredited a once proud association that now finds itself defending gay marriage, taking positions on United States foreign policy and promoting left leaning social policy in spite of the lack of science that would justify such public stands. What follows are just a few of the articles, speeches, and letters that illustrate NARTH's continuing battle to restore research and integrity to the APA.

So when activists say, "Doesn't the APA oppose NARTH's position on treatment and unwanted homosexuality?" we reply—take a look at what other non-science, political positions the professional mental health associations are taking these days. You might be surprised.[35]

In a clever political move, NARTH co-opted the language of individual rights from gay liberation movements. While gay activists press for nondiscrimination and equal treatment, NARTH claims to uphold the right to seek therapy for those who wish to change their sexual orientation, a right that it claims is being violated by the mental health establishment.

In 2015 NARTH responded to the increasingly difficult legal environment for ex-gay therapy with a reorganization. An official announcement described the changes that would take place:

In recent years NARTH has been increasingly involved in legal and professional efforts to defend the rights of clients to pursue change-oriented psychological care as well as the rights of licensed mental health professionals to provide such care. In this context, it has been alarming to encounter frequent distortions and omissions pertaining to the scientific record regarding change in sexual orientation and the harms alleged to occur from professional assistance with such change.

In order to respond to these important developments more clearly in our mission, the NARTH board voted in January of this year to create a new organization, titled Alliance for Therapeutic Choice and Scientific Integrity (ATCSI).[36]

The announcement claimed that NARTH would continue to function within ATCSI as "a separate Institute that will continue to focus on matters pertaining to the psychological care of clients with unwanted same-sex attractions and behaviors."[37] Even a cursory look at ATCSI's website reveals that this "new organization" is in reality NARTH operating under a new name. The ATCSI website reproduces large sections from the previous NARTH website. ATCSI also replicates the previous divisional structure of NARTH, with the "NARTH Institute" name placed on the research and clinical divisions. Apparently, desperate times—ex-gay therapy's rapidly diminishing scientific credibility—called for desperate measures.

Ex-Gay Ministries

If NARTH (and now ATCSI) has tried to represent the scientific face of the ex-gay movement, the more overtly religious side has been represented by an array of evangelical ex-gay ministries claiming to assist individuals in overcoming homosexuality through a combination of psychological and spiritual practices. Ex-gay ministries first arose in the United States in the early 1970s. This was a time when evangelicals were increasingly reaching out to those on the fringes of society. Former hippies and members of the counterculture joined the "Jesus movement" and began filling evangelical churches like Calvary Chapel in Costa Mesa, California. The first residential ex-gay ministry was Love in Action (later changed to New Hope), founded in 1973 in Marin County, north of San Francisco.[38] Nonresidential ex-gay ministries, some formally connected to churches and others independent, were cropping up around the United States at the same time. By 1976 there were enough ex-gay ministries to warrant a weekend conference. Out of this conference emerged Exodus International, which, as I mentioned, became the umbrella group for various local ex-gay ministries until its closing in 2013.

At first the ex-gay movement occupied a marginal place in American evangelicalism. Both leaders and congregations largely ignored the movement. The first sign that centrist evangelical leaders were warming to the ex-gay movement was a 1984 *Christianity Today* article titled "These Christians Are Helping Gays Escape from Homosexual Lifestyles."[39] Beneath the headline was the caption, "Where churches fail to reach out to homosexuals, ex-gays are setting up their own ministries and seeing results." The piece was labeled a news article, but it was a clear endorsement of the work of Exodus International and affiliated ministries and a call for congregations to get more involved in ex-gay ministry. A box at the end of the article gave the mailing addresses for Exodus and four affiliated ministries listed in the article. Significantly, the article described the ex-gay approach as a "third alternative" to gay rights activists on the one hand and "people who merely declare homosexual behavior a sin, and who do not express compassion" on the other hand. This third alternative was "demonstrating a scriptural way out of homosexuality."[40]

Five years later *Christianity Today* revisited the ex-gay movement with a trio of articles. The first was "Coming Out," in which senior writer Tim Stafford described his visit to an Exodus executive board meeting. Stafford noted some continued challenges for the ex-gay movement, but he ended with an endorsement of its work and a call for congregations to get involved. "Most congregations know nothing about the needs of homosexuals, and many don't want to know. Ex-gay ministries offer a way to respond. If the wider church were to embrace such ministries, it would see at close range the realism of what they do. If the church keeps them at arm's length, it will never know. They will be weaker. The rest of us will be, too."[41] Stafford's article was followed by "I Found Freedom," Colin Cook's testimony of how God helped heal him from homosexuality.[42] The third article in the series was "Homosexuality according to Science" by the evangelical psychology professor (and future NARTH leader) Stanton L. Jones. Jones attempted to refute scientific arguments used by pro-gay Christians while defending Christianity's historic condemnation of homosexual behavior.

In the 1990s centrist evangelical leaders increasingly embraced the ex-gay movement. InterVarsity Press had first dealt with the topic of overcoming homosexual attraction in John White's 1977 book *Eros Defiled: The Christian and Sexual Sin*.[43] In 1980 it published a booklet titled *Homosexual Struggle*, an autobiographical account of a young woman named "Nancy" who moved away from lesbianism with God's help.[44] Both publications suggested that it is possible for some people to move from homosexuality to heterosexuality, but neither book referenced the ex-gay movement. By 1993 InterVarsity Press was ready to publish its first book officially related to the ex-gay movement: Bob Davies (then executive director of Exodus) and Lori Rentzel's *Coming Out of Homosexuality: New Freedom for Men and Women*.[45] Many other books related to the movement would follow. Meanwhile, *Christianity Today* continued its positive coverage.

It took the evangelical right considerably longer to warm to the ex-gay movement. However, Focus on the Family eventually threw its support behind the movement by launching its Love Won Out ad campaign in 1998. According to Tanya Erzen, this public embrace hid considerable behind-the-scenes tensions:

> What the [Love Won Out] ad campaign finally brought to light was the shaky and often tenuous association between the ex-gay movement and more influential organizations like Focus on the Family. Although often lumped into the rest of the religious Right, Frank [Worthen] and other members of the ex-gay movement had for years sought to gain legitimacy or even a hearing with James Dobson and had been repeatedly ignored. Dobson and other leaders treated Frank and the ex-gays who had "come out of homosexuality" as a bit of an embarrassment. As emissaries from New Hope like [Mike] Haley and [John] Paulk joined Focus on the Family, it became politically expedient to use the message of change to revamp its anti-gay agenda. This time, instead of outright condemnation, Dobson could showcase John Paulk as proof that people could change into heterosexuals through Christian love.[46]

Erzen, who conducted an ethnographic study of the New Hope ministry, reveals another important feature of the movement: participants in ex-gay ministries don't necessarily embrace the views expressed by ex-gay leaders.

> Concentrating on individual testimonies illuminates the disparities between ground-level participants, ministry leaders, and Christian Right organizations. It also exposed why some men and women become disillusioned with ministries. The cynicism was borne out in the ways ex-gay men and women I talked to disassociated themselves from the politics of the Christian Right and even the leadership of the ex-gay movement. Some men and women in ex-gay ministries resent that the wider ex-gay movement showcases and distorts their stories to promote an anti-gay political agenda. Many ex-gays admit that although some changes in behavior and identity take place, it is probable that they will continue as "strugglers" their entire lives.[47]

Significantly, the evangelical left has never warmed to the ex-gay movement. Leaders in this wing of American evangelicalism have been divided over whether homosexual practice is a sin. But even those who believe that it is a sin advocate respectful dialogue with others, and they don't claim that acceptance of homosexuality is a threat to the church and society. The evangelical left has also consistently supported civil rights measures for gays and lesbians, many of which the Christian Right opposes as unnecessary, as unfair "special rights," as undermining the (heterosexual) family, or as infringing on religious freedom (which means the freedom of those who condemn homosexuality). While the evangelical left remains divided on the issue, the proportion of leaders who accept homosexual practice has steadily increased in recent years. The ex-gay movement thus remains an evangelical center-right project, though, as Erzen notes, there are major fault lines within the project.

The Evangelical Embrace of "Change"

It's one thing to believe that homosexual practice is sinful. It's another thing to believe that gays and lesbians should try to change their orientation. For Christians, there are at least two other options. One is to treat gays and lesbians as "others" to be condemned and shunned. This is the policy of the infamous Westboro Baptist Church, known for its protest banners proclaiming, "God hates fags." A less extreme version of this response came from evangelical right political groups such as the Moral Majority and Focus on the Family prior to 1998.

The second option is the position taken by the Roman Catholic Church, which considers homosexuality "objectively disordered" but has never endorsed ex-gay therapy. Courage is a Roman Catholic apostolate that ministers to "persons with homosexual desires" and operates with the support of the Roman Catholic hierarchy.[48] The FAQ section of its website describes its noncommittal stance regarding ex-gay or reparative therapy:

> Courage members are under no obligation to try to develop heterosexual attractions, because there is no guarantee that a person will always succeed in such an endeavor. Courage's aim is to help persons with same-sex

attractions develop a life of interior chastity in union with Christ. If any of our members wish to go to professionals to explore the possibility of heterosexual development, we will stand by them, by helping them to keep the deepening of their Catholic faith and obedience to Christ as their first priority. Courage itself does not provide professional therapy. Some of our members have found varying levels of heterosexual development to be a by-product of living a chaste life for a period of time; however, the goal and focus of Courage remains a life of interior chastity, humility, and holiness, which can be achieved by all, with God's grace.[49]

The website also reveals Courage's distaste for the "ex-gay" terminology: "Courage prefers to think of itself as a 'Pro-Chastity' ministry."[50] In practice, this "pro-chastity" stance means accepting that many if not most of those involved in its ministry will seek to lead celibate lives.

Why, then, do the evangelical center and right embrace a program to change gays and lesbians, rather than either of these two alternatives? Let's begin with the first alternative. Condemning gays and lesbians was strategically important to the evangelical right when it became more politically active in the early 1980s. Gays and lesbians were portrayed as part of a constellation of undesirable groups (including liberals, secular humanists, and abortion rights activists) that threatened the "traditional values" on which the United States was founded. More specifically, gay rights and the acceptance of the "gay lifestyle" were a threat to "the family," which supposedly formed the moral foundation of society. This hardline strategy helped mobilize rank-and-file evangelicals into supporting evangelical right organizations like Focus on the Family and the Christian Coalition. However, as social acceptance of homosexuality increased, along with the number of "out" gays and lesbians who were friends and family members of evangelicals, unqualified condemning of gays and lesbians was no longer a workable political strategy.[51] By the late 1990s Focus on the Family was ready to soften its message.[52] The new strategy, as exemplified by Focus on the Family's Love Won Out campaign, offered "compassion" and "hope" to those struggling to overcome homosexuality.

What about the Roman Catholic approach—expecting celibacy from gays and lesbians rather than trying to make them straight? This alternative is problematic because of two key features of evangelical culture.

First, the Roman Catholic tradition has always held lifelong celibacy in high esteem, eventually requiring it for clergy and those in religious orders, but evangelicals are heirs to a Protestant tradition that significantly devalued lifelong celibacy. Martin Luther famously denounced the monastic life as spiritually inferior to that of laypeople carrying out their vocations in society. Luther also abolished the celibacy requirement for clergy, and other branches of Protestantism later followed suit. More recently, evangelical leaders have presented strengthening "the family" as a core religious commitment. While evangelical leaders continue to push for sexual abstinence prior to marriage, lifelong celibacy is somewhat of a deviant lifestyle in the evangelical world. It is hardly surprising, then, that ex-gay ministries offer hope of not only reducing same-sex attraction, but also entering into "healthy" sex within heterosexual marriage.

There's another feature of evangelical culture that makes lifelong celibacy for gays and lesbians problematic. Some scholars call it "free will individualism." This is the widespread belief that individuals are responsible for their fate because God has given them free will. Evangelicals frequently apply this belief to individuals' eternal fates (heaven or hell), and also to their fates in this world (for example, wealth or poverty).[53] Applied to homosexuality, this means that individuals are responsible for the fact that they're homosexual, and they're capable of overcoming homosexuality if they have enough faith.[54] Once mainstream evangelical leaders recognized the "struggling" gays and lesbians in their midst, they naturally promised them that they could become not merely celibate gays but ex-gays.

The beginnings of the ex-gay movement in evangelicalism happen to coincide with a period of conflict in American psychiatry and psychology over whether to classify homosexuality as a pathological condition and/or one that can be overcome through therapy. Evangelicals have long struggled to validate their theology through science, so it's not surprising that evangelical leaders would become invested in this conflict. If homosexuality is a pathological condition, this can be used as evidence that it's contrary to God's will for people's lives. If even secular therapy can help overcome homosexuality, how much more so can therapy based in Christian practice?

One significant challenge for evangelical ex-gay leaders was that anti-gay theories were primarily rooted in the psychoanalytic tradition, which is poles apart from the world of evangelical theology. These theories needed to be translated into a form that was both understandable to evangelicals and consistent with their theology. This translation work was first undertaken by the British psychologist Elizabeth Moberly in her book *Homosexuality: A New Christian Ethic*, published in 1983. Moberly is Eastern Orthodox, but her work was written for a broad Christian audience and contains nothing that would be theologically objectionable to an American evangelical readership. In fact, she quotes the American evangelical ex-gay leader Kent Philpott along with the popular English evangelical John White. Moberly draws from the work of Bieber, Socarides, and others to assert that homosexuality is caused by difficulties in the parent-child relationship, especially in the early years of life. The relationship with the parent of the same sex is especially important: "From amidst a welter of details, one constant underlying principle suggests itself: that the homosexual—whether man or woman—has suffered from some deficit in the relationship with the parent of the same sex; and that there is a corresponding drive to make good this deficit—through the medium of same-sex or 'homosexual' relationships."[55] Consequently, therapy to overcome homosexuality involves overcoming the "same-sex deficit" through nonsexual relationships with members of the same sex.

Two aspects of Moberly's book suggest that the author's goal was to translate psychoanalytic theory for a Christian audience. The first is the absence of terms from Freudian theory such as "Oedipus complex," "penis envy," or "castration anxiety" that a Christian lay audience would find not only confusing but also possibly offensive. The second is the inclusion of Christian theology. Secular anti-gay psychiatrists refer to heterosexuality as the normal outcome of human biology without referring to a creator, whereas for Moberly, human biology reflects God's design and intention for adulthood—complementary relationships between men and women. Similarly, the path of human development isn't an accident of evolution but the result of "God-given laws for human growth."[56] Finally, she admits that psychologically based therapy is useful, but reminds her readers, "It is God who heals, and so our dependency on God is all-important."[57]

Following in the footsteps of Moberly was Joseph Nicolosi, one of the cofounders of NARTH. Like Moberly, Nicolosi took psychoanalytic theory about the pathological nature of homosexuality, removed the problematic Freudian terminology, and pitched his books to a religious audience. As a leader in NARTH, Nicolosi was responsible for representing the scientific face of the ex-gay movement. Consequently, his books have much less overt Christian content compared with those of Moberly. Still, there are frequent references to human "design" that imply the existence of a creator, as well as attention to the concerns of faith communities. "Most of the parents of prehomosexual children who come to us for help are people of religious faith—Catholic, Protestant, Mormon, Jewish—but a few, too, are secularists who intuitively sense that humankind is designed to be heterosexual."[58]

According to Tanya Erzen, Moberly was a "celebrity" at Exodus International meetings in the early 1980s. However, she discontinued her association when Exodus leaders refused to validate her claim that Nicolosi plagiarized her ideas.[59] Nicolosi maintained close ties with Exodus until the organization's demise in 2013. Both Moberly and Nicolosi continue to exert sizable influence over evangelical ex-gay theology.

The political strategy of condemning gays and lesbians, characteristic of the evangelical right during the 1980s, clearly fits into Hofstadter's definition of the paranoid style. This strategy posits the existence of a grand conspiracy of anti-Christian movements, including gay and lesbian activists, which threatens to undermine the moral foundation of society. But what of the ex-gay movement approach that emphasizes "compassion," "healing," and "hope" for those "struggling" with homosexuality? The important thing to recognize is that the language of compassion exists alongside, rather than fully replacing, the older language that depicts gays and lesbians as a moral threat. Again, the concept of free will individualism is central. Ex-gay leaders offer compassion to those gays and lesbians *who wish to change* (and, if they persist, will experience change). They claim that unrepentant gays and lesbians are willfully choosing a dysfunctional and immoral lifestyle. Moreover, gay rights movements are not only unnecessary (since homosexuality is a choice), but they threaten to corrupt major social institutions.[60] The supposed takeover of American mental health guilds by gay activists, resulting in the suppression of scientific evidence that homosexuality is a disorder, is of particular concern to ex-gay leaders.

The ex-gay project conforms to the paranoid style in another important way. As I discussed in the previous chapter, Hofstadter argued that paranoid movements frequently celebrate the renegade from the enemy cause. For the intelligent design movement, the renegades are former secular academics like Phillip E. Johnson who came to reject Darwinism. For the ex-gay movement, the renegades are, of course, ex-gays, along with the psychiatrists who formed NARTH in order to support them. Ex-gays not only show that "change" is possible but bear witness to the dysfunctional and unfulfilling nature of the "gay lifestyle."[61]

Hofstadter also observed that obsession with deviant sexual activity has frequently been a feature of paranoid movements:

> The sexual freedom often attributed to [the enemy], his lack of moral inhibition, his possession of especially effective techniques for fulfilling his desires, give exponents of the paranoid style an opportunity to project and freely express unacceptable aspects of their own minds. Priests and Mormon patriarchs were commonly thought to have especial attraction for women, and hence licentious privilege. Thus Catholics and Mormons—later Negroes and Jews—lent themselves to a preoccupation with illicit sex.[62]

It's impossible to read this description and not see the parallel with ex-gay leaders' depictions of "promiscuous" gays.

The Ex-Gay Literature: Religious and Scientific Arguments

Like intelligent design leaders, ex-gay leaders have written a vast number of books to promote their movement to a broad audience, especially their evangelical base. The ex-gay literature is significantly larger than the intelligent design literature. This isn't surprising, given the greater number of ex-gay leaders and the fact that the ex-gay movement predates the intelligent design movement by almost two decades. In my analysis I focus on a sample that includes many of the most popular ex-gay movement books.[63] These have been cited, recommended, and/or sold by major ex-gay ministries, *Christianity Today*, and Focus on the Family. The books are interrelated; the more recently published ones often cite the older ones, and many of the authors endorse each other's books.

We can group the authors of these books into several categories. First, there are psychiatrists or psychologists who have been associated with NARTH, including NARTH cofounder Joseph Nicolosi along with Stanton L. Jones, Mark A. Yarhouse, and Jeffrey Satinover. Other authors have been associated with ex-gay ministry organizations like Exodus International (prior to its closing). These include Andrew Comiskey, Joe Dallas, Bob Davies, Jeff Konrad, Elizabeth Moberly, John and Anne Paulk, and Leanne Payne. Thomas E. Schmidt and Robert A. J. Gagnon are both evangelical New Testament scholars, and Gagnon currently serves on the board of the Restored Hope Network.

Six of the authors—Comiskey, Dallas, Davies, Konrad, and the Paulks—identified themselves at the time of writing as ex-gay individuals who had successfully left behind the homosexual lifestyle. All of the authors, with three exceptions, are evangelicals. As I mentioned earlier, Nicolosi is a Roman Catholic who has clearly been influenced by evangelicalism. Moberly is Eastern Orthodox but is similarly influenced by evangelicalism. Satinover is an Orthodox Jew with unusually strong Christian sympathies. Satinover cites the New Testament in his writings. When he read the Christian apologist C. S. Lewis, he recounts, "I had the distinct impression that here was Truth—with a capital 'T.'"[64] All of the authors are from the United States except Moberly, who is from England.

In the previous chapter we saw that InterVarsity Press published the majority of the intelligent design literature. A more diverse group of publishers is responsible for the ex-gay literature. Still, InterVarsity Press is the single largest publisher of the books in this sample and demonstrates how the evangelical center has embraced the ex-gay movement.

Fundamental to all of this literature is the insistence that the Bible—and by extension authentic Christianity—condemns homosexual practice. This belief is so entrenched in mainstream evangelicalism that some books hardly bother to defend it. The books that do offer lengthier defenses of this belief are aimed at a broader audience that includes nonevangelicals, or else were written to provide evangelicals with arguments to use against liberal Christians who accept homosexual practice. Not surprisingly, the biblical scholars (Schmidt and Gagnon) offer the most elaborate defenses of this belief.

This literature also devotes considerable space to arguments related to science, in keeping with the ex-gay movement's goal of presenting itself as scientifically grounded. As I discussed in the previous chapter, in the traditional evangelical approach to science, science and the Bible form one truth and offer an alternative (and superior) scientific paradigm when mainstream science contradicts evangelical beliefs. We can see this approach at work in four specific features of the ex-gay literature. First, several of the authors challenge claims made by other Christians (including theologically liberal Christians) that new scientific knowledge about sexuality requires churches to reconsider their condemnation of homosexuality. Second, the authors all treat the Bible as a source of scientific data about human sexuality, including the origins and changeability of homosexuality. Third, several of the authors argue that data from medical and social scientific studies and from human anatomy confirm the Bible's teaching that homosexuality is contrary to God's will. Finally, the authors all reject the decisions of mainstream psychiatric and medical guilds to declassify homosexuality as an illness, and some authors explicitly declare that these guilds are practicing flawed science. Most of the authors instead affirm the work of NARTH. Let's examine each of these features in detail.

Countering the Use of Science by Christians Who Affirm Homosexuality

An increasing number of Christians, especially those in the liberal wings of mainline denominations, have reexamined or even repudiated Christianity's traditional condemnation of homosexuality. In addition to citing contemporary biblical scholarship, these Christians cite new scientific data on sexuality as justification.[65] Authors in the ex-gay movement are troubled by this trend because it frames anti-gay Christians as being out of touch with scientific reality. They therefore have to come up with a counterframing response. We'll examine two books that do just that.

Stanton L. Jones and Mark A. Yarhouse's book *Homosexuality: The Use of Scientific Research in the Church's Moral Debate* presents itself as a review of scientific research on homosexuality and a critical examination of how this research is used and misused in church debates. According to the authors,

> The scientific research on homosexuality is often cited very casually in these debates, especially in the study and support documents of the mainline Christian denominations. After the stem "Science says . . ." sweeping and inaccurate generalizations are often made. After such generalizations ethical conclusions are often thrown out that are only loosely tied to the supposed scientific findings.[66]

Joe Dallas frames his book *A Strong Delusion* as an attempt to confront the "Gay Christian Movement," consisting of the Metropolitan Community Churches (a denomination ministering primarily to gay, lesbian, bisexual, and transgender persons) and those in the mainline and evangelical churches who affirm homosexuality. Regarding MCC's leader Troy Perry, Dallas writes, "Troy Perry's assertion that 'scientific information, social changes, and personal experience are the greatest forces for change in the way we interpret the Bible' is unsettling. Social change and personal experience are irrelevant to truth; Jesus Christ, who is the same yesterday, today, and forever (Hebrews 13:8), is not known to follow social trends."[67]

The Bible as a Source of Data on Sexuality

American evangelicalism has traditionally insisted that the Bible is a factual document. The ex-gay literature adheres to this tradition by arguing that the Bible provides scientific data about human sexuality, including homosexuality. The two most common claims in these books are that the Bible reveals that (1) human sexuality has been corrupted by the Fall, with homosexuality being one result; and (2) homosexuals are capable of "change."

All of the ex-gay authors in this sample treat the Fall described in Genesis 3 as an event in human history. (This is in contrast to the liberal Christian interpretation that the Genesis story is a metaphorical narrative reflecting on the human condition, not a historical account.) For these authors the Fall is responsible for all sorts of failings in the area of

sexuality and gender relations and the inability of humans to fully conform to God's will. For example, Andrew Comiskey writes,

> Striving for wholeness in the arms or image of the same sex had proved
> to be a futile and confusing quest. The Genesis account helps explain this
> futility. God never intended for man or woman to seek completion in
> the same sex. Thus homosexual pursuit of erotic and emotional bonding
> violates something basic to our humanity. The Creator, in His inspired
> Scriptures, has shown that homosexual feelings and behaviors must be
> identified with the fall. Homosexuality is one of the many sexual disor-
> ders that have become woven into the fabric of sinful humanity.[68]

Statements about the "fallen" nature of humanity as the source of homosexuality can be found in most of the other books.

A second common claim in this literature is that the Bible (specifically 1 Corinthians 6:9–11) indicates that individuals are capable of leaving behind homosexual relations with the help of God. One example can
be found in Bob Davies and Lori Rentzel's *Coming Out of Homosexuality*:

> Furthermore, there is clear biblical evidence that God can change the life of
> a person involved in [homosexual] behavior. In 1 Corinthians chapter six
> the apostle Paul is addressing men and women in the church at Corinth. He
> lists many forms of behavior—including homosexual involvement—that
> will bar someone from God's kingdom (v.9). Then Paul makes an amazing
> statement: "And this is what some of you *were.*" (v. 11, emphasis added). Paul
> knew former homosexuals in the church at Corinth! So the message that
> homosexuality can be changed is not new; homosexuals have been experi-
> encing change since the Bible was written.[69]

Note the phrase "biblical evidence," which assumes the objective,
factual nature of the Bible. Several other books cite the same biblical
passage.[70] However, there are differences in how authors interpret the
passage. Authors associated with ex-gay ministries (Dallas, Davies, Konrad, and Anne Paulk) interpret the passage to mean that individuals who
call on God's help can expect to experience a reduction in their attraction to the same sex (that is, modify their sexual orientation), though

this may involve a long and difficult journey. In contrast, Gagnon, Jones, and Yarhouse, all of whom are academics, write that not all homosexuals can expect to substantially modify their sexual orientations in the direction of heterosexuality, but that all homosexuals can "change" by leaving behind homosexual relations, pursuing a celibate lifestyle if necessary.

As discussed earlier, for ex-gay leaders the belief that homosexuality is a changeable condition is closely associated with the belief that same-sex attraction results from an individual's choices over time. That is, life circumstances may encourage certain choices, but the individual is ultimately responsible for what he or she becomes. Several authors explicitly make this argument.[71] An example of this reasoning can be found in Jeff Konrad's book *You Don't Have to Be Gay*:

> I realize that the word *choice* upsets a lot of individuals, so let me explain. First, I'm not saying you woke up one day and chose to be sexually attracted to other men. With the discrimination and pain that so often accompanies the homosexual, who in his right mind would choose to be gay?
>
> What I am saying is that being gay is an acquired identity, an identity brought about through the misinterpretation of events and its subsequent responses. Many of my childhood experiences were beyond my control, but my responses were my own choices. An inappropriate response to a situation here, another one there—eventually they added up to a distorted image of myself . . . and for me, a homosexual identity.
>
> Since homosexuality is an acquired identity, it makes sense that you can choose to change your identity. As adults we can choose to respond to things in a healthy and mature manner rather than reacting in childish and foolish ways.[72]

The one book with a contrary perspective is Yarhouse's *Homosexuality and the Christian*.[73] Yarhouse writes that individuals are responsible for their choices regarding sexual behavior and identity (whether or not to identify as a "gay" person), but he denies that individuals are responsible for developing same-sex attraction. This is among the most recently published books in this literature, and it may be an attempt to steer the ex-gay movement in a somewhat different direction.

Scientific Proof That Homosexuality Is Contrary to God's Will

Several of the authors follow the evangelical tradition of using scientific data to prove that the Bible (along with a particular interpretation of it) is true. In this case, they offer medical and social scientific data as empirical evidence that homosexuality is contrary to God's will, as (they claim) the Bible clearly teaches. Three arguments along these lines are the most common: (1) homosexuals suffer from poor physical and mental health, consequences of pursuing a lifestyle contrary to God's creational intentions; (2) homosexuals (men in particular) are promiscuous and/or have unstable romantic relationships; and (3) the complementary sex organs of the human male and female are evidence that God intended men and women to be in complementary relationships.

The most thorough attempt to link homosexuality with ill health can be found in Jeffrey Satinover's *Homosexuality and the Politics of Truth*. Satinover reviews what he portrays as a highly politically charged debate in the field of psychiatry over whether homosexuality is an illness. He then concludes,

> A better way to determine the desirability or undesirability of homosexuality is to leave behind the circular thinking and self-serving rhetoric and instead examine the medical facts. As we will see in the next chapter, much detailed and sophisticated research shows that homosexuality is unequivocally associated with a large number of severe *medical* problems—even apart from AIDS.[74]

In the chapter that follows, titled "Is Homosexuality Desirable? Brute Facts," Satinover contends that homosexuality is associated with a number of health problems, including hepatitis, liver cancer, rectal cancer, and a high suicide rate. He also cites a study that he claims reveals that 40 percent of gay males regularly engage in anal sex without using a condom. He uses this data to conclude that "the incidence and intractability of anal intercourse in a gay population, even in the face of illness or death, suggests its central, compulsive role in the lifestyle."[75]

The word "compulsive" is significant, because what Satinover is trying to do is draw parallels between homosexuality and alcoholism. To say that homosexuality is an "undesirable" condition is part of a larger

argument—that homosexuality is contrary to God's will and has reper-
cussions, as the Bible reveals:

> The correlation between male homosexuality and disease has been rec-
> ognized for at least two thousand years. Thus the Apostle Paul, writing
> during the heyday of the Roman Empire when licentiousness was ram-
> pant, observed that "Men committed indecent acts with other men, and
> received in themselves [sometimes translated 'in their bodies'] the due
> penalty for their perversion."[76]

We can find similar claims in some of the other ex-gay books. For
example, in his book *Straight and Narrow?*, Thomas E. Schmidt uses statistics to argue that there are higher rates of physical and mental illnesses
among the homosexual population. Like Satinover, Schmidt thinks that
this is evidence that homosexual relations violate God's will: "Paul wrote
in Romans 1:27 that homosexuals 'received in their own persons the due
penalty of error.' It is not clear what he meant by 'penalty' in his time,
but it is hard not to make a connection between his words and the health
crisis we observe in our time."[77] Gagnon's book *The Bible and Homosexual Practice* cites Satinover's book and reiterates his conclusions.[78]
Finally, Jones and Yarhouse's book *Homosexuality* reviews mental health
data for homosexuals and offer a similar if more tentative claim:

> The scientific evidence points to a correlation of homosexuality with per-
> sonal distress, though not all homosexuals are distressed. Many pro-gay
> advocates view homosexuals who are distressed as the victims of societal
> prejudice rather than of anything inherently unstable about being gay or
> lesbian. But it might be instead that the homosexual condition is discor-
> dant, or out of alignment, with God's creational intent for human life and
> hence unlikely to foster the kind of sense of well-being that goes along
> with living a fulfilling life.[79]

Significantly, none of the authors is willing to say that AIDS was sent
by God as a punishment for same-sex relations. But several of them
suggest something similar: that contracting AIDS is a potential consequence of engaging in behavior that's contrary to God's will. This type
of claim is most clearly stated in Jeff Konrad's *You Don't Have to Be Gay*:

I certainly don't believe that AIDS is God's curse, judgment—or whatever—against homosexuals. I think AIDS, for the homosexual, is simply the consequence of their actions, not God's wrath or judgment upon them. . . . Because He created us, He knows what effects upon the body result from unnatural acts, abuse, and promiscuity. That's why He provided us with limitations and restraints, so we might live a rich, abundant life. If we follow the Bible as our owner's manual, we'll achieve such a life, but if we go against His laws, there are definite consequences.[80]

Besides claiming that homosexuals suffer from ill health, these authors invoke a second type of scientific evidence: studies showing a high rate of promiscuity and/or relational instability among homosexuals, particularly men. For example, Gagnon writes that "all the data for homosexual conduct indicates that it has a very poor track record so far as enduring monogamous relationships are concerned," and cites more than a dozen studies to support his claim.[81] Gagnon concedes that societal disapproval of same-sex relationships does play some role in this relational instability, but he insists that it's not a sufficient explanation:

Yet the ratios [of the number of sexual partners for homosexuals versus heterosexuals] are *so* disproportionate that two other significant factors must be involved. One is the obvious fact that homosexual unions do not produce children . . . and children (especially one's own biological children) *can* be a stabilizing factor in a relationship. However, this factor . . . does not explain why lesbians have far fewer sexual partners on average than homosexual men (though still higher than their heterosexual female counterparts). The most important factor probably has to do with the nature of male sexuality. As a general rule, men who are left to their own devices have great difficulty forming monogamous relationships. Men need to be "civilized" and "domesticated" into such unions by women.[82]

In other words, same-sex relational instability (particularly for homosexual males) happens because same-sex partners are violating the gender complementarity that God built in to creation. And in case the reader takes issue with Gagnon by noting monogamous same-sex couples that he or she knows, Gagnon reasserts the scientific foundation of his claims: "Yet the occasional anecdotal evidence [of monogamous same-sex couples] does not stack up against the cumulative statistical evidence culled from numerous scientific studies, let alone deal with the question of God's revealed design for sexuality in Scripture and the anatomical puzzle of same-sex coupling."[83]

Gagnon's arguments (and list of studies) build on similar conclusions reached by Schmidt, Satinover, and Jones and Yarhouse, all of whom he cites. Konrad also writes that homosexual promiscuity reveals that homosexual relations are contrary to God's design, citing a single study for support.[84] Comiskey claims that promiscuity is evidence that homosexual relations are contrary to God's design, but he cites no studies.[85] Finally, Moberly asserts without citing supporting evidence that homosexual relationships are unstable, a result of the fact that "there is no basis for permanence in the structure of the homosexual condition."[86]

A final piece of scientific evidence offered by some of the authors is the complementarity of human male and female sex organs, which several books argue is an empirical manifestation of the overall gender complementarity that God intends for humans. For example, according to Schmidt,

> The Genesis narrative affirms that male and female are different in correspondence to one another such that their union constitutes a completion. . . . And whether or not we regard sexual differences as symbolic of other differences between the sexes, physical complementarity is undoubtedly present. That is, the penis fits inside the vagina, and the fit is pleasurable to both partners.[87]

Gagnon similarly refers to "the witness of nature (to which the Bible points), that is, the complementarity of male and female sex organs as the most unambiguous clue people have of God's intent for gender pairing, apart from the direct revelation of the Bible."[88]

There's a potential weakness to this strategy of offering empirical evidence that homosexuality is contrary to God's intended order. Christians who are accepting of homosexuality often say that same-sex attraction is part of the natural order, and this is empirical evidence that God didn't intend all people to be heterosexual—in other words, "God created me (or others) gay." The ex-gay movement authors then have to explain why they think some kinds of evidence (disease, promiscuity, sex organs) are admissible when discerning God's will and another kind of evidence (same-sex attraction) is inadmissible. They accomplish this by attributing same-sex attraction to the Fall, as discussed above. Same-sex attraction may be "natural" with respect to the body after the Fall, but it's "unnatural" with respect to God's intended order.[89] For authors who cite complementary sex organs as evidence of God's will, the Fall corrupted human sexual desires but had no effect on human sexual anatomy.[90]

Rejecting Mainstream Psychiatry and Psychology

We've already seen how mainstream mental health and medical guilds came to reject the idea that homosexuality is an illness. In response, several ex-gay books attacked the scientific integrity of the American Psychiatric Association, claiming that its decision to declassify homosexuality as a mental illness was driven by politics rather than science.[91] This argument is most fully explicated in Satinover's book *Homosexuality and the Politics of Truth*. Satinover, a psychiatrist who has been associated with NARTH, writes that the APA's shift was a result of a well-organized campaign by gay activists:

> For better or worse, mental health professionals exert influence that greatly exceeds the actual wisdom we demonstrate. In the early years of "gay liberation," this reality was used for the fledgling gay activists' advantage. They anticipated that if the influential American Psychiatric Association (APA) could be convinced to redefine homosexuality, the other guilds would follow shortly thereafter and then so would the rest of society. Their plan was implemented with near-total success.[92]

According to Satinover, gay activists gained their victory in the APA "with no new scientific evidence," and relied instead on aggressive political tactics.[93] As a result, new research on homosexuality that could call the APA's stance into question is being stifled.

The authors who don't explicitly criticize the APA nonetheless all affirm that homosexuality is a psychological disorder. They offer similar descriptions of how an individual is led toward homosexuality: problems relating to parents (especially the same-sex parent), childhood trouble with same-sex peers, and/or sexual abuse can alienate an individual from his or her true, God-given gender identity.

*   *   *

To sum up, the ex-gay literature follows the American evangelical tradition of attempting to fuse the religious and the scientific. Ex-gay authors think that the Bible condemns homosexual practice and offers hope for change—and they think that their reading of the Bible is not only correct theology but also correct science. Like authors from the intelligent design movement, ex-gay authors insist that mainstream science (in this case, the APA) is peddling falsehoods while they offer scientific truth.

The Ex-Gay Movement's Identity Dilemma

The ex-gay movement faces the same impossible dilemma as the intelligent design movement: it has to present itself as scientifically credible (and therefore untainted by religious and political influences) and at the same time mobilize the support of Christian conservatives. The ex-gay movement's fight for scientific credibility is somewhat easier, because ex-gay (reparative) therapy was at one point embraced by mainstream psychiatry. In other words, the ex-gay movement seeks the restoration of an abandoned scientific paradigm rather than the more challenging job of replacing a dominant paradigm (evolution) with a new one (intelligent design). Additionally, the intelligent design movement must constantly fend off comparisons with the failed paradigm of creation science. No parallel exists for the ex-gay movement. As with the intelligent design movement, conservative Christian support was never guaranteed—the evangelical right ignored the ex-gay movement for two decades.

Ultimately, no movement can succeed at being accepted as science and religion at the same time. The best that movement leaders can do is convince themselves and their core followers, even if they fail in the broader society. Ex-gay leaders don't seem to be using the "discursive tacking" strategy favored by some intelligent design proponents, but they do mirror the intelligent design movement in their use of the division of labor and in having NARTH/ATCSI distinguish between supposed primary and secondary missions, just as the Discovery Institute does.

Division of Labor

Compared with the intelligent design movement, the ex-gay movement has a seemingly more robust division of labor, involving not only different authors but also different organizations. NARTH/ATCSI has been responsible for advancing the "pure science" frame, even if it has been far from consistent in adhering to this message. Evangelical ex-gay ministries, in contrast, have been openly religious. They sometimes use scientific arguments, but they never pretend to be *purely* scientific and are thus the primary carriers of the "religious crusade" frame.

A check of the NARTH website in 2006 revealed two statements that clearly represented "pure science" framing. The first statement was in a section labeled "Our Track Record": "NARTH welcomes the support of all lay organizations, including religious groups, which turn to us for scientific evidence which may support their traditional doctrines. We remain, however, a professional organization devoted to scientific inquiry."[94] Another section of the website contained a 2003 statement titled "NARTH and Civil Rights" that addressed legal cases related to civil rights for gays and lesbians. The statement again asserted the scientific focus of NARTH: "Recognizing that these legal issues and policies are complex—and wishing to maintain our status as a scientific organization—the Governing Board of NARTH has decided that, in most instances, it will not take a position on such issues."[95]

A check of the website in 2013 revealed that the "pure science" framing had been moved to the frequently asked questions section. Question 4 asks, "Is NARTH a religious organization?" The answer is, "No. It is a scientific and professional organization that includes highly qualified academics and fully licensed mental health professionals."[96] This question and answer were retained with minor editing on the NARTH Institute website following the 2015 reorganization.

NARTH/ATCSI has employed this "pure science" framing for two reasons. First, it needs to be recognized as a scientific organization in order to challenge the scientific claims of mainstream mental health guilds such as the American Psychiatric Association. Second, it has worked to counter gay-affirming programs in public schools, and it can do this more effectively if it's perceived as providing a scientific perspective.

In contrast to NARTH, the ex-gay ministries present their religious identities unambiguously on their websites. For example, prior to its demise, Exodus International described itself as "a nonprofit, interdenominational Christian organization promoting the message of *Freedom from homosexuality through the power of Jesus Christ.*"[97] The Restored Hope Network's mission statement is also unambiguously Christian: "Restored Hope is an inter-denominational membership governed network dedicated to restoring hope to those broken by sexual and relational sin, especially those impacted by homosexuality. We proclaim that Jesus Christ has life-changing power for all who submit to Christ as Lord; we also seek to equip His church to impart that transformation."[98]

There have been multiple links between NARTH (and later ATCSI) and the network of ex-gay ministries, indicating that they have been a united movement. First, some ex-gay ministry leaders have relied on arguments produced by NARTH and its leaders (especially Joseph Nicolosi) in their books. Second, some ex-gay ministry websites have included hyperlinks to the NARTH website. Third, Nicolosi has frequently attended ex-gay ministry conferences, including Exodus conferences prior to the organization's closing. Finally, Nicolosi helped produce booklets related to Focus on the Family's ex-gay ministry.

Distinguishing between Supposed Primary and Secondary Missions

Recall that the Discovery Institute attempts to manage the contradiction between its "pure science" and its "religious crusade" framing by distinguishing between a supposed primary mission (advancing science) and a supposed secondary mission (supporting religious organizations). The reality, of course, is that it does nothing to advance science, and supporting conservative Christianity is in fact its primary mission. NARTH (and later ATCSI) has suffered from the same contradiction and has used the same rhetorical strategy to manage it.

Before examining NARTH's use of this strategy, let's consider how the organization has used the "religious crusade" frame. In 2006 the NARTH website had a page devoted to its Interfaith Committee on Theological Concerns, the very existence of which was curious for a "scientific" organization. The page contained articles with titles such as "Catholic Schools, Teens, and Homosexuality: The Truth Will Set Them

Free," "The Bible Still Matters" (a strongly positive review of Gagnon's book *The Bible and Homosexual Practice*), and "Responding to Pro-Gay Theology."[99]

A check of the website in 2009 revealed that the religious content was still present, if less prominent. A tab on the main page titled "News Watch" led to a section titled "Theological Issues." Most of the earlier religious articles remained. Among the new articles was the transcript from a discussion sponsored by the Heritage Foundation (a think tank with close ties to the evangelical right) titled "Same-Sex 'Marriage' and the Fate of Religious Liberty."[100]

By 2013 NARTH had again reorganized its website. The home page listed several divisions: Clinical; Medical; Ethics, Faith & Family; and Education and Client Rights. The Ethics, Faith & Family page contained a featured video described as "Presentation on Biblical Hermeneutics in relation to homosexuality by Dr. Henry Virkler at the 2012 NARTH Conference in Orlando, Florida." This was accompanied by an opinion piece by R. Albert Mohler Jr., president of Southern Baptist Theological Seminary, titled "The Homosexual Agenda: Religious Liberty under Fire." The piece warned about the danger that homosexual activists pose to the liberty of Christian (meaning conservative Christian) churches:

> [Homosexual activists] will not rest until all organized opposition to their behavior and lifestyle is silenced. There can be no question that the Christian church represents the greatest threat to the normalization and celebration of homosexual behavior. Thus, the church and Christian believers must be silenced if the homosexual activists are to have their way.[101]

These two features and other religiously oriented content were retained after the 2015 reorganization, when the Ethics, Faith & Family division became part of ATCSI.

Delivering conservative Christian messages has clearly remained an important task of the NARTH/ATSCI websites. We can see efforts to downplay the significance of these messages in NARTH's statements about its mission and identity. Let's consider again NARTH's statement about its "track record": "NARTH welcomes the support of all lay organizations, including religious groups, which turn to us for scientific evidence which may support their traditional doctrines. We remain, however, a professional organization devoted to scientific inquiry." Not only does this statement frame support for religious groups as being of secondary importance, but it suggests a very specific manner in which this support take place—providing scientific evidence. Additionally, it suggests that NARTH passively receives attention from religious groups ("which turn to us").

Let's also consider the complete answer to the question "Is NARTH a religious organization?" (changed in 2015 to "Is the Alliance or the NARTH Institute a religious organization?")[102] from its FAQ list. The first part of the answer reads: "No. It is a scientific and professional organization that includes highly qualified academics and fully licensed mental health professionals. Any number of organizations and individuals including religious organizations may use our knowledge base and professional training and presentations."[103] Here, NARTH again frames itself as a scientific organization that passively receives attention from religious organizations. From there, the answer shifts to consideration of the client, whose possible religious motivation is an individual matter rather than an indication of NARTH's own religious orientation:

> NARTH affirms the right of religious belief and diversity for clients as well as therapists. Respect for religious diversity requires that mental health professionals give as much weight to religious belief as to sexual identity in offering ethical therapeutic services. Some critics have falsely accused NARTH of simplistic attempts to promote change, such as "praying away the gay." This reflects a lack of understanding of the therapeutic relationship as well as a lack of understanding of change. Sometimes people who lack understanding feel it is an easy matter to make changes in homosexual orientation, when it almost always requires high motivation and effort—as with changing many other aspects of life. However, the spiritual motivation and experiences of a given individual as well as religious organizational support can be a very important component in assisting people with their change process.[104]

That NARTH's leaders would create such a long-winded answer to such a simple question is surely a red flag that they're being less than straightforward. In any case, this elaborate framing strategy can't hide the obvious: NARTH/ATCSI is very much enmeshed in conservative Christianity. Far from passively receiving attention from religious groups, it's an active partner with evangelical ministries in advancing the ex-gay movement agenda. But the impossible goal of trying to be a scientific organization and a religious organization at the same time forces its leaders, just like those of the Discovery Institute, to engage in deceptive rhetoric.

Managing Failure

One constant that we can see throughout the four-decade-long history of the ex-gay movement is repeated attempts to manage failure. Despite the best efforts from leaders and members alike, same-sex attractions remain impervious to change. Rank-and-file members in ex-gay ministries fail to turn straight, and many of the movement's leaders who define themselves as ex-gay have had public failings or have abandoned the movement and embraced their homosexuality. For example, Exodus leader Michael Bussee abruptly left the movement when, en route to speak at a church with an Exodus volunteer with whom he had worked for several years, the two men realized that they were in love.[105] Focus on the Family ex-gay spokesman John Paulk created headlines in 2001 when he was spotted in a gay bar.[106] In 2013 Paulk finally renounced the ex-gay movement and issued an apology to gay community. Somewhat like the leader of a religious sect that has incorrectly predicted the end of the world, ex-gay leaders have had to take steps to maintain the plausibility of their movement when promised ends have failed to materialize.[107]

The primary response of ex-gay leaders to inconvenient realities has been to lower expectations over time. When Exodus was first starting, leaders were filled with great optimism that anyone who put their faith in God could be changed completely from homosexual to heterosexual. As Frank Worthen proclaimed at a 1978 Exodus meeting, "God will not take a person half-way and then abandon them. God would do a complete work."[108] By the 1990s ex-gay leaders were no longer promising complete change. Rather, they said that while a substantial reduction in same-sex attraction was possible, ex-gay individuals should be prepared for a lifelong struggle. There were open disagreements between ex-gay leaders (discussed earlier in the review of the ex-gay literature) concerning what proportion of ex-gays would develop sufficient attraction to the opposite sex to make heterosexual marriage a realistic option and what proportion would have to opt for lifelong celibacy.

The expectation of lifelong struggle is the central theme of Andrew Comiskey's 2003 book *Strength in Weakness: Healing Sexual and Relational Brokenness*. A previous book had chronicled Comiskey's transition from homosexuality to heterosexual marriage, but this book opens with an admission of his continued homosexual temptations. While on vacation in Manhattan he found himself receiving unwanted attention from gay men who wondered whether he and his wife were a couple: "The assertiveness of the homosexuals we encountered caused me to work harder to assert who I was and what I stood for, and that was good. But at the same time—I have to admit—these overtures were appealing to me. Against the sophisticated backdrop of Manhattan, the homosexual lifestyle appeared highly seductive."[109]

The ex-gay movement's lower expectations were forced by experience, but they happened to fit well with the evangelical belief that all people remain "sinners" even after becoming born again in Christ, and Christians are therefore continually dependent on God's grace. Comiskey resorts to this framing immediately after the above anecdote:

I have discovered that God does not free me from all of my weaknesses. Rather, he frees me to cry out to him as I struggle to do what is right. Then he is faithful to release his power again and again and again. When submitted to God, our weaknesses have holy purposes. They challenge the limitations of our self-reliance. And they remind us—more often than we would like—of our need for the strength God can provide.[110]

This approach is not without hazards. The evangelical world thrives on clear-cut conceptual distinctions, on black and white categories. Once outright condemnation became inappropriate, the natural response of evangelical leaders to the existence of gays was to turn them into ex-gays. But if individuals continue to "struggle" with homosexual attraction, then in what sense are they ex-gays? It's not a big conceptual leap from acknowledging the "struggle" of ex-gays to realizing that sexual orientation is unchangeable and questioning the ex-gay movement's project.

In addition to lowering expectations, ex-gay leaders try to maintain the movement's plausibility by citing research studies that, they claim, prove the efficacy of ex-gay (reparative) therapy. One such study was conducted by Joseph Nicolosi of NARTH and titled "A Survey of Sexual-Orientation Change." It was released to the public in 1997, though, significantly, it was never published in a journal.[111] Also widely touted by ex-gay leaders is Robert Spitzer's 2003 journal article "Can Some Gay Men and Lesbians Change Their Sexual Orientation? 200 Participants Reporting a Change from Homosexual to Heterosexual Orientation."[112]

Responding to widespread criticism of these and other studies supporting ex-gay therapy, the NARTH-affiliated psychologists Stanton L. Jones and Mark A. Yarhouse conducted yet another study, presented in their book *Ex-Gays? A Longitudinal Study of Religiously Mediated Change in Sexual Orientation*. The authors go to considerable lengths to explain that their study is scientifically rigorous and provides convincing evidence that ex-gay therapy can work. The acknowledgments section of the book addresses one significant obstacle to scientific acceptance: the fact that the book was published by InterVarsity Press and not a secular academic press. The authors turn to familiar conspiracy theory, arguing that the book was shunned for purely political reasons rather than because of its low scholarly quality: "[Our literary agent] found door after door slammed in his face because of the topic of study and likely fallout for a publisher committed to such a project."[113]

Christianity Today supported Jones and Yarhouse with two companion articles praising the study. The first article, "An Older, Wiser Ex-Gay Movement," framed the authors' modest expectations for change (individuals continue to struggle with same-sex attraction, and some opt for celibacy) as part of a larger maturation of the ex-gay movement, which now offers "realistic hope for homosexuals."[114] The second article was labeled "news" and titled "The Best Research Yet."[115] Predictably, the study got a much more critical reception from those outside the Christian Right world. Gay bloggers quickly found flaws with the study, while psychology journals found the study unworthy of review. Jones and Yarhouse eventually launched a website (www.exgaystudy.org) related to their study. Among the website's sections was one responding to the many criticisms the study received. Few scholars go to this length to defend their work. However, nothing less than the scientific credibility of ex-gay therapy was at stake.

Despite these efforts, the ex-gay movement continues to experience high rates of defection. In fact, ex-gay leaders face considerable "counterframing" from disgruntled former participants in ex-gay ministries who form the "ex-ex-gay" movement. Of course, the biggest blow to the ex-gay movement was the defection of Exodus leaders. Ex-gay leaders and their supporters mainly responded by attacking Alan Chambers's theology, accusing him of straying from core evangelical commitments. But there was little they could do to refute Chambers's experience that ex-gay therapy simply failed to work for Exodus's numerous clients.

Selective Skepticism of Psychological Theories

In contrast to intelligent design leaders, ex-gay leaders tend to avoid references to postmodern theory.[116] Instead of a selective embrace of postmodernism, we find a selective skepticism of psychological theories. Ex-gay leaders reject any psychological theories that contradict their view that homosexuality is a curable illness. They argue that these theories, which currently dominate major mental health and medical guilds, are the result of pro-gay "politics" rather than scientific data. In contrast, they uncritically accept psychological theories that are consistent with their view of homosexuality, and label such theories scientifically sound.

Joe Dallas, former president of Exodus International, openly acknowledges this type of selective skepticism of the field of psychology, and in fact recommends it to his readers:

> The fact that much of today's psychology is polluted with anti-Christian teaching should not scare us away from the field itself. It should make us cautious, even skeptical at times, but not unwilling to examine what it has to offer that is of merit. There's nothing wrong with psychological theory per se, unless and until it usurps the authority of scripture or becomes the end-all and be-all solution to human problems.
>
> Here is a simple test to determine whether or not a psychological theory is valid: If it contradicts the Bible, reject it outright. It's false. If it's not spelled out in Scripture, but doesn't contradict it either, at least

accept its possibility. It might be true. If it's in the Bible, affirm it as absolute truth.[117]

Dallas's advice may be persuasive for an evangelical audience, but speaking openly about using the Bible as a litmus test for scientific truth hardly advances the credibility of the ex-gay movement in the wider society. It has been up to the leaders of NARTH/ATCSI, as carriers of the "pure science" frame, to make the same case using less explicitly Christian language. As discussed earlier in the review of the ex-gay literature, NARTH leaders did this by criticizing the American Psychiatric Association's decision to remove homosexuality from the *DSM*, claiming that the decision was the result of pro-gay politics rather than science. In making this claim, NARTH leaders depended heavily on the account of the APA controversy provided in Ronald Bayer's book *Homosexuality and American Psychiatry*, citing Bayer's arguments concerning the political motives of the pro-gay faction in the APA. But in doing so, they blatantly distorted the book's contents. Bayer's thesis is that the question of whether homosexuality is "a disease given in nature" can't be answered by science. "The status of homosexuality is a political question, representing a historically rooted, socially determined choice regarding the ends of human sexuality. It requires a political analysis."[118] In other words, Bayer argues that *both sides* of the APA debate on homosexuality were motivated by politics rather than science. NARTH leaders seized on the half of Bayer's thesis that supports their case, citing it as authoritative truth. They pretended that the other half of Bayer's thesis, which would have called into question NARTH's status as a scientific organization, does not exist. Of course, NARTH leaders were free to criticize any parts of the book with which they disagreed. But admitting that they agreed with only half of the book would have prevented them from using it as an authoritative source of truth, and would have exposed their practice of selective skepticism described here.[119]

Selective skepticism explains ex-gay leaders' love-hate relationship with the psychiatrist Robert Spitzer. Recall that Spitzer was instrumental in the APA's decision to declassify homosexuality as an illness, drawing the scorn of those who would later become leaders of the ex-gay movement. However, when he was approached at the 1999 APA annual meeting by an ex-gay protester, someone who claimed that he had successfully changed his sexual orientation, Spitzer became interested in scientifically testing whether such change was possible.[120]

In 2003 Spitzer published the results of his study in the *Archives of Sexual Behavior* (the official journal of the International Academy of Sex Research) in an article titled "Can Some Gay Men and Lesbians Change Their Sexual Orientation? 200 Participants Reporting a Change from Homosexual to Heterosexual Orientation."[121] He recruited individuals for the study who claimed to have sustained some change in homosexual orientation for at least five years following reparative therapy. These individuals were informed of the study by ex-gay religious ministries (43 percent), by NARTH (23 percent), or by therapists from whom they had received reparative therapy. The study utilized ten self-report measures to access sexual orientation before therapy and at the time of the study (after therapy). Spitzer claimed that the data from the self-reports indicated that the therapy did produce a significant (though not complete) shift in sexual orientation away from homosexuality: "It can be seen that there was a marked reduction [in homosexual orientation] on all change measures. This was not only on the three measures of overt behavior and sexual orientation self-identity, as critics of reparative therapy might expect, but also on the seven variables assessing sexual orientation itself."[122]

The remainder of that same issue of the *Archives of Sexual Behavior* was devoted to articles and essays responding to Spitzer's study. The *Journal of Gay and Lesbian Psychotherapy* also devoted an issue in 2003 to responses to the study. Psychologists and psychiatrists reviewing Spitzer's study identified several major methodological flaws. Some took issue with the highly self-selected, nonrepresentative nature of the sample. Some questioned whether individuals' memories of their pretherapy experience were accurate, suggesting that a longitudinal study (one with pre- and post-therapy interviews) would have been more accurate. Finally, some questioned the reliability of the self-report data, given that many of these individuals were motivated (for religious and other reasons) to provide proof that reparative therapy works.

Several ex-gay leaders wrote response essays too. Predictably, these all treat Spitzer's study as methodologically sound. Joseph Nicolosi's essay, "Finally, Recognition of a Long-Neglected Population," reiterates his view that the gay male lifestyle is marked by immaturity in comparison to that of men in heterosexual marriages. He argues that "respect for client diversity" requires that reparative therapy be made available for those who want it.[123] Mark A. Yarhouse's essay, "How Spitzer's Study Gives a Voice to the Disenfranchised within a Minority Group," similarly invokes pluralism while defending Spitzer's methodology.[124]

By 2012 Spitzer was ready to shift his position again, admitting that his study was methodologically flawed and apologizing to the gay community. An article on the NARTH website titled "All the Talk about the Spitzer Study" blamed Spitzer's change of heart on political pressure from gay activists and affirmed the scientific soundness of his earlier research:

> There has been a lot of internet chat lately about Dr. Robert Spitzer, his decade old study of change, and regrets he might be having about getting involved with research on unwanted homosexuality. Dr. Spitzer, a kind and thoughtful man, is now approaching his 80th birthday. Sadly, his study published in the Archives of Sexual Behavior in October 2003 on evidence for effectiveness of reorientation therapy brought down the public scorn and personal harassment of the gay political lobby in full force. For almost a decade he has been personally attacked and his scholarship has been questioned. Regrets? We can be sure that touching this modern "third rail of politics" (it used to be social security and old age benefits) has brought Spitzer little peace at the end of a long career as a respected academic and researcher.
>
> However, research has little to do with politics, feelings, or regrets. It is really about science.[125]

In sum, ex-gay leaders commend Spitzer as "scientific" when he agrees with them and criticize him as "political" when he doesn't.

We should also consider the ex-gay movement's reliance on Freudian psychology. Freud was a staunch atheist and considered religion an "illusion" that assists the psychologically weak, so he's an odd figure for religious conservatives to embrace. In fact, if Christian Right leaders consider Darwinism to be a threat to traditional morality based on its supposedly atheistic implications, they should be even more strongly opposed to the Freudian tradition, as Freud was much more hostile to Christianity than Darwin ever was. Moreover, Freud's concept of penis

envy—that girls eventually realize that their bodies are incomplete because they don't have penises—contradicts the Christian Right position
that both male and female bodies are the product of God's design.

Freud has come in for a lot of criticism, and so has the discipline of
psychoanalysis more broadly. I can't provide a full summary here, but it's
important to note that not everyone thinks that Freudian concepts are
supported by empirical data.[126] Some feminist critics have been especially skeptical of Freud's concept of penis envy, and rightfully so.[127] One
need not be a psychiatrist to see this concept as blatant male chauvinism
masquerading as scientific truth.[128] Yet penis envy has played a central
role for anti-gay psychoanalytic theorists.

Neither the atheistic orientation nor the scientific inadequacy of
Freudian theory is of any consequence to ex-gay leaders. Because the
psychoanalytic tradition eventually came to view homosexuality as both
pathological and curable, ex-gay leaders have been willing to accept this
tradition uncritically. Only then could they present their religiously
based views on homosexuality as grounded in science.

The common pattern in all of this is that ex-gay leaders condemn
their opponents as "political" while ignoring their own very obvious political motivations. A startling illustration of this hypocrisy can
found on the cover of Jeffrey Satinover's book *Homosexuality and the
Politics of Truth*.[129] Here we find a statement declaring it "the best book
on homosexuality written in our lifetime," attributed to "*Congressional
Record*, May 1996." According to Satinover's website, the quote came
from Representative Robert Dornan (Republican from California).[130] A
book denouncing the politicization of truth displaying an endorsement
by a politician—and one known more for inflammatory rhetoric than
thoughtful reflection—would strike any sensible person as completely
bizarre. But apparently this is all quite normal for ex-gay leaders operating in the paranoid style.

Creationist Assumptions

All of the major writers associated with the ex-gay movement endorse
the creationist belief that the human body is a product of God's
design.[131] They also embrace the Christian Right belief in gender
complementarity—that God designed men and women for different,

complementary social roles. This includes sexual complementarity (marriage between one man and one woman), the evidence for which, they believe, is revealed in the complementary sexual organs of men and women. For these writers, the Fall was a historical event that caused homosexuality and other sins, though it didn't undo the gender complementarity or alter sexual organs. For anyone who embraces evolution and recognizes that human bodies have been shaped by a long process of natural selection, these arguments completely lack credibility.

Let's consider the biological categories of male and female. Ex-gay writers often describe sex categories as though they were something designed for humans. They were not. The biological categories of male and female evolved long before humans existed and are found widely (along with other sex categories, such as hermaphrodites) in the animal and plant worlds.

As for the complementary fit between human male and female sexual organs, this is the expected outcome of natural selection. Far from being rare or surprising, as ex-gay writers seem to imply, complementary fit can be found in *every* extant species of mammal. After all, any species of mammal whose typical members were physically unable to copulate would immediately go extinct. Only by ignoring basic evolutionary biology can ex-gay leaders pretend that human sex organs provide empirical support for their religious doctrine.

An additional problem with the Christian Right's belief in gender complementarity is the existence of intersex people, those whose bodies don't fit neatly into the "male versus female" dichotomy. This group includes those whose external genitals, internal reproductive organs, sex chromosomes, and/or sex-related hormones aren't typical of either males or females. The social science literature on intersex people notes that Western societies have largely denied their existence, and doctors frequently perform surgery on the genitals of intersex newborns in order to assign them to either the male or female category.[132] In recent years intersex individuals have increasingly pressed for recognition and self-determination. Ex-gay leaders, like other leaders in the Christian Right, have responded to intersex people by ignoring their existence. This behavior is not surprising. Admitting that intersex people exist would be tantamount to admitting that God has *not* assigned every individual to a male or female body and the accompanying social role. In other words, it would cast into doubt all of the Christian Right's beliefs about gender complementarity.

Let's now turn to belief in the Fall. For many theologically conservative Christians the Fall serves as a catchall explanation for phenomena that they don't want to attribute to God—suffering, evil, natural disasters, and so on.[133] Belief in the Fall is usually based on a literal reading of Genesis 3, which describes Adam and Eve disobeying God by eating fruit from the tree of the knowledge of good and evil. Some Christian writers like C. S. Lewis have opted for a semi-literal reading.[134] This involves seeing Adam and Eve not as two individuals but as literary symbols representing the entire human race, while still insisting that the Fall was a real historical event with negative consequences for the Earth. However, most critical biblical scholars would see both of these readings as problematic.[135] The scholarly consensus is that Genesis is a text written in the language of myth (or metaphor) rather than history. In any case, the Fall is not an event that can be historically or scientifically verified. Ex-gay writers thus confuse theological speculation with science when they argue that homosexuality was caused by the Fall.

A more realistic alternative to viewing homosexuality as a negative consequence of the Fall is to recognize that it's a natural variation in sexuality. Both bisexuality and exclusive homosexuality have been well-documented in the animal world.[136] Homosexuality was once considered an evolutionary paradox since it discourages reproduction, but more recent genetic theories have had little difficulty accounting for it.[137] Unfortunately, these scientific insights are unacceptable to Christian Right leaders, who cling to both creationist beliefs and negative views of homosexuality.

Lies, Damn Lies, and Statistics

Let's turn to ex-gay writers' use of statistical data in their attempt to prove that homosexual relations are contrary to God's will. This effort to use science to substantiate evangelical beliefs is reminiscent of Phillip E. Johnson's highly flawed "theistic realism" project discussed in the previous chapter. Both efforts are based on a fundamental misunderstanding of what science can and can't do.

Ex-gay writers use data on numbers of sexual partners to portray gays and lesbians as more "promiscuous" than heterosexuals and their relationships as more "unstable." I won't get into the details of the statistics cited by each ex-gay writer, but the overall pattern is rampant misuse of statistics, to the point where the work of these writers would be immediately rejected if subjected to peer review by social scientists. For example, some writers attempt to draw statistical inferences from studies with nonrepresentative samples.[138] Some writers ignore the statistical margin of error (confidence interval) that can invalidate comparisons between straight and gay/lesbian samples.[139] These writers tend to focus on the mean number of sexual partners and ignore the wide variation among straight, gay male, and lesbian populations. But these technical errors aren't the main problem. Behind ex-gay writers' use of statistics related to sexual behavior is the assumption that monogamy (one sexual partner for life) represents an objective standard of "success" against which groups of people can be tested with mathematical precision. Of course, these writers are really measuring conformity to typical evangelical sexual mores, mores that many people reject. People can't "fail" a test that they aren't interested in taking.

Ex-gay writers tend to downplay the effects of social context, and pretend that there's a single, eternal "heterosexuality" to be compared with a single, eternal "homosexuality." And they almost completely ignore bisexuality, which contradicts their dichotomous sexual categories.[140] Looking at heterosexual behavior across cultures and historical periods, we can see that polygamy has been more common than monogamy. Polygamy in the Hebrew scriptures (Old Testament) is an embarrassing problem to be explained away for those who proclaim that the biblical standard is marriage between "one man and one woman." In contemporary American culture, there's evidence that both heterosexual and homosexual patterns continue to evolve. Studies of heterosexual college students have found that "dating" has increasingly been replaced by "hooking up."[141] The nationwide legalization of same-sex marriage and increasing adoptions by gay couples are undoubtedly having some impact on gay and lesbian sexual patterns, the details of which are yet unknown.[142] In any case, the various studies of sexual behavior that ex-gay writers cite are at best merely snapshots of particular times and places.

These arguments become even more problematic when we focus specifically on lesbians. Ex-gay writers admit that their statistics show that lesbians have fewer sexual partners than gay men. Following their own logic, this would indicate that lesbian relationships are less out of alignment with God's will than gay male relationships. Of course, this conclusion would be theologically unacceptable to ex-gay writers, so they ignore the implications of their quantitative approach to sexual morality.

Turning to ex-gay writers' discussions of gay and lesbian health, we again find invalid statistical arguments, including the frequent use of nonrepresentative samples. But these technical errors pale in comparison with a more serious problem with using health as a measure of alignment with God's will. Let's put aside the issue of sexuality and consider, broadly speaking, which populations tend to be the healthiest. One obvious tendency is that wealthy people have better health than the poor. So if health is an indication of alignment with God's will, then Catholic social teachings have things backwards—God has a preferential option for the rich, not the poor. We also find healthier populations in advanced, industrialized countries than in developing countries, with the exception being the wealthy elite in the latter countries. In the United States we find better overall health among whites and Asian Americans than among blacks, Latinos, or Native Americans. Apparently the first two groups are following God's will better than the latter three, or else racial equality is not one of God's priorities. Somewhat puzzling is the fact that life expectancy at birth is higher in the very secular country of Sweden (81.28 years) than in the more religious United States (78.62 years).[143] But statistics don't lie. Somehow the Swedes must be following God's will, even though very few of them go to church.

The obvious problem with all of this is that there are perfectly good nonreligious explanations for differences in health between different populations. For example, there are vast difference in access to health care. And not everyone has the information, access, and money necessary for a healthy diet. Bringing conformity to God's will into the equation is entirely unnecessary. Likewise, a host of nonreligious factors (from social stigma to the specific characteristics of the HIV virus) can explain whatever health differences may exist between straight and gay populations. Most ex-gay writers acknowledge these nonreligious factors but then invoke God anyway.

Finally, we should consider ex-gay writers' approach to the AIDS epidemic. As I discussed earlier, no writer claims that God sent AIDS as a punishment for homosexuality. Rather, some suggest that AIDS is the "consequence" of living a life contrary to God's will. This rhetorical sleight of hand doesn't change the fact that these writers are portraying AIDS as a form of divine punishment and incorrectly presenting AIDS as a "gay disease." AIDS strikes people of all sexual orientations. People practicing heterosexual monogamy can contract the disease from an infected partner. And the disease is transmitted in ways other than sexual contact, such as blood transfusion or birth from an infected mother. Once again, lesbians confound ex-gay writers' arguments—while gay men have a relatively high rate of infection with AIDS, lesbians have a lower rate than straight women. In fact, according to the Centers for Disease Control, "Transmission of HIV between women who have sex with women (WSW) has been reported rarely."[144] Using ex-gay writers' own logic, this is empirical evidence that, while God disapproves of male homosexual relations, God is unconcerned about lesbianism. Why else would there be "consequences" for the first type of behavior and not for the second?[145]

In sum, ex-gay writers attempt to use statistical data as scientific evidence that their anti-gay theology is true. But their arguments contain so many flaws that these efforts are anything but convincing. File this under "trying too hard."

Conclusion

As Christian Smith has argued, American evangelicalism has long gained strength by engineering feelings of embattlement, by finding various "others" who are viewed as threats.[146] The groups that are cast in this role, such as Catholics and communists, change over time as circumstances demand. When Christian Right leaders succeeded in making the "defense of the family" a primary evangelical concern in the 1980s, this opened the door for gays and lesbians to be cast in the role of "other" and to move from curious deviants to powerful threats—in other words, to become the objects of paranoid-style imagination.

The ex-gay movement is just one of several approaches to paranoid-style fear of homosexuality. But it's the approach most compatible with the evangelical belief in free will individualism, that people are ultimately responsible for their destinies. And it has the added bonus of ex-gays themselves, people who can provide classic evangelical testimonies of being saved from sin and tell frightening stories of the "homosexual lifestyle" they once embraced. Finally, as social acceptance of homosexuality increased, along with the number of "out" gays and lesbians, this approach became more palatable than the unrestrained condemnation found among some Christian Right leaders. No wonder the ex-gay movement succeeded in becoming the hegemonic approach to homosexuality in American evangelicalism.

What makes the ex-gay movement paranoid *science* is its leaders' desire to make their theological beliefs credible by wrapping them in the language of psychoanalysis, as well as marshaling statistical data as evidence that violating God's will (as they understand it) has negative consequences. To explain the rejection of their ideas by mainstream mental health and medical guilds, they have had to craft a conspiracy theory, a classic paranoid-style move. By performing careful surgery on Ronald Bayer's *Homosexuality and American Psychiatry*, they can claim that the book reveals how mainstream psychiatry has been taken over by "political" gay activists, with the result being the suppression of anti-gay "science."

In their study of evangelical elites' responses to homosexuality between 1960 and 2009, the sociologists Jeremy Thomas and Daniel Olson conclude that there is a modest trend toward increasingly gay-tolerant positions. They predicted that as this liberalizing trend continues it will "likely cause substantial conflict within evangelicalism and could potentially lead to division and schism as more progressive evangelicals fall into increasing disfavor with more conservative evangelicals."[147] The closing of Exodus International and the subsequent condemnation of this action by leaders from the evangelical center and right would seem to confirm this prediction. Additionally, surveys of younger (millennial generation) evangelicals have shown them to be significantly more tolerant of homosexuality than their elders, a trend that is causing more than a little alarm among evangelical leaders.[148] The ex-gay movement will likely face a shrinking base of support in the future. Unfortunately, we should not expect its demise quite yet. Evangelicals, especially those in the conservative wing, feed off of feelings of embattlement. The defection of ever more evangelical leaders and laypeople will likely spur the remaining ex-gay leaders to fight even harder and embrace the paranoid style even more tightly.

*   *   *

For ex-gay leaders, the acceptance of homosexuality is undermining the moral foundation of American society. In contrast, Christian Right leaders committed to a conservative bioethical agenda are focusing on a dangerous future that must be prevented. Unless we protect human dignity by banning practices such as embryonic stem cell research, germline human genetic engineering, and euthanasia, American society will step onto a slippery slope to dystopia.

3

"Our Way or a Brave New World"

Christian Right Bioethics

After Charles Colson died in April 2012, obituaries in major news outlets like the *New York Times* and the Associated Press told readers the colorful tale of his transformation. Once President Nixon's "hatchet man" who engineered "dirty tricks" to bring down political opponents, Colson became a born-again Christian just as the Watergate investigation was closing in on him. After serving time in prison, he began his signature Prison Fellowship ministry, which sought to rehabilitate prisoners and offenders and became a model for other faith-based ministries to prisoners. Most obituaries also mentioned his leadership in the Christian Right, including his efforts to bring Catholics and evangelicals together to advance conservative morality in the political sphere.

There was more to Colson's story, but it was ignored by the mainstream media. In the final years of his life Colson devoted himself to what he saw as the greatest moral challenge of the twenty-first century: preventing biotechnology from corrupting American culture and destroying human dignity. He co-led the Council for Biotechnology Policy with Nigel M. de S. Cameron. Colson and Cameron also coedited the 2004 book *Human Dignity in the Biotech Century: A Christian Vision for Public Policy*, which brought together major evangelical and Catholic advocates for a conservative bioethical agenda.

The mainstream media's neglect of this significant part of Colson's career reflects a larger dynamic. Opponents of embryonic stem cell research occasionally get media coverage, but in general, the Christian Right's movement to advance conservative bioethics is much less well known than the other three movements featured in this book. Leaders in this movement frequently complain that rank-and-file evangelicals haven't taken up the broad range of bioethical issues with the same passion that they bring to the issue of abortion. These leaders have written several important books and essays, but the movement lacks the sprawling popular literature of the intelligent design and ex-gay movements. Additionally, the Christian Right's bioethics movement is not as well institutionalized as the other three movements. Colson's Council for Biotechnology Policy doesn't seem to be currently operating. The Center for Bioethics and Human Dignity at Trinity International University (Deerfield, Illinois) provides the most visible institutional hub for the movement, but it's hardly a powerhouse when it comes to engineering strategy. The Discovery Institute also contributes to the movement, but while its Center for Science and Culture lists nearly forty directors, fellows, and advisors supporting intelligent design, the "Program on Human Exceptionalism" supporting conservative bioethics is mostly the work of Wesley J. Smith, with a few other fellows listed as "additional contributors to the program."[1] Finally, in contrast to intelligent design or the ex-gay movement, the Christian Right's movement to advance conservative bioethics lacks a recognizable label used by either insiders or outsiders. In other words, normally market-savvy Christian Right leaders have done a poor job of marketing this movement. Of course, all of this could change in the future. As bioethical issues like human genetic engineering move from the theoretical to the concrete, bioethical debates will almost certainly command increasing public attention. The Christian Right is likely to step up its efforts.

As with intelligent design and the ex-gay movement, support for the movement comes from both the evangelical center and the evangelical right. InterVarsity Press and *Christianity Today* are two major institutions from the evangelical center that have supported the movement, while Focus on the Family and the Family Research Council are two major institutions from the evangelical right that have done likewise. In comparison to the other three movements featured in this book, the movement to advance conservative bioethics has substantially more Roman Catholic leaders. This reflects connections with the anti-abortion movement, which has been a common cause of evangelicals and Roman Catholics since the 1980s. Leaders in the evangelical left embrace a variety of positions on bioethical issues. However, even those holding more conservative positions tend to do so without the absolutism, dualism, and appeals to fear—in other words, features of the paranoid style—found among Christian Right leaders. Consequently, the evangelical left is not involved in this movement.

The Christian Right's bioethics agenda focuses on three main issues. The first is the treatment of embryos, which, according to Christian Right leaders, deserve protection starting at "the moment of conception." In addition to the obvious opposition to abortion, this involves opposition to embryonic stem cell research, any type of human cloning, and in vitro fertilization. The second issue is the technological modification of human bodies, which Christian Right leaders believe should be limited. Consequently, they oppose germline human genetic engineering (modifications to the human genome that would be passed on to descendants) and cybernetic enhancements. The third issue is euthanasia.[2] Christian Right leaders not only oppose medical aid in dying (also known as physician-assisted suicide) but also advocate the long-term use of life support for those in persistent vegetative states. Christian Right leaders' approaches to all three issues follow from their belief in human exceptionalism.

Few people would dispute that embryonic stem cell research, human genetic engineering, and euthanasia are important ethical issues that deserve serious reflection. It's certainly possible to make a reasonable case for caution in any of these arenas, given the uncertainty of consequences, the limits of current scientific knowledge, and/or the ambiguity of real-life situations. But as we know by now, Christian Right leaders have little tolerance for uncertainty or ambiguity. Instead they prefer to believe that they possess the certain and clear truth revealed by God. What's more, their beliefs about bioethics are shaped by the same paranoid style that shapes their thinking in other areas related to science.

The paranoid style is apparent in four aspects of their bioethical thought. First, they employ a dualism that contrasts their certain truth with the errors and foolishness of their opponents. Second, they employ an additional dualism that contrasts their own goodness with the evil intentions of at least some opponents. Third, they claim to be engaged in a high-stakes struggle. Their opponents threaten not simply to do harm but to undermine human dignity and destroy the moral foundation of society. Finally, their bioethical arguments depend heavily on the slippery slope fallacy. Specifically, they argue that compromising with their opponents is foolish and will only cause society to slide into the type of dystopia depicted in Aldous Huxley's novel *Brave New World*. Only the heavily restrictive approach advocated by Christian Right leaders can prevent disaster.

The paranoid nature of these arguments is obvious enough that writers associated with the movement occasionally anticipate criticism and insist that they're not being paranoid (or alarmist).[3] Furthermore, several of these writers are undoubtedly aware that the slippery slope argument is regarded as a type of logical fallacy, but they still resort to it. For example, in a seminal essay for the movement titled "The Return of Eugenics," the conservative theologian Richard John Neuhaus had this to say:

> I am sometimes asked whether I "believe in" the slippery slope, as though it requires an act of faith. I believe in the slippery slope the same way I believe in the Hudson River. It's there. There is no better metaphor to describe those cultural and technological skid marks which are evident to all who have eyes to see.[4]

Wesley J. Smith quotes from this essay and asserts that, while some see slippery slope arguments as exercises in alarmism, "Richard John Neuhaus has it right."[5]

Stem Cell Research: Basic Issues

According to the National Institutes of Health (NIH), stem cells are "cells that have the ability to divide for indefinite periods in cultures and give rise to specialized cells," and specialized cells are those found in the various tissues in an organism.[6] Of particular interest to researchers are human embryonic stem cells, which are derived from the inner cell mass of human embryos in the blastocyst state (beginning four days after fertilization). Embryonic stem cells are *pluripotent*, that is, "capable of giving rise to most tissues of an organism."[7] Research with human embryonic stem cells could potentially help scientists to understand better how human development works and to make drug testing more effective. But of greatest interest is their use for cell therapies. According to the NIH, "Pluripotent stem cells, stimulated to develop into specialized cells, offer the possibility of a renewable source of replacement cells and tissue to treat a myriad of diseases, conditions, and disabilities, including Parkinson's and Alzheimer's diseases, spinal cord injury, stroke, burns, heart disease, osteoarthritis, and rheumatoid arthritis."[8] Adult stem cells can be found in some types of tissue in adults and children. These cells are *multipotent*, giving rise to cells that have a particular function (for example, blood cells).[9] Adult stem cells are also important for research and medical applications, but scientists consider them to be less promising than embryonic stem cells. Most scientists involved in this research advocate utilizing both types of human stem cells.

Cell therapies would be made possible by a practice known as therapeutic cloning. This would involve replacing the DNA-containing nucleus of a donor egg cell with the nucleus of one of the patient's somatic cells (cell other than sperm or egg) in a process known as somatic cell nuclear transfer. The resulting embryo, which would be a genetic clone of the patient, could be harvested for embryonic stem cells. Therapeutic cloning, which would have the aim of providing medical treatment, differs from reproductive cloning, which has the aim of using the embryo to produce a baby who would be genetically nearly identical to the somatic cell donor.

The moral complication comes from the fact that harvesting embryonic stem cells requires the destruction of the embryo. Existing embryonic stem cell lines used in research are derived from leftover embryos created for in vitro fertilization treatments and from aborted fetuses. Therapeutic cloning, in contrast, would involve the creation of new embryos. The different views of embryonic stem cell research follow from different understandings about the beginnings of human life. If human life begins at "the moment of conception," then all embryos are human persons and destroying embryos constitutes murder. If the embryo becomes a human person at some later stage of development, then an early embryo may demand some degree of respect, but destroying it would not constitute murder.

Most scientists working in embryology don't try to answer the question of when human life begins, as this is a philosophical question not subject to empirical verification.[10] Among bioethicists outside the Christian Right, many have doubts that human personhood starts with the beginning of conception. The bioethicist Thomas Shannon discusses these views in relation to debates over abortion, the moral status of the fetus, and the use of fetal tissues and organs for medical therapies in the United States:

First, there is growing recognition that fertilization is a process that takes about a day to complete rather than being a sharply defined moment. Thus the beginning of a particular human life is not as clearly demarcated as previously thought. Additionally, there seems to be a growing consensus around the fact that individuality—the inability of an organism to be divided into whole other organisms—comes after the process of restriction—which commits each cell to becoming a particular body part—occurs. There is about a two-week time period in which the pre-implantation embryo, while manifesting a unique genetic code, is not an individual for it can be divided either naturally into twins or triplets or artificially into individual cells each of which can become a whole other being. Third, there is a degree of consensus that while not necessarily a person in the full sense, the pre-implantation embryo is entitled to some measure of respect because it is living, shares the human genome, and has a strong potential (though not a present reality) for personhood.[11]

Thus, for many bioethicists, early embryos have an ambiguous status, a view at odds with that of the Christian Right.

Science doesn't clearly indicate that human life begins at "the moment of conception" (the phrase itself being problematic given that fertilization is not an instantaneous process), and the Bible doesn't teach it either. In fact, the Bible says absolutely nothing about the fertilization process, for one simple reason: no one in the ancient world knew that human egg and sperm cells existed. It took the invention of the microscope many centuries after the Bible was completed before humans had even a basic understanding of fertilization. Yet this doesn't stop Christian Right leaders from insisting that their views concerning the beginning of human life represent the clear teaching of the Bible.[12] To understand how this situation came about, we should start with the origins of evangelical opposition to abortion.

From Abortion to Embryonic Stem Cells

Given how strongly the evangelical world opposes abortion, many readers will be surprised to learn that this commitment is only a few decades old. The 1973 Supreme Court *Roe v. Wade* decision legalizing abortion throughout the United States received only limited criticism from evangelical leaders. Many evangelical leaders even welcomed the decision.[13] The anti-abortion movement that emerged immediately after the decision was spearheaded by Catholics, with little evangelical involvement. However, by the 1980 election, opposition to abortion had become a major feature of evangelical politics, one that was embraced (at least rhetorically) by Ronald Reagan as he courted evangelical voters. What happened in the intervening years to bring this about?

The historian Randall Balmer lifts the veil on the startling about-face in his book *Thy Kingdom Come: How the Religious Right Distorts the Faith and Threatens America*. Balmer, who identifies himself as a "lover's-quarrel evangelical" and generally holds moderately liberal political views, was inexplicably invited in 1990 to a conference of the Ethics and Public Policy Center, an organization associated with the evangelical right. Balmer recounts a session featuring Paul Weyrich, one of the architects of the Christian Right's political resurgence:

> Let's remember, he said animatedly, that the Religious Right did not come together in response to the *Roe* decision. No, Weyrich insisted, what got us going as a political movement was the attempt on the part of the Internal Revenue Service (IRS) to rescind the tax-exempt status from Bob Jones University because of its racially discriminatory policies.[14]

At issue was the university's policy forbidding interracial dating. This ran afoul of federal regulations that prevented institutions that practiced racial segregation from qualifying as a charitable institution. For leaders like Weyrich, this action by the federal government against an evangelical school represented an assault on the evangelical subculture. Balmer then describes the startling tale of how the defense of Bob Jones University led to the war against abortion:

> During the following break in the conference proceedings, I cornered Weyrich to make sure I had heard him correctly. He was adamant that, yes, the 1975 action by the IRS against Bob Jones University was responsible for the genesis of the Religious Right in the late 1970s. What about abortion? After mobilizing to defend Bob Jones University and its racially discriminatory policies, Weyrich said, these evangelical leaders held a conference call to discuss strategy. He recalled that someone suggested

that they had the makings of a broader political movement—something that Weyrich had been pushing for all along—and asked what other issues they might address. Several callers made suggestions, and then, according to Weyrich, a voice on the end of one of the lines said, "How about abortion?" And that is how abortion was cobbled into the political agenda of the Religious Right.[15]

It's one thing to try to use an issue to mobilize people, and quite another to succeed as well as the Christian Right did with the issue of abortion. Surveys since the 1980s have consistently shown high levels of opposition to abortion on demand among evangelical laypeople.[16] What explains the evangelical world's embrace of the anti-abortion movement? Three factors seem likely. First, Christian Right leaders linked abortion to the broader issue of sexual morality, a longtime evangelical concern that was pushed to the fore in the wake of the sexual revolution of the 1960s and 1970s. Demand for abortion was portrayed as one of many negative consequences of failing to follow God's plan to practice sexuality only within heterosexual marriage. Second, Christian Right leaders linked acceptance of abortion to feminists, a group that they opposed for denying the gender complementarity taught in the Bible.[17] Third, the issue of abortion gave evangelicals a new opportunity to contrast themselves with the immoral broader culture. Evangelicals would be people who "respect life" when others fail to do so.[18]

Once evangelical leaders had made protecting unborn life one of their priorities, it was necessary to have a clear demarcation of when life begins, given evangelicals' distaste for ambiguity. The sociologist John H. Evans describes the shift that took place among evangelicals: "Evangelicals and fundamentalists lost their previous reticence to being active in politics and became involved in social movements concerning social issues like abortion, school prayer, the equal rights amendment, and so on. And, to put it simply, conservative Protestants adopted the Catholic arguments about life beginning at conception."[19]

Adopting this stance on the beginning of life meant that evangelicals had to make at least two significant theological modifications. Unlike Catholics, evangelicals hold the Bible to be the only source of doctrinal authority. So, while the Roman Catholic hierarchy cited its own teaching authority as the justification for its stance that life begins at conception, with various biblical citations used in an explanatory role, evangelical leaders cited the same Bible verses as the sole basis for their belief. Second, evangelical leaders had to delink the issue of abortion from the issue of artificial contraception. Catholic pro-life activists have long sought a legal ban on birth control pills based on the belief (whether scientifically correct or not) that they sometimes act as abortifacients—that is, that they promote the expulsion of an embryo if they fail to prevent ovulation.[20] Given that married evangelicals widely used birth control pills, and that the Roman Catholic Church had faced a backlash from laypeople over its stance on artificial contraception, evangelical leaders would have faced a political disaster if they had come out against birth control pills.[21] Instead, they opted for the highly unusual practice of claiming scientific ignorance.

We can find a good example of this on one of Focus on the Family's websites intended to provide advice for Christian living. A question on the site asks for advice on birth control: "What is your opinion on the use of birth control? We're a newly married young couple trying to make up our minds about the best way to approach contraception, but we're getting mixed messages from our friends, family members, and physicians."[22] The first part of the response acknowledges the diversity of beliefs regarding the matter: "As you've discovered, the question of birth control can be a touchy and controversial subject, especially within the Christian community. We realize that believers from different faith backgrounds have drawn very different conclusions in this area, and as a non-denominational family outreach we don't feel it's our place to force our opinions on anyone."[23] The response eventually addresses the specific topic of birth control pills but doesn't provide a definitive answer:

> Birth control pills have become controversial because *some* of them are believed to function as abortifacients on *some* occasions. This is a complex matter, partly because there are many different formulations of oral contraceptives. . . . The most commonly prescribed oral contraceptives contain both estrogen and progesterone. These, and Depo-Provera injections, appear to work by suppressing ovulation, in which case they can be regarded as true contraceptives, since they function by preventing the union of sperm and egg. The majority of physicians with whom we have consulted do not believe that these pills or Depo-Provera have an aborti-

facient effect. A minority, however, feel that this possibility does exist and that women should be informed about it.[24]

Note that admitting uncertainty is in sharp contrast to Focus on the Family's approach to other scientific matters such as evolution or homosexuality, where it is not at all hesitant to force its opinions (presented as *facts*) on American society. The answer concludes by leaving proper action to the discretion of individuals: "On the whole, we would suggest that contraception is an issue that should be approached with generous amounts of prayer and plenty of wise counsel from friends, parents, older adults, pastors, and trusted medical professionals."[25] As unusual as this approach was, it successfully defused what could have been an explosive issue. Other Christian Right organizations followed similar approaches.[26]

With the advent of embryonic stem cell research, Christian Right leaders once again had an issue directly connected to their belief that life begins at "the moment of conception." But there was little concern over political backlash from the rank and file (in marked contrast to the issue of birth control pills). The choice for evangelical leaders was clear: oppose all human embryonic stem cell research, since the destruction of human embryos constitutes murder. However, Christian Right leaders soon found that mobilizing evangelicals around this issue, like they had on abortion, would be impossible. Unlike abortion, embryonic stem cell research had no symbolic connection to the maintenance of conservative norms regarding sex or gender. Even more importantly, the pro-life movement had routinely used pictures of late-term fetuses in order to frame opposition to abortion as "saving babies."[27] It was much harder to use this frame when the "baby" at issue was a small clump of cells. In recent years even nominal opposition to embryonic stem cell research has eroded among evangelicals. A 2008 Pew Research study found that 57 percent of white evangelicals opposed embryonic stem cell research.[28] A follow-up study in 2013 found that the figure had dropped to 38 percent.[29]

Arguments against Embryonic Stem Cell Research and Cloning

The Christian Right's opposition to embryonic stem cell research and cloning is based on the insistence that human life begins at "the moment of conception" for those naturally conceived and at the moment of somatic cell nuclear transfer for cloned embryos. Consequently, a major task of Christian Right leaders in this area is to refute those scientists and bioethicists who call into question these beliefs. They start by asserting that the Christian Right's view of conception is an indisputable scientific fact. We can find an example of this in the position statement on human cloning produced by the Center for Bioethics and Human Dignity at Trinity International University:

> Regardless of one's views on abortion and personhood of the human embryo, human embryos are unequivocally human beings and therefore should not be subject to destructive research. An international consensus now recognizes that human embryos are biologically human beings beginning at fertilization and acknowledges the physical continuity of human growth and development from the one-cell stage forward.[30]

An endnote lists six standard textbooks in human embryology that supposedly demonstrate this claim. Other Christian Right sources discussing conception follow this same strategy and cite similar textbooks in the attempt to prove that "human life begins at conception" is the consensus scientific view. However, a perusal of these textbooks quickly reveals that Christian Right leaders are misrepresenting them.[31] Embryologists generally avoid philosophical questions about when human life begins, and embryology textbooks focus instead on technical description. In other words, the "international consensus" among scientists is a fabrication.[32]

The disability activist Joni Eareckson Tada takes a less academic approach but also uses the language of "fact" to support the Christian Right's view of conception: "Whether you believe that the soul inhabits a tiny human embryo—which I'm convinced it does—is almost beside the point. The fact is, it's *human*. It's not a goat or a rat or a chicken embryo. It is human, and each of us began our journey on this planet as one of those embryos."[33]

A second response to opponents, reminiscent of the intelligent design and ex-gay movements, involves claiming that those who disagree with the Christian Right's position are motivated by politics and financial interests rather than the pursuit of scientific truth. William Saunders of the Family Research Council uses this strategy in an essay titled "The Human Embryo in Debate." Of particular concern to him is the term "pre-embryo" used by some scientists to refer to the period immediately following conception. He argues that scientists invented this term to obscure the fact that early embryos are human beings:

> The term *pre-embryo* was developed and used largely, if not exclusively, to mislead; to hide scientific facts about the beginnings and unity of human life; to bolster support for a new reproductive technology; and to obtain funding for experiments on human embryos. . . . Though the term *pre-embryo* has been rejected by science, the central idea behind it—the dehumanizing of the early embryo in order to justify its destruction—lives on.[34]

Saunders further proclaims that, given the indisputable fact that human life begins at conception, there's no justification for a scientific debate: "It is time to end the debate about the human embryo. This 'debate' merely cloaks an ideological and political agenda. The human embryo *is* a human being. As such, he is entitled to our complete respect. He may not be sacrificed on the altar of scientific progress or on the altar of 'compassion' (for others)."[35]

According to Christian Right leaders, scientists and bioethicists are also dishonest when they claim that there is a distinction between therapeutic cloning and reproductive cloning. If even the earliest of human embryos is a human person, then all cloning is reproductive (that is, leading to the creation of a new human). As Nigel M. de S. Cameron succinctly puts it, "We should note that all cloning is in fact 'reproductive,' and none is 'therapeutic' to the clone."[36]

These leaders emphasize the scientific arguments for recognizing that early embryos are human persons, but they also offer a number of religious arguments for Christian audiences. They rely on the same biblical proof texts used by Catholics and evangelicals in the pro-life movement, such as Jeremiah 1:4–5 ("Now the word of the Lord came to me saying,

'Before I formed you in the womb, I knew you, and before you were born I consecrated you'") and Psalm 139:13 ("For it was you who formed my inward parts; you knit me together in my mother's womb").[37] They also refer to the doctrine that humans, and only humans, are created in the image of God and argue that this applies to all stages of human life, including early embryos. Finally, they refer to the doctrine of the incarnation, that God took human form in the person of Jesus, as proof that humans are created in God's image from conception. As Tada writes, "Jesus became human at the moment Mary's egg became miraculously fertilized. At one point in his life, Jesus was an embryo. So Christians can have no doubt that the tiniest human being is a person in God's image."[38]

For the Christian Right, once we recognize that human embryos are persons, then the immorality of embryonic stem cell research and all types of human cloning becomes clear. Charles Colson states the matter bluntly:

> Research cloning creates an embryonic human being—someone who bears the image of God—in order for it to be "disaggregated" for medical purposes. That is a polite way of saying that it is pulled to pieces for its stem cells. The embryo is killed for the benefit of a sick person who is different from the embryo only because he or she is older. It is barbaric and has been correctly characterized as "high-tech cannibalism."[39]

William Saunders takes the argument even further, contending that embryonic stem cell research violates the Nuremberg Code and, in arbitrarily deciding who is worthy of life, parallels the activities of the Nazis:

> The [Nazi] idea of "racial hygiene" is discredited today, and I doubt any reader would defend such views. However, notice what the corollary is: Assuming that embryos are human beings, there is no morally significant difference between the people killed by the Nazis in their euthanasia centers and extermination camps and those embryonic human beings being destroyed currently. If each is a human being, *each is a life worthy of life.* Thus the same ethical standard must be used to judge actions by third parties that affect their well-being.[40]

Consequently, the Christian response to biotechnology should be to speak the truth to American society and remind them of what the Bible teaches about being human.

Christian Right leaders take their claims even further: not only is embryonic stem cell research immoral in and of itself, they say, but it sets American society on a slippery slope toward accepting even worse types of biotechnology. These leaders agree that the United States should enact a "comprehensive ban" covering all types of human cloning. A ban that covers only reproductive cloning, as allies of the biotechnology industry propose, would fail to achieve its goal. The most extensive discussion of this issue can be found in Discovery Institute fellow Wesley J. Smith's book *Consumer's Guide to a Brave New World*. According to Smith, embryonic stem cell research would inevitably lead to "designer babies" and a new era of eugenics. "Big Biotech" will not accept any limits on cloning research:

> Explicit or implicit scientism drives many [supporters of cloning research] to fervently oppose *any* prohibitions on scientific research based on the moral values of society—particularly if they believe these to be founded in religion. Add the quest for riches through biotech entrepreneurship into the equation, backed as a fallback position with tax dollars, and the stage is set for the emergence of a dehumanized future.[41]

Finally, Christian Right leaders insist that embryonic stem cell research is unnecessary for medical purposes, since research with adult stem cells is much more promising. They claim that developing medical therapies based on embryonic stem cells is hindered by a wide range of problems, including tumor formation, tissue rejection, and the need for massive numbers of human egg cells.[42] As early as 2004 they claimed that, in contrast, the efficacy of adult stem cell therapies was already well established.[43] A 2013 report by the Family Research Council reiterated these arguments: "Adult stem cells have been successful in healing human beings for many years, treating dozens of diseases and disorders, whereas [embryonic stem] cells have yet to show proven success in treating a single human being."[44] Why, then, has there been a widespread perception that embryonic stem cell research is necessary? They blame the combination of duplicitous scientists and biotech entrepreneurs and a gullible media that spreads misinformation.

The Dangers of Eugenics and Transhumanism

Charles Colson and Nigel Cameron once reflected on the expanding biotechnology agenda, "Beyond cloning and embryo research lies the sinister question of 'germline' genetic engineering—making inheritable changes in human genes."[45] They and their colleagues saw this phenomenon as "sinister" for two reasons. First, it lets humans "play God." Second, like therapeutic cloning, it represents the beginning of a slippery slope. At the end of the slope is a new era of eugenics even worse than that unleashed by the Nazis.[46] Note that Christian Right leaders don't raise similar objections to gene therapies, which unlike genetic engineering don't produce inheritable changes to the human genome.[47]

Given their belief that humans are unique in being created in the image of God, Christian Right leaders think that reengineering the human genome is equivalent to becoming our own creators and usurping God's role.[48] According to Joni Eareckson Tada, this misuse of technology is the same type of behavior condemned in the biblical story of the Tower of Babel:

> The Babel principle represents rebellious technology, intended to enable humans to take over from God. It led to the scattering of nations and the curse of enmity and division that has plagued the world ever since. Yet thousands of years later, in a form that could never before have been imagined, we see the Babel bug returning. Human technology has grown so potent that we think we have no need of God; it claims powers over our own species that will enable us to recreate ourselves in our own image.[49]

These leaders see a cruel irony in this quest to become like God: it destroys rather than enhances human dignity by reducing humans to mere products. Since humans are unqualified to play the role of creator, reengineered humans become, in Cameron's words, "commodity rather than creation."[50]

Christian Right leaders also worry that human germline genetic engineering, once started, will be impossible to control. The inevitable result will be a new era of eugenics. Indeed, genetic enhancement will not only be possible but will become an obligation. As Wesley J. Smith puts it, "Like some surrealistic game of keeping up with the Joneses, the race to breed ever more intelligent, beautiful and talented children would grow progressively more extreme."[51]

They also warn that in this new era of eugenics, biotechnology companies will seek patents on human genes. C. Ben Mitchell, a bioethics professor at Trinity Evangelical Divinity School, warns that we will no longer own our bodies: "The answer to the question, who owns my genes? may seem obvious. 'I own my genes,' one might respond. But this is less than clear. Once our genes are removed from our bodies, they are up for grabs. Genes and other human tissues may become patentable property under the present patent system."[52] Tada is even more certain of the danger: "The biotech industry wants to be able to own human beings. They have already patented genes; now they want to be able to patent human embryos and fetuses on which they have experimented. It begs the question: Whose life *is* it anyway?"[53]

Biotechnology companies seeking profits are not the only group Christian Right leaders blame for advocating human germline genetic engineering. Equally dangerous is the transhumanist movement. Transhumanists seek to use technology to take control of human evolution, overcoming current limits on human physical and intellectual capabilities and culminating in the creation of a posthuman species. For Christian Right leaders such goals ignore the dignity of humans as uniquely created in God's image. According to Smith, "In essence, transhumanism is futuristic misanthropy."[54] Smith and others warn that, while this movement may seem extreme, we shouldn't underestimate its potential to do great harm.

C. Christopher Hook of the Mayo Clinic (and a senior fellow at the Center for Bioethics and Human Dignity) writes that transhumanists are interested in more than just genetic engineering. They also seek to use cybernetic technology, merging the human with the machine, to overcome the limits of biological human bodies. He speculates on the future if this "borgification of humanity" is not prevented:

> We live in a society that is motivated increasingly by competition and personal gain, and less by any idea such as what is best for human nature or

our destiny, particularly as it relates to a nature as a created being responsible to a Creator. A significant number of individuals will actively pursue
these enhancements, undergoing every upgrade. Those who refuse to be
enhanced will find themselves considered Luddites and as backwards and
inferior. They may even be considered harmful to the larger collective in its
goals of integration and control. Discrimination is unavoidable.[55]

In other words, cybernetic enhancements will move down the slippery
slope from choice to obligation.

In sum, Christian Right leaders see proposals to reengineer the
human race as threats to human dignity, much like embryonic stem cell
research. If enacted, such proposals would inevitably bring us to a dystopian future like that of Huxley's *Brave New World*.

Euthanasia's Slippery Slope

Christian Right leaders see a third threat to human dignity in the chang-
ing medical approaches to death, particularly the legalization of medical
aid in dying, also known as physician-assisted suicide (PAS),[56] and the
allegedly loosening standards regarding the withdrawal of life support.
Among the earliest Christian Right treatments of the topic was Joni
Eareckson Tada's 1992 book *When Is It Right to Die? Suicide, Euthanasia,
Suffering, Mercy.* Wesley J. Smith addressed the topic in his 1997 book
Forced Exit: The Slippery Slope from Assisted Suicide to Legalized Murder.
Smith updated his book in 2003 and again in 2006, with the final edition bearing the new title *Forced Exit: Euthanasia, Assisted Suicide, and
the New Duty to Die.* Focus on the Family, the Family Research Council,
and the Center for Bioethics and Human Dignity have all released statements condemning PAS.

Tada's *When Is It Right to Die?* combines autobiography with theological reflection and social commentary. Tada insists that, despite the
trials of being a quadriplegic for twenty-five years, her life is worth living. Those with similar struggles should, as she does, trust that God is
in control until the day they are united with God: "Be patient. Don't give
up. This life's not over yet. It will get better. One day you will enjoy the
most perfect exit. 'But God will redeem my life from the grave; he will
surely take me to himself.' Psalm 49:15."[57]

Tada admits having been tempted to commit suicide, but, she believes, these temptations come from the devil: "The Tempter. Murderer from the beginning. Father of lies. The devil's goal is to destroy your life, either by making your existence a living nightmare, or by pushing you into an early grave. Take heed: If you have ever been enticed to prematurely end your life, then you've been listening not just to something but to someone."[58] The devil whispers lies such as "no one cares," "I can't live with the depression," or "nothing awaits me after death."[59] The devil hates human bodies because each one is created in the image of God.

According to Tada, if suicide is contrary to God's will, the same can be said of mercy killings, both as "active euthanasia" and as "passive euthanasia":

> God clearly opposes *active* euthanasia, whether it be plunging a sword into the bleeding body of a king on a battlefield, or plunging a syringe full of phenobarbital into the veins of a dying patient. The prohibition against murder in the Ten Commandments logically includes murder of the self. Mercy killing and suicide contradict the legitimate self-love of "love your neighbor as *yourself*."[60]

She admits that the Bible contains no accounts of "passive euthanasia," or withdrawing medical treatment to cause death. "But it's not hard to imagine that had King Saul been rescued by paramedics and put on life support, only to have some Amalekite unplug them, God would have frowned."[61] God owns our bodies. Consequently, "any means to produce death in order to alleviate suffering is never justified."[62]

Tada also makes the case for sustaining the lives of those in persistent vegetative states. She criticizes secular perspectives on such people, which miss the ways God may be actively working in their lives. Accordingly, Christians are called to oppose this type of secular thinking:

> Admittedly, a truckload of arguments for "pulling the plugs" of respirators or feeding tubes can be stockpiled against the needs of people in comas or vegetative states: medical expenses, quality of life, family stress, patient suffering, the precedence of court rulings, and the pressure from

the public. But it is for these very reasons that we should "Stop evaluating by what the world thinks about them or by what they seem to be like on the outside," as it says in 2 Corinthians 5:16 [The Living Bible].[63]

Tada believes that legalized euthanasia would harm not only the relevant individuals but also the moral fabric of American society. She invites readers to imagine a hypothetical scenario in which voters approve a state initiative permitting a terminally ill patient to request a lethal injection from his or her doctor: "Just picture the Brave New World that it created. In fact, imagine the headlines if euthanasia *were* legalized in this country."[64] She then elaborates on hypothetical headlines such as "Physicians are cast in the role of killer, not healer," "Standard medical care is being seriously undermined," and "The character of a helping society is beginning to disintegrate."[65] She imagines that in such a society, "vulnerable people, such as the poor, the senile, and those uninsured, are being pressured into euthanizing themselves in order to relieve the economic burden they place on society."[66] Moreover, "discrimination against elderly and disabled people is beginning to run rampant—terms such as 'useless victim' and 'unfortunates to be pitied' reveal a growing cynicism and bigotry."[67]

Lest anyone think that her "Brave New World" scenario is far-fetched, Tada insists that "all this is beginning to happen" in the Netherlands.[68] "Although euthanasia is not legalized in Holland, the courts are turning a blind eye to thousands of terminally ill patients who are being euthanized by physicians. Some reports indicate that half the doctors in Holland who offer 'aid in dying' have killed conscious patients without bothering to get consent."[69] She argues that the same thing could happen in the United States given the hotly emotional and dynamic nature of the issue of euthanasia:

No, I'm not being a doomsday prophet when I say that legalizing the right to die is like taking a crowbar to Pandora's box. Pry that lever under the lid with a single law and you've opened the whole box, exposing the entire population to "equal protection for being killed." Once legalized, the logical end of euthanasia is sheer terror. So why even get behind it in the first place?[70]

According to Tada, these disastrous results aren't surprising. Only by obeying God's laws can we build a better society.

Tada elaborated further on these views in her 2006 book *How to Be a Christian in a Brave New World*, cowritten with Nigel M. de S. Cameron. There she ties the issue of euthanasia to the other major issues in the Christian Right's bioethics agenda: embryonic stem cell research and human genetic engineering. She also takes aim at one of the Christian Right's main enemies in the area of bioethics, the Princeton University professor Peter Singer. Of greatest concern is Singer's view that some humans should not be recognized as "persons," including those in persistent vegetative states. "Already, [Singer's] warped ethics are influencing hospital boards, hospices, and state institutions, not to mention students at Princeton University. Psalm 10:2 appears to describe well Dr. Singer's kind of ethic: 'In his arrogance the wicked man hunts down the weak, who are caught in the schemes he devises.'"[71] Christians, according to Tada, must oppose this kind of ethic, following God's example by defending the weak and vulnerable.

In contrast to Tada, Wesley J. Smith avoids theological arguments in order to appeal to a broad audience. In fact, he repeatedly points out that opposition to legalized euthanasia is not limited to Christians, and he dismisses the idea that conservative Christian campaigns against legalization would impose religious beliefs on others who don't share them. Here we see parallels with the division of labor strategy employed by the intelligent design movement, not surprising given that Smith is a fellow at the Discovery Institute.

The final version of *Forced Exit* was published more than eight years after medical aid in dying became legal in Oregon and before any other states had legalized it. The book opens with an emotionally charged account of the suicide of Smith's friend Frances. Frances did not suffer from a terminal illness, but life circumstances had left her severely depressed. She began to envision suicide as the answer to her problems. "Frances's suicide was not an act born of impulse or momentary despair. She had planned it for years. Indeed, almost from the moment I met her in Los Angeles in 1988, she had spoken enthusiastically about how empowering and ennobling it would be for her to take her own life."[72] According to Smith, the aftermath of Frances's death failed to match the idealistic picture she had painted: "Frances's death was not noble and uplifting, as she had fantasized. We miss Frances and mourn her loss, but she has not left behind the sweet garden of memory she fervently believed (hoped) her death would create. . . . [M]ost of us felt angry, betrayed and empty in the wake of her self-destruction."[73]

Smith then recounts reading through her suicide file and finding several issues of the Hemlock Society's newsletter:

> As I read the material, my jaw dropped. The documents seemed scur-
> ~~more~~ than pro-suicide propaganda extolling
> npowering experience.
> —allegedly letters from
> licides, and/or advocacy
> s had an almost religious
> tracts from some bizarre
>
> nanasia as "death fundamen-
> ces's thinking. Such people,
> euthanasia for the terminally
> moted for the 'hopelessly ill'
> ne 'hopelessly ill' are disabled
> rail elderly."[75]
> ger, whom he considers among
> ially evil and dangerous influ-
> g Singer's book *Rethinking Life*
> *onal Ethics*, Smith provides yet
> ader comparing an opponent to
>
> called the *Mein Kampf* of the eu-
> any of the euphemisms common
> wledges euthanasia for what it is:
> rd about how pervasive these death

practices have become ... y and, unlike his fellow death fundamentalists, is quite candid about their destructiveness to the concept that all human life is inherently equal, a degeneration he celebrates and I condemn.[76]

Smith sees high stakes in the fight over legalized euthanasia, making it comparable to the issues of embryonic stem cell research and human genetic engineering. Widespread legalization would put American society on a slippery slope toward a Brave New World (a claim also made earlier by Tada). The result would be no less than the destruction of the moral fabric of society:

> Legalized euthanasia would not occur in a vacuum. The abandoning and anti-community values it represents would undoubtedly ripple throughout our culture and be adopted by the many structures of society, and would likely usher in a new era in which exercising personal autonomy and maximizing self-determination would become the culture's overriding purpose, rather than an important *part* of a broad mix of values that make up a healthy, balanced and free society. Our duties and responsibilities to community and to each other would be eclipsed, sacrificed on the altar of individual fulfillment. We would become so many islands, interacting but isolated, individuals placed side by side with few mutual commitments.[77]

Furthermore, the people who would be most endangered by legalized euthanasia would be those made vulnerable by physical or mental illness, as well as members of less socially advantaged groups such as the poor, the less educated, and racial minorities.

Again echoing Tada, Smith points to the Netherlands as an example of a society that has descended to the bottom of the slippery slope. In a chapter titled "Dutch Treat," Smith writes that guidelines in the Netherlands meant to limit the scope of euthanasia have always proven to be useless. The initial idea was for euthanasia to be a rarely used safety value to prevent needless suffering. Unfortunately, a very different situation has emerged:

> Instead of the medical establishment's managing and controlling death, the reverse seems to have occurred: The death imperative is controlling the practice and ethics of Dutch medicine. In the last thirty years Dutch doctors have expanded euthanasia practice exponentially, going from killing the terminally ill who ask for it, to killing the chronically ill who ask for it, to killing the depressed who have no physical illness who ask

uplifting, as she had fantasized. We miss Frances and mourn her loss, but she has not left behind the sweet garden of memory she fervently believed (hoped) her death would create. . . . [M]ost of us felt angry, betrayed and empty in the wake of her self-destruction."[73]

Smith then recounts reading through her suicide file and finding several issues of the Hemlock Society's newsletter:

> As I read the material, my jaw dropped. The documents seemed scurrilous to me—nothing more than pro-suicide propaganda extolling self-destruction as a morally correct and empowering experience. Most of the newsletters had stories in them—allegedly letters from satisfied readers—of warm and successful suicides, and/or advocacy pieces by euthanasia proponents. The articles had an almost religious tone that made me feel as if I were reading tracts from some bizarre death cult.[74]

Smith goes on to describe proponents of euthanasia as "death fundamentalists" and blames them for warping Frances's thinking. Such people, he argues, are not content with legalized euthanasia for the terminally ill: "Legalizing hastened death is now promoted for the 'hopelessly ill' or 'desperately ill,' as well as the dying. The 'hopelessly ill' are disabled people, those with chronic illnesses, the frail elderly."[75]

Like Tada, Smith singles out Peter Singer, whom he considers among the "death fundamentalists," as an especially evil and dangerous influence on American society. In discussing Singer's book *Rethinking Life and Death: The Collapse of Our Traditional Ethics*, Smith provides yet another instance of a Christian Right leader comparing an opponent to a Nazi:

> *Rethinking Life and Death* can fairly be called the *Mein Kampf* of the euthanasia movement, in that it drops many of the euphemisms common to pro-euthanasia writing and acknowledges euthanasia for what it is: killing. Indeed, Singer is straightforward about how pervasive these death practices have become in our society and, unlike his fellow death fundamentalists, is quite candid about their destructiveness to the concept that all human life is inherently equal, a degeneration he celebrates and I condemn.[76]

Smith sees high stakes in the fight over legalized euthanasia, making it comparable to the issues of embryonic stem cell research and human genetic engineering. Widespread legalization would put American society on a slippery slope toward a Brave New World (a claim also made earlier by Tada). The result would be no less than the destruction of the moral fabric of society:

> Legalized euthanasia would not occur in a vacuum. The abandoning and anti-community values it represents would undoubtedly ripple throughout our culture and be adopted by the many structures of society, and would likely usher in a new era in which exercising personal autonomy and maximizing self-determination would become the culture's overriding purpose, rather than an important *part* of a broad mix of values that make up a healthy, balanced and free society. Our duties and responsibilities to community and to each other would be eclipsed, sacrificed on the altar of individual fulfillment. We would become so many islands, interacting but isolated, individuals placed side by side with few mutual commitments.[77]

Furthermore, the people who would be most endangered by legalized euthanasia would be those made vulnerable by physical or mental illness, as well as members of less socially advantaged groups such as the poor, the less educated, and racial minorities.

Again echoing Tada, Smith points to the Netherlands as an example of a society that has descended to the bottom of the slippery slope. In a chapter titled "Dutch Treat," Smith writes that guidelines in the Netherlands meant to limit the scope of euthanasia have always proven to be useless. The initial idea was for euthanasia to be a rarely used safety value to prevent needless suffering. Unfortunately, a very different situation has emerged:

> Instead of the medical establishment's managing and controlling death, the reverse seems to have occurred: The death imperative is controlling the practice and ethics of Dutch medicine. In the last thirty years Dutch doctors have expanded euthanasia practice exponentially, going from killing the terminally ill who ask for it, to killing the chronically ill who ask for it, to killing the depressed who have no physical illness who ask

for it, to killing newborn babies in their cribs because they have birth defects, even though they cannot possibly ask for it. Dutch doctors also engage almost routinely in nonvoluntary euthanasia without significant legal consequence—even though such homicides are regarded as murder under Dutch law.[78]

What about Oregon? Smith claims that it's impossible to know how well the Death with Dignity Act, the law legalizing PAS in Oregon, is working. This he blames on "a bureaucratic stonewall," the result of which is that "no independent investigations [are] conducted by the state into actual assisted suicide deaths" and that no "attempts [are] made beforehand to ensure that the guidelines are followed."[79] Nevertheless, he shares several alleged cases of PAS that failed to adhere to proper protocols. He also cites the annual reports from the Oregon Health Department (OHD) showing that most patients were *not* taking advantage of the Death with Dignity Act as a "last resort" because of "severe, un-relenting and intolerable suffering," as proponents of the act had promised.[80] Rather, the survey of patients showed that they were concerned with losing autonomy (87 percent), decreased ability to participate in activities that make life enjoyable (84 percent), perceived loss of dignity (80 percent), losing control of bodily functions (59 percent), and being a burden on family, friends, or caregivers (59 percent). According to Smith, these are all issues that require loving attention from caregivers, friends, and relatives rather than suicide assistance. He concludes that Oregon is indeed heading down the slippery slope. "The OHD studies warn us that Oregon has started down the same destructive path that was blazed by the Netherlands. It is clear for those who want to see: As-sisted suicide is not only bad medicine but even worse public policy."[81]

Like Tada, Smith expresses concern about the treatment of those in persistent vegetative states. In particular, he writes that the "euthana-sia consciousness" seeping into American culture has shifted attitudes about providing such patients with food and water delivered via feed-ing tubes. According to Smith, this was once considered humane care, "basic nonmedical services that each human being is absolutely entitled to receive in a medical setting: warmth, shelter, cleanliness and such."[82] But more recently, "such care has been redefined as medical treatment, creating a vehicle to intentionally end the lives of cognitively disabled people while retaining the pretense of ethical medical practice."[83] Smith cites the work of Richard John Neuhaus and blames the shift on bioethicists, who he argues were concerned with managing costs and driven by the ethic of personal autonomy. "In the end, as Neuhaus wrote, what once was unthinkable policy becomes the starting point for the slide down the next portion of the slippery slope." Note that Smith's account of the medical world is the inverse of that offered by some of the Christian Right's opponents, who blame religious conservatives for promoting burdensome care of patients in persistent vegetative states.[84]

Smith titles his concluding chapter "Hospice or Hemlock—The Choice Is Ours." Here he makes the case that legalizing euthanasia is unnecessary. Euthanasia proponents may claim to be responding to uncontrollable human suffering, but they're working from a false premise: "This is fact: Nearly all pain can be effectively treated and controlled, including pain associated with arthritis, cancer, AIDS and multiple sclerosis."[85] He goes on to insist that euthanasia is not required for "death with dignity," since this is provided by hospice care. As anticipated in the chapter title, he draws a sharp contrast between the two choices:

> The message of hospice is that each patient is valuable and important, and that dying is a basic stage of life that is worth living through and growing from—until death comes through natural processes. . . . The euthanasia philosophy is just the opposite. By definition, euthanasia is a statement that life is not worth living and not worth protecting. Worse, the euthanasia philosophy claims that the answer to dying, disability or other "hopeless illness" is to induce death artificially and "get it over with." No wonder the world's most notable hospice professionals disagree with the hemlock approach.[86]

For Smith, as for other Christian Right leaders, the message that "life is not worth living" must be defeated before it destroys American society.

Why the Slippery Slope Is Slippery Logic

As I discussed previously, slippery slope arguments have long been recognized as a type of logical fallacy. They're virtually absent from academic writing in social science fields such as sociology and history, fields that study social change. Given the centrality of these arguments for the Christian Right's bioethics agenda, it's worth discussing in some detail why they're flawed and why they're more suitable for paranoid science than for legitimate social science analysis.

When they're applied to societies (as opposed to individuals), slippery slope arguments imply a set of assumptions about how social change works.[87] First, social change moves in only one direction, and is difficult or impossible to reverse. This is the "slope" portion of the concept. Second, once change has begun, it will always continue to move in the same direction and can't be stopped. This is the "slippery" portion of the concept. Third, there is a clearly marked threshold that, if crossed, places society on the slope and begins the change process. Usually, a slippery slope argument is given as a warning, with the assumption that the threshold has not yet been crossed, and society is currently in a "safe zone" of stability.

Each of these assumptions is problematic. Taken together they lead to a grossly inaccurate picture of how social change occurs. For an example of how slippery slope logic can fail, let's consider a 1986 article that attempted to predict how "permissive" abortion laws would affect American society. Sidney Callahan is a psychologist and ethicist who describes herself as a "pro-life feminist."[88] In her article "Abortion and the Sexual Agenda: A Case for Pro-Life Feminism," she writes that "women can never achieve the fulfillment of feminist goals in a society permissive toward abortion."[89] Permissive abortion laws in the wake of *Roe v. Wade* have placed American society on a slippery slope, creating an environment that's detrimental to women.[90] For one thing, men will fail to take responsibility for pregnancies: "Traditionally, many men have been laggards in assuming parental responsibility and support for their children; ironically, ready abortion, often advocated as a response to male dereliction, legitimizes male irresponsibility and paves the way for even more male detachment and lack of commitment."[91] Another effect of legalized abortion is that the state will be less inclined to fund day care and child support or to require workplaces to accommodate women's maternity since permissive abortion sends the message that pregnancies and children are a woman's private responsibilities: "More and more frequently, we hear some version of this old rationalization: if she refuses to get rid of it, it's her problem. . . . The larger community is relieved of moral responsibility."[92] The result is that abortion rates will climb ever higher as abortion moves from being a choice to being an obligation. (Note the parallel with Wesley J. Smith's warning that the right to die will become the duty to die.)

> With more abortion there is more abortion. Behavior shapes thought as well as the other way round. One tends to justify what one has done; what becomes commonplace and institutionalized seems harmless. . . . Finally, through the potency of social pressure and force of inertia, it becomes more and more difficult, in fact almost unthinkable, *not* to use abortion to solve problem pregnancies. Abortion becomes no longer a choice but a "necessity."[93]

Did Callahan's vision of a slippery slope, with runaway abortion rates intertwined with societal changes harmful to women, come to pass? Hardly. Abortion rates have fallen in the years since the article was written. The Guttmacher Institute, which tracks abortion in the United States, found that "in 2011, the U.S. abortion rate reached its lowest level since 1973."[94] Many states do have restrictions on abortion, such as requiring waiting periods or prohibiting "partial-birth" abortions, but access to abortion remains mostly intact. In any case, abortion rates have fallen in states with the least restrictive abortion laws along with rates in other states. And to the extent that governments have cut funding for day care or child support, this has been part of a larger move to shrink welfare spending of all kinds. The strongest advocates for these cuts have been Republicans, most of whom declare themselves "pro-life" on abortion.

Further flaws in Callahan's logic show up when we take a longer historical view of abortion in the United States. In her book *Abortion and the Politics of Motherhood*, the sociologist Kristin Luker describes the early American republic as having few legal restrictions on abortion:

> At the opening of the nineteenth century, no statute laws governed abortion in America. What minimal legal regulation existed was inherited from English common law tradition that abortion undertaken before quickening was at worst a misdemeanor. Quickening, as that term was understood in the nineteenth century, was the period in pregnancy when

a woman felt fetal movement . . . between the fourth and sixth month of pregnancy. Consequently, in nineteenth-century America, as in medieval Europe, first trimester abortions, and a goodly number of second trimester abortions as well, faced little legal regulation.[95]

Because only the pregnant woman could reliably tell when quickening had occurred, even this minimal regulation was probably infrequently enforced.

The legal picture shifted dramatically in the middle of the nineteenth century as physicians successfully fought to criminalize abortion. According to Luker, this anti-abortion crusade was not motivated by religious beliefs, but rather by the desire of physicians to increase the status of their profession (at a time when they did not enjoy their present level of respect):

The "regular" physicians, who tended to be both wealthier and better educated than members of other medical sects, therefore sought to distinguish themselves both scientifically and socially from competing practitioners. Support of anti-abortion activity was admirably suited to this need. By taking an abortion stand, regular physicians could lay claim to superior scientific knowledge, based on the latest research developments and theories (usually from abroad) to buttress their claim that pregnancy was continuous and that any intervention in it was immoral. . . . The abortion issue thus gave them a way of demonstrating that they were both more scientifically knowledgeable and more morally rigorous than their competitors.[96]

The legal picture shifted again as "second-wave" feminists began to push for abortion rights in the 1960s, culminating with the 1973 Supreme Court *Roe v. Wade* decision.

If we look at the whole picture, the history of abortion in the United States appears less like a slippery slope than like a sticky pendulum. Rather than one-directional change toward increased acceptance of abortion, American society has alternated between increased and decreased acceptance. Rather than unstoppable change, we find periods of change punctuated by periods of stability. Finally, the *Roe v. Wade* decision did not take American society across a threshold that had never been crossed, but returned abortion regulation to a state roughly comparable to where it had begun. To be clear, I'm not arguing that all examples of social change follow this "sticky pendulum" pattern. And I'm not saying that abortion will necessarily continue to follow this pattern in the future. Social change is complex and unpredictable. The slippery slope fallacy posits certainty about the future where none is warranted.

Indeed, Callahan's wildly inaccurate reading of social trends is a good example of a long-term hazard that social movements face when they rely on slippery slope arguments: having predictions falsified. Consider that opponents of same-sex marriage long argued that legalization would be a slippery slope leading to churches being forced to perform these marriages, to legalized polygamy, and even to marriage between people and animals.[97] As the legalization of same-sex marriage has failed to produce any of these scenarios, opponents have faced decreasing credibility.[98] The same fate could very well be in store for opponents of medical aid in dying.

What about the claim that a slippery slope has occurred in the past based on a pattern of change? In contrast to those working in the physical or biological sciences, historians can't conduct controlled experiments in which a single variable is manipulated while all others are held constant. We can't simply demonstrate that factor x is responsible for y occurring in history. Competent historians will admit the uncertainty of their causal claims. Those using past events to justify a political agenda, like Wesley J. Smith, ignore the uncertainty of their claims.

An additional problem with applying a slippery slope argument to a past trend is that proving that a real change has taken place may not be as straightforward as claimed. At minimum, we would need empirical data that are equivalent in nature (an "apples to apples" comparison) from two points in time. With this in mind, let's consider Smith's claim that Oregon is on a slippery slope as a result of the Death with Dignity Act. According to Smith, proponents of the Death with Dignity Act claimed prior to the law's implementation that only those facing unbearable pain would utilize the law. However, data from the Oregon Health Department's reports indicate that patients were primarily motivated by other factors, such as "losing autonomy," "decreased ability to participate in activities that make life enjoyable," and "perceived loss of dignity." It's immediately obvious that Smith doesn't have data that are equivalent in nature. The earlier data consist of alleged political arguments made by particular individuals campaigning for the proposed law.[99] The latter data consist of the motivations reported by the patients themselves after the law took effect. These are two different groups of people operating in two different contexts. At most Smith has shown that some of those who campaigned for the Death with Dignity Act were dishonest with the public (an unfortunate but hardly uncommon phenomenon in American politics). He hasn't shown that a change has occurred over time. To accomplish that, he would need to compare data from the early years of the Death with Dignity Act with data from later years and demonstrate that motivations for utilizing the law have shifted from concerns about unbearable pain to other factors. In fact, an examination of the data indicates that no such shift has occurred.

In sum, despite the insistence by Richard John Neuhaus (echoed by Wesley J. Smith) that the slippery slope is as real as the Hudson River, it remains a fallacy. Christian Right leaders are addressing bioethical issues that can legitimately be debated. However, because they consistently rely on the slippery slope fallacy, their entire bioethics agenda is at odds with scientific and social reality.

Is Oregon the New Netherlands? And Is the Netherlands as Bad as the Christian Right Claims?

In its fight against legalizing PAS in the United States, the Christian Right likes to use the Netherlands as Exhibit A. This country provides proof, they claim, that the slippery slope is real. Dutch society has moved from allowing voluntary euthanasia to allowing doctors to perform nonvoluntary euthanasia. Any state that chooses to legalize PAS will inevitably follow the same path. Moreover, legalized euthanasia will destroy the moral fabric of a society. Smith claims that legal guidelines "allow the Dutch people to ignore reality and pretend that killing can be controlled."[100] According to Smith, "the Dutch have proved that once killing is accepted as a solution for one problem, tomorrow it will be seen as the solution for hundreds of problems."[101]

However, a number of scholars have challenged this negative portrayal of euthanasia in the Netherlands. In their essay "Thirty Years' Experience with Euthanasia in the Netherlands," the Dutch medical ethicist Johannes J. M. van Delden and his coauthors take issue with the slippery slope arguments. Citing studies of Dutch euthanasia undertaken in 1990, 1995, and 2001, they find that the annual number of euthanasia deaths has remained relatively stable. They acknowledge that the existence of nonvoluntary euthanasia (0.8% of euthanasia cases in 1990 and 0.7% of cases in 1995 and 2001) is a serious problem that is "obviously not justified by the principle of respect for patient autonomy."[102] Nonetheless, they maintain that these cases fail to prove the existence of a slippery slope:

> Before 1991, Dutch commentators on euthanasia talked exclusively about cases that fell within the narrow definition of acts carried out at the patient's request. Only later did the existence of the cases of acts *without* explicit request of the patient become known, giving the impression that the Dutch had begun with hastening death on request and had ended up doing so with nonvoluntary cases.
>
> This, however, is not necessarily true. We simply do not know whether life-terminating acts occurred without the patient's request less or more frequently in the past. What we do know is that the occurrence did not increase in the decade between 1991 and 2001.[103]

The Christian Right's portrayal of euthanasia in the Netherlands looks even more problematic in light of comparative data from other European countries. In their article "End-of-Life Decision-Making in Six European Countries: Descriptive Study," Agnes Van der Heide and her coauthors survey doctors involved in ending a patient's life between June 2001 and February 2002 in Belgium (Flanders), Denmark, Italy (four areas), the Netherlands, Sweden, and Switzerland (German-speaking part). The authors note the differing legal regulations concerning "euthanasia" (defined narrowly as a physician directly administering the means of death to a patient) and assisted suicide in the six countries.[104]

> Both practices are prohibited in Sweden, Denmark, and Italy. In Switzerland, assisted suicide is allowed if it is done without any self-interest, for doctors and other citizens, whereas euthanasia is forbidden. In the Netherlands, euthanasia and assisted suicide were both prohibited at the time of our study, but doctors were not prosecuted if they acted in ac-

cordance with an officially enacted notification procedure that included several guidelines for prudent practice. Euthanasia was also prohibited in Belgium at the time of our study, but a new law that allowed euthanasia under certain conditions had already been discussed; the legal status of doctor-assisted suicide was (and is) uncertain.[105]

If the slippery slope view were correct, we would see high rates of nonvoluntary euthanasia ("ending of life without the patient's explicit request") in the Netherlands and Switzerland, comparatively lower rates in Belgium, and little or no incidence in the remaining countries of Denmark, Italy, and Sweden. This is not the case. The rates of nonvoluntary euthanasia among total deaths are highest in Belgium (1.5 percent) and Denmark (0.67 percent). The Netherlands and Switzerland sit in the middle of the pack with 0.60 percent and 0.42 percent, respectively. The lowest rates are in Sweden (0.23 percent) and Italy (0.06 percent). Italy is clearly the outlier. In the remaining countries we see no relationship between the legalization of (physician-administered) euthanasia and/or assisted suicide and the incidence of nonvoluntary euthanasia. Once again, the Christian Right's portrayal of the Netherlands and the slippery slope theory are refuted by the empirical data.

Yet another challenge to the negative portrayal of the Netherlands comes from the philosopher and medical ethicist Margaret P. Battin and her coauthors in their article "Legal Physician-Assisted Dying in Oregon and the Netherlands: Evidence concerning the Impact on Patients in 'Vulnerable' Groups." They examine data from both Oregon and the Netherlands to test the argument by opponents that legalized assisted dying leads to abuse of people in vulnerable groups. They admit that the available data can't provide a conclusive picture, but they contend that thus far there is no evidence of such systematic abuse: "Rates of assisted dying in Oregon and the Netherlands showed no evidence of heightened risk for the elderly, women, the uninsured (inapplicable to the Netherlands, where all are insured), people with low educational status, the poor, the physically disabled or chronically ill, minors, people with psychiatric illnesses including depression, or racial ethnic minorities, compared with background populations."[106] The one vulnerable group that could have a heightened risk was people with AIDS. However, the absolute number in Oregon was small (six people with AIDS in the first nine years of the Death with Dignity Act), while the Dutch data were inconsistent.[107]

Suppose that evidence emerges demonstrating that the legalization of euthanasia in the Netherlands has led to undesirable outcomes. Does this mean that other regions that adopt similar policies will inevitably follow the same path? Social scientists would answer this with a firm no. Regardless of how bad (or not so bad) Dutch society may be, it represents *a single case study* of the trajectory euthanasia can take in a society. It can't provide a universal picture of euthanasia because each geographic entity (country, state, and so forth) is different along a wide range of cultural, economic, and social variables. Only when we collect data from a large number of geographical entities will a reliable picture emerge. To use an analogy from the medical world, treating Dutch society as if it provides a universal picture of euthanasia would be comparable to declaring a drug safe or unsafe after a clinical trial involving a single patient. Human bodies are not all alike. Real clinical trials require large numbers of patients before researchers can draw any conclusions from them.

Why, then, are Christian Right leaders so fixated on the Netherlands? Most Americans know little about Dutch society. This gives the Christian Right the chance to make inaccurate claims about euthanasia in the Netherlands (straw person fallacy), and then to warn that the same outcome awaits any states, including Oregon, foolish enough to legalize PAS.

Not that Oregon has been completely ignored by PAS opponents, either within or outside the Christian Right. Opponents have raised a number of concerns about Oregon's Death with Dignity Act, including inadequate data collection by the state of Oregon, the possibility of "shopping" for a doctor who will grant a PAS request, and the practical difficulty of limiting PAS to those who will die within six months, as the law stipulates.[108] Not surprisingly, these objections have been rebutted by proponents of assisted dying, as have alleged cases of patients being pressured into ending their lives.[109] In the final analysis, there is currently no convincing evidence that Oregon's Death with Dignity Act has led to widespread nonvoluntary euthanasia.

Recall that for Wesley J. Smith, the slippery slope of legalized voluntary euthanasia will lead to more than just nonvoluntary euthanasia.

He claims that euthanasia is incompatible with hospice care, so it's appropriate to ask whether the hospice industry in Oregon has suffered a severe decline relative to hospice in other states.[110] There's no evidence that this is the case. On the contrary, Oregon's hospice industry seems to have adapted well to practicing care under the Death with Dignity Act. The Oregon Hospice Association makes the following statement on its website:

> Oregon's Death With Dignity Act went into effect in 1997. It no longer matters whether physician-assisted dying should or should not be permitted. It is a legal option in Oregon. Oregonians need not choose *between* hospice and physician-aid in dying. Dying Oregonians can choose *both* from among the options on the end-of-life continuum of care. . . . The Oregon Hospice Association supports patient choice.[111]

Note that the last sentence contradicts Smith's claim that the hospice industry is solidly opposed to PAS.

A 2001 survey of hospice workers in Oregon provides further evidence of Smith's error. Among hospice social workers, 72 percent supported the Death with Dignity Act, 13 percent opposed, and 5 percent were neutral. Among hospice nurses, 48 percent supported the law, 36 percent opposed, and 16 percent were neutral.[112] Additionally, as the Oregon Hospice Association statement details, hospices in Oregon provide patients with psychosocial assessments to screen out those patients who don't qualify for life-ending medication due to mental health issues. In other words, the hospice industry works with Oregon's system of medical aid in dying to prevent abuses. Clearly, Smith's "hospice versus hemlock" argument represents a false choice fallacy contradicted by empirical evidence.

We should also consider Tada and Smith's overarching claim that legalized euthanasia will destroy the moral fabric of society. It's this type of grand claim that defines the paranoid style described by Hofstadter. Has this occurred in the state of Oregon? Christian Right leaders don't even try to make this case—a wise decision. They may be able to exploit Americans' ignorance about Dutch society to portray the Netherlands as a moral wasteland. But a similar attempt with the state of Oregon (as well as other states that have legalized PAS more recently) would bring instant ridicule, and justifiably so. The best that these authors can do is predict that signs of moral degradation will appear soon. As with other predictions based on slippery slope logic, this one will become increasingly less credible over time.

Moral Hypocrisy

Tada and Cameron's book *How to Be a Christian in a Brave New World* includes this dedication at the beginning: "To George W. Bush, Forty-third President of the United States, defender of the dignity of human life; with deep respect and appreciation." Bush earned this accolade for his decision to ban federal funding of stem cell research that would involve the destruction of additional human embryos. The authors include a quote from Bush invoking the Christian Right's favorite literary reference to describe biotechnology: "We have arrived at that brave new world that seemed so distant in 1932, when Aldous Huxley wrote about human beings created in test tubes in what he called a 'hatchery.'"[113] The book implies that Tada played some role in swaying the president: "Back in 2002, when President Bush finished his inspiring speech against cloning and the abuse of technology, I [Cameron] watched him step down from the podium and give [Tada] a hug."[114] Other Christian Right leaders such as Charles Colson and Wesley J. Smith have similarly described Bush as a moral exemplar.[115]

Anyone with even a cursory knowledge of George W. Bush's political career knows that portraying him as a "defender of the dignity of human life" is laughable. He was responsible as president for launching not one but two wars. Bush's war in Iraq was sold to the American public on the far-fetched argument that Saddam Hussein was somehow connected to the September 11 attacks, and on false intelligence regarding (nonexistent) weapons of mass destruction. His administration's "war on terrorism" involved the use of torture, euphemistically dubbed "enhanced interrogation." As governor of Texas he was famously enthusiastic about the death penalty and dismissed the very real possibility of innocent people being wrongly executed. The Christian Right's idealized portrayal of Bush shows its willingness to overlook real assaults on human dignity for anyone who supports its paranoid bioethics agenda.

This is not the only case of moral hypocrisy in the Christian Right's bioethics movement. Several movement leaders argue that money from the biotechnology industry is corrupting bioethics. The most strident criticism comes from Wesley J. Smith, whose book *Consumer's Guide to a Brave New World* complains repeatedly about "Big Biotech":

> But the lure of great wealth provides a powerful incentive to hold self-justificatory beliefs and embark on morally questionable endeavors. Indeed, the biotechnology industry has coalesced into one of the nation's most powerful special interests—Big Biotech—which spends tens of millions of dollars each year in contributions to public relations and political campaigns. It works tirelessly to influence public opinion and convince government officials and regulators to accept the official biotech view that—with the exception (for now) of bringing a cloned baby to birth—researchers should be allowed virtually a free hand.[116]

Charles Colson made similar arguments:

> The debates over today's biotech revolution and the public policy that must be put into place bring us back to foundational truth. This is no easy matter since there is big money invested in this revolution and potential fortunes to be made. In light of the enormous amount of money behind biotech, we have to insist that we are not against scientific progress. We simply want that progress tied to moral truth. Without that connection, we will end up creating the ultimate *Brave New World*, where we can decide ahead of time what a person is going to be and where human dignity, human freedom and human rights are things of the past.[117]

If the Christian Right really is concerned about big money corrupting morality, why focus only on the biotech industry? What about Big Oil, Big Banking, Big Agra, Big Telecom, and so on? The fact is that Christian Right leaders, like most other American conservatives, strongly support free market capitalism. Various Christian Right organizations have long depended on support from business leaders, and Smith's Discovery Institute is no exception. In light of all of this, Smith's and Colson's displays of economic populism are completely unconvincing.

Christian Right leaders believe that they're the moral guardians of American society, and that advancing a conservative bioethical agenda is a significant part of this role. But with this kind of moral hypocrisy, they hardly seem qualified for the role.

Conclusion

Embryonic stem cell research, human genetic engineering, and euthanasia are all issues that deserve serious ethical reflection. Unfortunately, this kind of reflection is incompatible with a paranoid vision that, as Hofstadter described, focuses on preventing a nonexistent vast conspiracy from destroying society rather than on conducting accurate analyses. Even the occasional use of logical fallacies is a worrisome sign of a lack of intellectual rigor. But the Christian Right's entire bioethics agenda depends on the slippery slope fallacy. Once we understand that the slippery slope is more mirage than Hudson River (notwithstanding Neuhaus's claims), it becomes clear that Christian Right leaders have nothing of substance to contribute to bioethical debates.

Ethical analysis of all kinds should be grounded in a careful consideration of empirical reality. For bioethics, this should involve consideration of both biological and sociological facts. However, the clear pattern in the Christian Right's bioethics is to bend the facts to justify its paranoia-driven agenda. Whether they argue that there's a scientific consensus that life begins at the "moment of conception" or that members of marginalized social groups are the ones most likely to utilize PAS, Christian Right leaders demonstrate their characteristic contempt for reality.

Their misuse of *Brave New World* provides further evidence of how little reality matters to them. Huxley's novel makes nuanced arguments concerning the dangers of humans' pursuit of pleasure and the possible culture of triviality that can result. In the hands of Christian Right leaders, however, the novel becomes a blunt weapon for attacking anyone who disagrees with them. "Brave New World" becomes an epithet for any world not dominated by conservative Christian values. This is ironic. Huxley's religious views, a blend of agnosticism and Hindu-inspired mysticism, hardly resembled conservative Christianity. It's particularly ironic that Christian Right leaders invoke the novel to condemn euthanasia. Huxley, who was diagnosed with cancer of the larynx, famously turned to euthanasia to end his suffering. The attractiveness of *Brave New World* to Christian Right leaders obviously lies in its portrayal of a dystopian society ruined by the misuse of technology. For those who see biotechnology as a threat to their religious values, the novel is a perfect vehicle for advancing a paranoid vision of the future—that is, once they replace the real Huxley with a virtual one.[118]

*   *   *

Christian Right leaders involved in intelligent design, the ex-gay movement, and bioethics all apply human exceptionalism to the human body. Intelligent design proponents also extend the exceptionalism to the Earth, which they portray as a "privileged planet" designed to facilitate scientific discovery by humans. The final movement discussed in this book takes the privileged status of humans' planetary home a step further, claiming that God designed the Earth to be immune from environmental hazards like anthropogenic climate change. Those who argue otherwise are opposing the will of God.

4

Seeing Red over Green Evangelicals

The Crusade against Environmentalism

For more than two decades, E. Calvin Beisner has been a leading evangelical critic of the environmental movement. A former professor at evangelical colleges and a longtime fellow at the pro–free market Acton Institute for the Study of Religion and Liberty, Beisner used to engage his opponents in the evangelical world with debate and dialogue.[1] He described himself as a "friendly critic" of those evangelicals who embraced environmentalism.[2] In his 1997 book *Where Garden Meets Wilderness: Evangelical Entry into the Environmental Debate*, he claimed to have had only limited criticisms of the theological, biblical, and ethical views of evangelical environmentalists: "On the majority of theological issues—especially those at the defining center of the Christian Faith—evangelical environmentalists have maintained orthodoxy while addressing environmental concerns that have, for the most part, been brought to public attention from outside the evangelical or even the broadly Christian camp. They are to be commended for this." He claimed to be especially appreciative of the ways evangelical environmentalists pushed back against "New Age" criticisms of Christianity.

In 2010 any semblance of respect for evangelical environmentalists vanished, replaced by a new hardball approach. Five years earlier, Beisner had been instrumental in the formation of the Cornwall Alliance for the Stewardship of Creation (originally called the Interfaith Stewardship Alliance), the de facto leader of the evangelical opposition to environmentalism and featuring many prominent figures from the evangelical right. The Cornwall Alliance was now ready to unveil its new initiative: Resisting the Green Dragon. Accompanying the launch of the website (www.ResistingTheGreenDragon.com) was a twelve-part DVD series and discussion guide targeting evangelical churches, schools, and small groups, plus a companion book. The DVD case featured the picture of a menacing, metallic dragon with a gaping mouth and a globe for an eyeball. The DVD trailer showed rapidly moving images associated with environmentalism (a tree hugger, a Greenpeace banner) and the political world (the White House, a European Communist Party banner) accompanied by an ominous beat while the evangelical radio personality Janet Parshall summarized the case against environmentalism:

> In what has become one of the greatest deceptions of our day, radical environmentalism is striving to put America and the world under its destructive control. This so-called Green Dragon is seducing your children in our classrooms and popular culture. Its lust for political power now extends to the highest global levels and its twisted view of the world elevates nature above the needs of people, of even the poorest and the most helpless. With millions falling prey [sound of a clock ticking begins] to its spiritual deception, the time is now to stand and resist.

No longer was evangelical environmentalism, frequently known as the creation care movement, a theologically sound movement in need of some minor corrections. As various speakers testified, it was a movement that "totally neglects spiritual welfare of men and women and looks at creation as though it were an end in itself." It was guilty of defining the gospel as "just social justice," and evangelicals should reject its example lest they "sell the gospel down the river." The series creators were clear: environmentalism was a tool of Satan and completely incompatible with authentic Christianity.

Resisting the Green Dragon is the paranoid style *par excellence*. All three of the Christian Right movements we've examined so far clearly fit within the paranoid style, but none can match the extreme rhetoric of the contemporary evangelical anti-environmental movement. Just how did it come to be the "champion" of paranoia among Christian Right movements challenging science? This chapter will tell the story.

American Evangelicals and the Environment in the Twentieth Century

Unlike human origins and sexual morality, the environment doesn't have a long history as a significant concern for American evangelicals.

Interest in the environment as a theological issue began to build slowly among evangelical leaders during the 1970s and 1980s, mostly in the evangelical left. By the 1990s a sufficient number of American evangelical leaders had embraced environmentalism that they began to form organizations related to this concern. The most prominent of these was the Evangelical Environmental Network (EEN), founded in 1993. Among the EEN's principal early leaders was Ron Sider, president of Evangelicals for Social Action. Sider was considered a "center-left" figure combining centrist evangelical views on abortion and homosexuality with typical evangelical left views on economic justice. Still, early supporters of the EEN came mostly from the evangelical left. As the 1990s progressed and the issue of climate change drew increasing attention from secular environmentalists and scientists, creation care remained primarily an evangelical left priority.

Meanwhile, the 1990s witnessed a growing movement to deny the existence of anthropogenic (human-induced) climate change.[3] Several books detail the features of this movement, including James Hoggan's *Climate Cover-Up: The Crusade to Deny Global Warming*, Chris Mooney's *The Republican War on Science*, Naomi Oreskes and Erik Conway's *Merchants of Doubt: How a Handful of Scientists Obscured the Truth on Issues from Tobacco Smoke to Global Warming*, and Michael Mann's *The Hockey Stick and the Climate Wars: Dispatches from the Front Lines*.[4] Funding for the climate change denial movement comes from corporations that might see reduced profits if there are efforts to reduce greenhouse gases, especially those in the fossil fuel and automotive industries. These corporations work with pro–free market think tanks whose members fear that efforts to curb climate change will bring increased government regulation of markets. Their strategy is not to provide proof that anthropogenic climate change isn't occurring, but simply to cast doubt on its existence. This has often involved conspiracy theories that portray climate scientists as overstating the certainty of their climate predictions either for financial gain (in the form of increased grant money) or out of arrogance. Leaders of this movement understand that if Americans can be convinced that the science behind climate change is unsettled, then they will object to government policies designed to curb greenhouse gases. These efforts have been highly successful, fueled by the same suspicion of scientific elites that makes creationism an enduring phenomenon in the United States.

As the climate change denial movement gained traction during the 1990s, the evangelical right became increasingly vocal in its support, essentially becoming the religious wing of a previously secular movement. Beisner and others from the evangelical right echoed the arguments of those in the secular world denying climate change, questioning both mainstream climate scientists and the wisdom of interfering in markets, and then added distinctly religious arguments. These centered on a particular reading of Genesis, according to which the Earth was created for the benefit of humans, who are to exercise "dominion." Inherent in this institutional arrangement was a division of labor. Since the secular wing of the denial movement adhered to scientific and economic arguments, the evangelical right was freed from having to employ a "pure science" frame. Beisner and his colleagues could employ the language of religious crusade without qualification.

At the end of the 1990s Beisner and his colleagues in the Acton Institute organized a major effort to counter the Evangelical Environmental Network. Acton's president, Father Robert Sirico, described the effort this way:

> In light of these contemporary confusions about the true nature of stewardship, and because this concept is so central to the concerns of the Judeo-Christian religious tradition and of the free society, the Acton Institute for the Study of Religion and Liberty has committed herself to articulating a vision of environmental stewardship informed by sound theological reflection, honest scientific inquiry, and rigorous economic thinking. To this end, the Institute brought together twenty-five clergy, theologians, economists, environmental scientists, and policy experts in West Cornwall, Connecticut, October 1999, to discuss the aspects of this problem and to lay the intellectual groundwork for further inquiry.[5]

Out of this meeting emerged the Cornwall Declaration on Environmental Stewardship, which was finalized in 2000. Those involved also formed a new organization called the Interfaith Council for Environmental Stewardship (ICES), which Sirico described as "a broad-based coalition of individuals and organizations committed to the principles espoused in the Cornwall Declaration."[6] Framing the effort as interfaith was significant because the Evangelical Environmental Network worked with a larger organization known as the National Religious Partnership for the Environment, which included Catholic, mainline Protestant, and Jewish participants. However, like other enterprises involving the Christian Right, the ICES was dominated by evangelicals, with politically conservative Catholics and Jews playing a secondary role. An indication of this evangelical (or at least Christian) dominance appeared in the "Our Beliefs" section of the Cornwall Declaration, where each item in the list of beliefs was preceded by a cross shape instead of the usual bullet. The Cornwall Declaration echoed many of the claims that Beisner had been making for several years. It contested the science supporting the existence of anthropogenic climate change, affirmed humans as God-appointed stewards of the Earth, and hailed the virtues of free markets.

The Battle for the Evangelical Center

At the start of the twenty-first century the evangelical left was committed to fighting climate change, the evangelical right strongly denied that climate change was a problem, and the evangelical center had yet to choose sides. This quickly changed as several high-profile centrist evangelical leaders were persuaded to take up the cause of climate care. The first of these was Richard Cizik, then vice president for governmental affairs of the National Association of Evangelicals (NAE). Katharine Wilkinson describes Cizik's "conversion" in her book *Between God and Green: How Evangelicals Are Cultivating a Middle Ground on Climate Change*. According to Wilkinson, Cizik had a conversation at Oxford University in 2002 with Sir John Houghton, the recently retired chairman of the scientific arm of the Intergovernmental Panel on Climate Change and a British evangelical. Houghton made the biblical case for Cizik and other American evangelicals to take action against climate change. Cizik's experience paralleled that of John Wesley, the founder of Methodism, who reported his heart being "strangely warmed" while attending a Moravian meeting on Aldersgate Street in London.

> Like John Wesley's famous Aldersgate experience in 1738, in the course of their exchange, Cizik suddenly felt his heart "strangely warmed" and

experienced a conversion to climate change that echoed his conversion to Christ two decades earlier. . . . Sensing that God had intervened in his life at this crucial moment, Cizik departed Oxford with a passionate commitment to climate care, soon to become a leading advocate for the cause across the Atlantic.[7]

David Neff, editor-in-chief of *Christianity Today*, also joined the cause of fighting climate change and worked with Cizik to support the efforts of the Evangelical Environmental Network. EEN leader Jim Ball worked hard to persuade still more centrist leaders to lend their support.[8]

Meanwhile, opponents of creation care on the evangelical right were honing their own efforts. In 2005 Beisner and his colleagues formed a new organization called the Interfaith Stewardship Alliance alongside the existing Interfaith Council for Environmental Stewardship. Why two organizations with similar names? It appears that the older organization was not very active, requiring a new organization to take aggressive action against creation care. This became clearer in 2007 when the Interfaith Council for Environmental Stewardship was renamed the Cornwall Alliance for Environmental Stewardship, while the Interfaith Stewardship Alliance was renamed the Cornwall Alliance for the Stewardship of Creation.[9] The Cornwall Alliance for the Stewardship of Creation, the newer organization, was given the www.cornwallalliance. org website. The older organization seems to have had only a token existence by that point. Moreover, Beisner revealed in a 2013 lecture that the "interfaith" label was either inauthentic or short-lived for the newer organization: "The Cornwall Alliance [for the Stewardship of Creation] is a network of evangelical theologians, scientists, and economists."[10] By 2015 the Cornwall Alliance website described the organization as "an evangelical voice promoting environmental stewardship and economic development built on Biblical principles."[11]

In 2006 members of the growing coalition supporting creation care launched a new campaign known as the Evangelical Climate Initiative, along with a statement titled "Climate Change: An Evangelical Call to Action."[12] Several claims in the statement are worth noting. First, evangelicals are called to address a wide variety of social issues. Although the authors were "proud of the evangelical community's long-standing commitment to the sanctity of human life," they didn't want evangelicalism to be "a single-issue movement." Second, there is solid scientific evidence that anthropogenic climate change is real. Third, the consequences of climate change will hit the world's poor the hardest. Fourth, efforts to combat climate change are part of the proper stewardship of the Earth mandated by the Bible.

A significant feature of the statement was its recommendations for reducing carbon dioxide emissions. It acknowledged the positive actions being taken at all levels of society, including "state and local governments, churches, smaller businesses, and individuals." Additionally, there were clear efforts to attract the evangelical center, which tends to be suspicious of government regulation of the economy. The first of these was a nod to market-based solutions: "In the United States, the most important immediate step that can be taken at the federal level is to pass and implement national legislation requiring sufficient economy-wide reductions in carbon dioxide emissions through cost-effective, market-based mechanisms such as a cap-and-trade program." The second was the framing of large corporations, including fossil fuel companies, as partners rather than adversaries in this effort: "We also applaud the steps taken by such companies as BP, Shell, General Electric, Cinergy, Duke Energy, and DuPont, all of which have moved ahead of the pace of government action through innovative measures implemented within their companies in the U.S. and around the world." The authors of the statement seem to have strategically ignored the role of fossil fuel companies in funding the climate change denial movement.

These efforts to attract more centrist evangelical leaders bore fruit. Among those who eventually endorsed "Climate Change: An Evangelical Call to Action" were prominent megachurch pastors Rick Warren of Saddleback Church and Bill Hybels of Willow Creek Community Church. NAE president Leith Anderson also endorsed the statement, an important display of support for Cizik.

Leaders in the evangelical right would not let this play for the evangelical center go unchallenged. In March 2007, twenty-five leaders sent a letter to the NAE board asking them to either restrain Cizik or encourage him to resign.[13] Among those signing the letter were James Dobson, chairman of Focus on the Family, Tony Perkins, president of the Family Research Council, and Alan Chambers, president of Exodus International.[14] None of the twenty-five signers were members of the NAE; they justified their concern by insisting that "our organizations interface with [the NAE] regularly and consider it to be an important Christian institution in today's culture." The letter made several key arguments. First, it contended that the existence of anthropogenic global warming was "a subject of heated controversy" and that the NAE "lacks the expertise to settle the controversy." It cited the work of Beisner's Interfaith Stewardship Alliance as presenting a credible case for skepticism of global warming. Second, it accused Cizik and others of using the issue of global warming to shift emphasis away from "the great moral issues of our time, notably the sanctity of human life, the integrity of marriage and the teaching of sexual abstinence and morality to our children." Third, it accused Cizik of speaking in a way that was "divisive and dangerous," especially when he labeled his opponents "the old guard." Fourth, it took issue with Cizik's willingness to discuss population control as a means of combating global warming: "We ask, how is population control going to be achieved if not by promoting abortion, the distribution of condoms to the young, and even by infanticide in China and elsewhere?" Finally, the letter insisted that Cizik's actions were endangering the very definition of "evangelical," moving it away from its previous association with "conservative views on politics, economics and biblical morality."

According to David P. Gushee, the NAE responded at its March 2007 board meeting by ignoring the evangelical right letter and affirming its existing broad policy agenda. "This polite but firm response to Dobson helped to establish, perhaps once and for all, that there is an independent evangelical center with its own vision that cannot be bullied or dictated to by the evangelical right."[15] However, Cizik's personal victory would prove to be short-lived. During an interview on National Public Radio's *Fresh Air* in December 2008, he stated that he was "shifting" and now supported same-sex civil unions.[16] This stance is not out of place in the evangelical left, but it's sharply at odds with the evangelical center's views on homosexuality. Cizik was quickly forced to resign from his NAE position. However, by then creation care had become firmly entrenched among centrist evangelical leaders. The NAE couldn't tolerate any softening of its condemnation of homosexuality, but it continued to support efforts to fight climate change.

Explaining the Evangelical Climate Change Fault Line

As we've seen, the intelligent design, ex-gay, and conservative bioethics movements all involve a coalition of center and right evangelical leaders, with leaders from the evangelical left uninvolved or even opposed. Climate change is the one issue related to science where a left and center coalition contends against the evangelical right.[17] What explains this unique situation? Based on his encounters with the evangelical right, Gushee concludes that its rejection of climate science stems from more than its alliance with the Republican Party:

> I am convinced that these forces [contributing to climate change skepticism] are fundamentally theological, not economic or political, though these latter factors do play a major part. Beisner, at least, expresses considerable distrust of mainstream science, trusts the free market implicitly and distrusts government regulation entirely, adheres to an archaic version of dominionist theology of creation, and holds fast to a hyper-Calvinist theology related to God's sovereignty (over against human responsibility) for what happens in human affairs.[18]

There are two main problems with Gushee's explanation. First, distrust of mainstream science (also known as real science) is hardly limited to the evangelical right. The intelligent design, ex-gay, and conservative bioethics movements, all of which have the support of the evangelical center, are based on paranoid-style distrust of mainstream science. Gushee, an advocate of the evangelical center and sometime critic of the evangelical right, is clearly unwilling to acknowledge how much the center and right have in common in relation to science. Second, while Beisner can be described as having a "hyper-Calvinist" theology, the same can't be said of the entire evangelical right, and certainly not of its Catholic, Jewish, and secular supporters in the fight against climate science.

The sociologist Laurel Kearns offers an alternative explanation: that the most significant factor for the climate science opposition is "economics and the support of free enterprise and capitalism."[19] This appears to be a more credible explanation, given that a shared economic ideology is the main factor uniting the religious and secular branches of the climate change denial movement. Centrist evangelical leaders also tend to support free markets, but their support is less fervent than that of evangelical right leaders. Centrist leaders were consequently open to accepting creation care as long as its proponents framed it in fairly market-friendly terms, which is exactly what the authors of the Evangelical Climate Initiative chose to do. For the diehard supporters of free markets in the evangelical right, creation care involved too many unacceptable compromises.

The Cornwall Alliance's support for free market capitalism appears to be more than just theoretical. Some liberal advocacy groups have sought to expose the financial ties between the Cornwall Alliance and the business interests funding the secular climate change denial movement. A 2010 report by ThinkProgress highlighted ties between the Cornwall Alliance and an anti-environmental group called the Committee for a Constructive Tomorrow (CFACT) and found that the latter group "is funded by at least $542,000 from ExxonMobil, $60,500 from Chevron, and $1,280,000 from the Scaife family foundations, which are rooted in wealth from Gulf Oil and steel interests."[20] A report released the same year by the People for the American Way's Right Wing Watch cited the ThinkProgress report and added further details: "Beisner is a CFACT board member and an 'adjunct fellow' of the Acton Institute, which is primarily funded by groups like ExxonMobil, the Scaife foundations and the Koch brothers. Beisner is also an adviser to the Atlas Economic Research Foundation, which is financed by the oil-backed Earthart Foundation, the Koch brothers, and ExxonMobil."[21] Whatever the exact amounts of money flowing into the Cornwall Alliance, such ties are hardly surprising. There is a long history of Christian Right leaders working with corporate backers. And since the Cornwall Alliance clearly operates as the religious wing of the broader climate change denial movement, we should expect it to share funding sources with its secular counterparts.

The Cornwall Alliance: Core Beliefs before the Green Dragon

In this section we'll look at the theological, economic, and scientific beliefs expressed by Cornwall Alliance leaders prior to the launch of the Resisting the Green Dragon campaign. Even though these leaders spun conspiratorial theories about climate scientists and claimed that environmentalism was having a negative impact on the world, they had yet to embrace the paranoid style (according to Hofstadter's definition) by subscribing to a grand conspiracy that threatened the foundation of society.

Dominion Theology

The theological foundation of the Cornwall Alliance's fight against environmentalism is the belief that men and women were created in God's image, were given a privileged place among creatures, and were commanded by God to exercise stewardship (or dominion) over the Earth. Beisner and other leaders emphasize that this stewardship involves following God's wishes rather than our own and is therefore not "anthropocentric" or "speciesist" (the ethicist Peter Singer's derogatory term for privileging humans over other animals). As one Cornwall Alliance essay insists,

> People, alone among the creatures on earth, have both the rationality and the moral capacity to exercise stewardship, to be accountable for their choices, to take responsibility for caring not only for themselves but also for other creatures. To reject human stewardship is to embrace, by default, no stewardship. The only proper alternative to selfish anthropocentrism is not biocentrism but theocentrism: a vision of earth care with God and his perfect moral law at the center and human beings acting as his accountable stewards.[22]

According to this theology, humans are commanded as God's image-bearers to improve the condition of the Earth: "Earth and all in it, while 'very good' (Genesis 1:31), were not as God intended them to be. They need filling, subduing, and ruling."[23] This divine mandate predates the Fall and God's subsequent cursing of the Earth. After the Fall and Curse, the mandate became more pressing as humans were tasked with helping to redeem the Earth. According to Beisner, "It is legitimate, therefore, for Adam's race, particularly under the redeeming rule of Christ, to seek to transform cursed ground back into blessed ground."[24] Beisner contrasts this view with that of most environmentalists, who wrongly idealize nature untouched by humans.

The mandate to improve the Earth means that extracting resources doesn't constitute exploiting nature, as environmentalists believe. And we don't need to worry about running out of resources.
Using the resources that God provided is exactly what humans are
meant to do, and there will always be enough. Beisner summarizes
this perspective:

> For generations people have worried about the world's running out of
> various resources—especially energy resources. Yet, paradoxically, the
> long-term price trends of all extractive resources—animal, vegetable, and
> mineral (including energy resources)—are downward. . . . I say "paradox-
> ically," because falling prices indicate falling scarcity, which is precisely
> the opposite of what we intuitively expect as people consume finite re-
> sources. What explains this paradox? It is the combination of the Curse-
> reversing effects of redemption and the creative aspects of the image of
> God in man—the latter enhanced by the former.[25]

Related to this, Cornwall Alliance leaders say there's no need to fear
population growth, given the divine mandate to fill the Earth. Environmentalists, who see humans primarily as consumers rather than pro-
ducers, wrongly believe that a growing human population will exhaust
the Earth's resources. But the Bible teaches that people are a blessing,
not a curse. According to Beisner, "The human race is not the population explosion but the population blossom; not the population boom
but the population bloom; not people pollution but the people solution;
not cancer but an answer."[26] Nor should we fear that a growing population will produce excessive pollution. Human ingenuity is exactly the
resource needed to produce a cleaner environment. Societies that make
the transition from an industrial economy to a service and technology-
oriented economy see pollution decline. Based on these beliefs, Beisner
paints a bright picture of our environmental future:

> People all over the world can expect a cleaner, safer, more healthful, more
> beautiful environment for our children's future. Not automatically. No,
> it will take lots of intelligent, hard work and lots of good, moral choices.
> But those are what God made people to do, and they are what Christ's
> redeeming work is enabling us to do despite our fall into sin.[27]

God Designed and Sustains the Earth

For Cornwall Alliance leaders, those who believe in catastrophic anthropogenic climate change are failing to accept what the Bible teaches about the Earth. They make two specific claims related to this issue. First, they maintain that God designed a robust Earth that cannot be easily harmed by human activity. Those who warn about the dangers of climate change, and especially of the "runaway greenhouse gas effect," assume a fragile climate system that is contrary to what the Bible teaches: "The Biblical worldview instead suggests that the wise Designer of Earth's climate system, like any skillful engineer, would have equipped it with balancing positive and negative feedback mechanisms that would make the whole robust, self-regulating, and self-correcting."[28]

Their second claim is that God actively sustains the Earth and has promised not to allow worldwide ecological disaster:

> Among [God's] promises are two that are particularly relevant to fears of dangerous manmade global warming: (1) that natural cycles necessary for human and ecosystem thriving (summer and winter, planting and harvest, cold and heat, day and night) will continue as long as Heaven and Earth endure (Genesis 8:22), and (2) that flood waters will never again [after the time of Noah] cover the Earth (Genesis 9:11–12, 15–16; Psalm 104:9; Jeremiah 5:22).[29]

The second promise "would seem to preclude the kind of catastrophic sea level rise envisioned by global warming alarmists."[30]

Cornwall Alliance leaders contend that the irrational fear of natural catastrophes is ultimately rooted in "the absence of the fear of the Lord."[31] Such fears will continue, despite the lack of a true scientific basis, until people repent and fear the Lord.

Fighting Climate Change Will Hurt the Poor

Recall that one of the creation care movement's primary arguments is that climate change will cause the most harm to the world's poor. The Cornwall Alliance directly challenges this claim, portraying itself as the one helping the poor, and environmentalists as wealthy elitists who are trying to block the path out of poverty. The title of the Cornwall Alliance's 2006 report, "A Call to Truth, Prudence, and Protection of the Poor" (followed in 2009 by an expanded version called "A Renewed Call to Truth, Prudence, and Protection of the Poor"), was clearly chosen to highlight this positive framing of its own activities and its negative "counterframing" of its opponents.

The Cornwall Alliance's case rests on the claim that the poor need to consume fossil fuels both to improve their daily lives and to make economic development possible:

> What impoverished people desperately need is abundant, affordable electricity—most easily achieved by using fossil fuels like coal, petroleum, and natural gas. However much these might emit real pollutants (not CO_2, which is essential to all plant growth and not a pollutant, but nitrous oxide, mercury, soot, and others), they are tremendously cleaner and safer than wood and dung.[32]

Unfortunately, environmentalists committed to fighting "alleged manmade global warming" prevent the poor from obtaining electricity from fossil fuels, proposing the impractical alternatives of solar, wind, and biofuels.[33] Environmentalism "largely has become a preoccupation of rich Westerners" who don't consider the impact their activism has on the poor.[34] In contrast, members of the Cornwall Alliance follow the Bible's command to "remember the poor."[35]

Climate Change Skepticism

As we've seen, evangelical supporters of creation care accept the consensus view of climate scientists that anthropogenic climate change is a real phenomenon that will cause great harm to the planet if it's not controlled. In contrast, Cornwall Alliance leaders and their allies in the evangelical right follow the lead of the secular climate change denial movement; they insist that there's no convincing scientific evidence that human activity is affecting climate.

Beisner laid out the main features of this case in his 1997 book *Where Garden Meets Wilderness*. According to Beisner, environmentalism is grounded in emotional manipulation rather than scientific facts:

An important weakness of much environmentalism is its tendency to present false or highly debatable claims of environmental problems and their significance as if they were unquestionably true. Usually, environmentalists use such claims to frighten people into accepting a message of environmental crisis, after which they will be more likely to embrace policy recommendations environmentalists make.[36]

Unfortunately, evangelical environmentalists uncritically accept the claims made by their secular partners and then "pass them along to their fellow believers with the added moral authority of Scripture."[37] This further promotes the crisis mentality.

To illustrate this problem among evangelical environmentalists, Beisner focuses on a 1995 membership recruitment letter by the Christian Society of the Green Cross. Among the letter's claims is that CO_2 has increased 26 percent since pre-industrial times, which will lead to higher temperatures. Beisner responds with a barrage of purported scientific facts ("purported" being the operative word) that indicate that increasing CO_2 levels pose no threat to the planet and may even be beneficial. This includes the claim that most of the increase in global average temperatures between 1880 and 1990 was attributable to natural causes and that the CO_2 increase will cause "little or no rise in sea levels, some benefit to agriculture because of longer growing seasons and increased water use efficiency . . . and less need for heating in the winter (thus reducing energy consumption)."[38]

In a move that mirrors some postmodernist and deconstructionist writings, Beisner refers to Thomas Kuhn's concept of "paradigm shifts" in scientific fields.[39] Beisner writes that the beliefs of the majority of climate scientists, who fear the effects of anthropogenic climate change, will eventually be replaced by the minority who share his skepticism:

As Thomas Kuhn argued in *The Structure of Scientific Revolutions*, a reigning scientific paradigm tends to dominate academia and publishing for decades while a small number of scientists nibble away, often unaware of each other, at bits and pieces of it. At some point, usually not gradually and piecemeal but suddenly and wholesale, the reigning paradigm collapses and is replaced by a new orthodoxy and the process repeats itself. . . . Such a transition seems imminent in the environmental debate as evidence mounts against the conventional doom-and-gloom view.[40]

Beisner adds his disappointment that those scientists who are Christians, "who are used to being minorities and confronting the bias of secular scientists," ignore the lessons from Kuhn and instead trust in the objectivity of the currently dominant scientists.[41]

Finally, Beisner claims that the financial interests of environmental organizations and climate scientists lead both groups to support a crisis perspective. He cites the large number of environmental organizations whose sole reason for existence is to alert people to environmental crises and propose solutions: "Without news of crises, fund raising (leading environmental organizations raised over $400 million in 1991) plummets. They have a vested interest, therefore, in supporting scholars whose work generates the 'right' results."[42] Additionally, many scientists feel a desperate need for funding, and they know that few donors will fund research on nonproblems: "[Donors] want to fund research on crises, the bigger the better. This creates a strong natural incentive for researchers to look for evidence of problems and ignore contrary evidence."[43]

Later documents by the Cornwall Alliance reiterate these claims and add a few updates. The alleged bias of climate scientists is not just about obtaining research funds but also about a lack of courage to dissent: "The temptation to use the 'likely results' criterion (which modelers use routinely to judge their models) as a cover for politically expedient results and the desire never to be an outlier are powerful human impulses to which scientists are not immune."[44] In addition to criticizing the broad field of climate science, the Cornwall Alliance also focused on one specific group, the United Nations Intergovernmental Panel on Climate Change (IPCC), and charged it with political bias: "The IPCC is a loosely organized, highly politicized group of scientists, bureaucrats, and governmental representatives first assembled in 1988 with the explicit mandate to build the scientific case for anthropogenic global warming—a mandate that has heavily shaped its findings."[45] A third new tactic is to cite the Global Warming Petition Project, also known as the Oregon Petition. This was an effort to collect names of scientists opposed to the Kyoto Accords, which were intended to address climate change. The petition has drawn widespread ridicule from opponents, who point out that only an extremely small percentage of signers are trained in climate science, and also that the petition relies on the fraudulent inclusion of names.[46] Ignoring these criticisms, the Cornwall Alliance uses the petition as evidence that a scientific "consensus" on anthropogenic global warming doesn't exist:[47]

> Meanwhile, the very reality of the consensus remains debatable, as evidenced by surveys of relevant scientific literature . . . and climate scientists . . . and the willingness of over 31,000 American scientists to sign a statement claiming, "There is no convincing scientific evidence that human release of carbon dioxide, methane, or other greenhouse gases is causing or will, in the foreseeable future, cause catastrophic heating of the Earth's atmosphere and disruption of the Earth's climate. Moreover, there is substantial scientific evidence that increases in atmospheric carbon dioxide produce many beneficial effects upon the natural plant and animal environments of the Earth."[48]

In several ways, the Cornwall Alliance's campaign against mainstream climate science parallels the other Christian Right movements covered in this book. Intelligent design leaders have also cited Kuhn to bolster their claims that mainstream scientific opinions will soon be overturned. Both intelligent design and ex-gay leaders condemn "politicized" science that is suppressing the truth. And science-by-petition is a tactic that has been used by the intelligent design movement, as well as by creation scientists, to attack evolution.[49]

The Cornucopian Connection

To better understand the Cornwall Alliance's anti-environmentalism stances, we need to consider the long-standing debate within economics over the effects of population growth. The pessimistic perspective on population originated with Thomas Malthus, an economist and clergyman in the Church of England writing in the early part of the nineteenth century. Malthus believed that human population tends to grow exponentially while agricultural production tends to grow arithmetically, leading to catastrophic shortages. Malthus was also known for harsh attitudes toward the poor; he insisted that helping the poor would only increase their population. Since Malthus viewed contraception as immoral, he favored controlling the population through late marriages and sexual restraint. Later forms of "neo-Malthusianism" abandoned some of Malthus's harsher ideas but retained the belief that "human population growth is a key problem because it tends to dangerously exceed natural resource carrying capacity, threatening malnourishment, aggravated poverty, and environmental deterioration."[50] Many environmental movement leaders espouse forms of neo-Malthusianism.

Other economists have been more optimistic about population growth, claiming that it's nonproblematic or even beneficial. Karl Marx and Friedrich Engels argued that capitalism, not population growth, was the root cause of poverty and other problems associated with industrialization. Once the capitalist order was overthrown and replaced by socialism, the "forces of production" would be freed to create a world of plenty. Marx and Engels's vision of the future seems to assume that some source of clean, easily attainable energy, which obviously did not exist in the nineteenth century, would emerge to enable production. Another significant critic of Malthus was the twentieth-century Danish economist Ester Boserup, who wrote that Malthus greatly underestimated the extent to which human ingenuity could be used to increase agricultural production, and that population growth drives such innovation.

In the late twentieth century a school of economic thought known as "cornucopianism" emerged, which borrowed some of Boserup's ideas but went significantly beyond her. These economists saw positive effects from population growth, and were staunchly committed to free market capitalism (obviously rejecting the Marxist tradition). Cornucopians claimed that as long as free markets are permitted to flourish, technological innovation will lead to adequate supplies of resources and a cleaner environment. A key principle for cornucopians is *substitution*—new resources (substitutes) can be found to meet growing demand, as when fossil fuels replaced wood as the primary source of energy. Substitution prevents scarcity from emerging with population growth. The most prominent cornucopian was Julian Simon. In his 1981 book *The Ultimate Resource*, Simon praised the power of human ingenuity to improve living conditions.[51] Increasing population means more human ingenuity and should be welcomed, not feared. The book's main arguments were stated boldly on its cover: "Natural resources and energy are getting *less* scarce. Pollution in the U.S. has been decreasing. The world's food supply is improving. Population growth has long-term benefits."

Like most academic debates, the economic debate over the effects of population growth includes many moderate positions, which reject both the neo-Malthusian and the cornucopian extremes. In one of his few references to this debate, Beisner implies that he embraces a moderate position:

> [There is] a common problem with facts (or alleged facts) about environmental degradation: a propensity for doomsayers to pick numbers at the scary end of the spectrum while paying little attention to evidence that those numbers may be vastly exaggerated. (At the same time there is a tendency for the doomsayers' critics—often called cornucopians—to pick numbers at the benign end of the spectrum while paying little attention to evidence that those numbers may be vastly minimized. The proper aim for both parties should be truth.)[52]

Of course, Beisner is no moderate, and neither are his colleagues in the Cornwall Alliance. Their economic arguments draw heavily from cornucopian writings. For example, the seventy-six-page Cornwall Alliance article "A Renewed Call to Truth, Prudence, and Protection of the Poor" cites Julian Simon ten times, always treating his claims as uncontestable truth. It cites the cornucopian political scientist Bjørn Lomborg fourteen times in a similarly uncritical manner. In fact, Cornwall Alliance leaders go well beyond traditional cornucopian thought by adding divine action. Simon's faith in humans led him to believe that it was unlikely that they would cause catastrophic climate change. Cornwall Alliance leaders' faith in God leads them to believe that catastrophic climate change is impossible because God simply won't allow it.

Enter the Green Dragon

Having lost the battle for the leaders of the evangelical center, in 2010 the Cornwall Alliance made an aggressive play for the evangelical rank and file. The Christian Right has a long history of using paranoid-style rhetoric in attempts to motivate evangelical laypeople. The Resisting the Green Dragon campaign is a case study in the paranoid style, using rhetoric that is extreme even by Christian Right standards in order to scare laypeople away from creation care. The campaign's twelve-part DVD series features appearances by a who's who of the evangelical right, including Tom Minnery from Focus on the Family, Tony Perkins from the Family Research Council, Richard Land from the Southern Baptist Convention's Ethics and Religious Liberty Commission, and Wendy Wright from Concerned Women for America. The DVD sessions feature provocative titles such as "Rescuing People from the Cult of the Green Dragon," "The Green Face of the Pro-Death Agenda: Population Control, Abortion and Euthanasia," and "Threats to Liberty and the Move toward a Global Government." The companion book by the South African-born physicist and "lay theologian" James Wanliss was titled *Resisting the Green Dragon: Dominion Not Death*. Wanliss did not attempt to cover the breadth of topics included in the DVD series, but he compensated by using even more heated rhetoric. The campaign was engineered with the assistance of the Heritage Foundation, a think tank with close ties to the evangelical right.[53]

The Resisting the Green Dragon campaign repeated many of the arguments found in earlier writings by Beisner and the Cornwall Alliance. For example, it continued to portray mainstream climate science as highly flawed. It still treated Julian Simon as an infallible authority on economic matters. The campaign also incorporated three claims that hadn't appeared in the Cornwall Alliance's writings, though they'd been circulating among evangelical opponents of environmentalism. These new claims relied heavily on the paranoid style. In fact, their portrayal of the environmental movement matched Hofstadter's description of the paranoid style's central image: "a vast and sinister conspiracy, a gigantic yet subtle machinery of influence set in motion to undermine and destroy a way of life."[54]

The first new claim was that environmentalism is completely incompatible with Christianity. As the title of the campaign indicates, environmentalism is to be identified with Satan. It's a religion that worships the Earth and competes with Christianity. The proper response of Christians is therefore "resisting," not embracing. Here we see the Manichean worldview associated with the paranoid style, as well as an example of the false choice fallacy. And since Cornwall Alliance leaders accuse the environmental movement of using Christians to hide its true (Satanic) nature, we also have paranoid-style conspiracy theorizing. This is a departure from Beisner's earlier position, which recognized and even commended a distinctly evangelical approach to environmentalism based in the Bible rather than "New Age" or "pagan" religion.

Wanliss repeats this first claim throughout his book, always with the same sneering tone. In a section titled "Green Religion," he writes that environmentalism provides an alternative religion for those who reject the Christian heritage of Western civilization: "It is a religion with a vision of sin and repentance, heaven and hell. It even has a special vocabulary, with words like 'sustainability' and 'carbon neural.' Its communion is organic food. Its sacraments are sex, abortion, and when all else fails, sterilization. Its saints are Al Gore and the IPCC."[55] Christians should remain hopeful that God will expose and defeat his foe:

> When the light exposes the unholy religious foundations of environmentalism, like the bones of a rotting carcass, no more disguise will be possible. No painted face, no fluffy illusions, no amount of bright semantic gymnastics, will morph the Green Dragon into anything other than what it is—an avowed enemy of humanity and of the greatest lover of humanity [God]. No semi-naked Hollywood celebrity bunnies draped over its foul form can deny its native evil. No precious perfumes can mask its vile vapors, its dark cloud of pantheistic pollution. We will not mourn its passing.[56]

The Green Dragon of environmentalism will face defeat in the long term, the argument goes, but in the short term it has successfully "penetrated the church with anti-human and anti-Christian ideas."[57] Environmentalism is strongest among the mainline churches, which Wanliss condemns for "having steadily pared every Biblical doctrine to the point that they whittle down Christianity to mere feelings."[58] Having traded authentic Christian belief for conformity to the world, these Christians are naïve about the dangers of environmentalism. But Wanliss expresses concern that environmentalism has even lured evangelicals. Not surprisingly, he singles out Richard Cizik for criticism:

> Perhaps one cannot fault the motives of folks like Cizik; unlike the mainstream environmentalist for whom humans are scum, Green Evangelicals

argue that we should save the environment because unless we act collectively and immediately the end is nigh for mankind. Unfortunately, they adopt the narrative of the Green Dragon and espouse the most radical solutions to environmental changes that are not—despite the hysterics—a crisis, often not even a problem. Unfortunately, Cizik is increasingly less an ambassador of Christ than of the Green Dragon. . . . Bleeding heart evangelicals have swallowed apocalyptic nightmares of the Green Dragon hook, line, and sinker.[59]

This quote also contains the second new claim introduced by the Resisting the Green Dragon campaign: that environmentalists hate humans. Cornwall Alliance leaders contrast this alleged perspective with the biblical proclamation that humans were created in God's image and therefore have worth and dignity. Again, we see the typical paranoid-style dualism. This claim also sets up the environmental movement as a threat to society, fulfilling another key feature of the paranoid style. This argument goes well beyond earlier concerns that environmentalists value nature more than they value humans.

This second new claim was emphasized in DVD session 9, which is titled "The Green Face of the Pro-Death Agenda: Population Control, Abortion, and Euthanasia." Charmaine Yoest, president of Americans United for Life, contrasted the environmental worldview with the Christian worldview of the pro-life movement. The former worldview sees humans as "parasites" and argues that "life is not worth living." The latter worldview sees humans as "possibilities" and argues that "your life can make a difference." Wanliss's book makes the same case, but in even starker terms:

Past decades have witnessed the accelerating ascent of what one could call, in its ugliest manifestation, the environmentalist death cult. It appears environmentalists believe that smart people have fewer children, and the wisest have none at all. From the writings and public declarations of prominent environmentalists it is clear the ethos of the movement fosters deep animus and hostility toward humanity. They hate humans. They hate them for being fruitful and multiplying. They hate them for having dominion over the other creatures, and for modifying nature. They reject the idea of humanity's special place in the world, and that God made man in his image. They spew disapproval of modern civilization. As we will see, they worship the wild wasteland and idolize nature.[60]

Significantly, Cornwall Alliance leaders place some of the blame for environmentalism's anti-human views on Darwinism, which, they claim, devalues humans by portraying them as mere animals. In Wanliss's words, "Modern environmentalism and Darwin's dangerous idea are coupled like a nest of writhing snakes."[61]

The third new claim from Resisting the Green Dragon is that environmentalists seek a totalitarian global government in order to impose their agenda on others. Again, we see the paranoid-style belief that the social order is threatened. Since Cornwall Alliance leaders believe that environmentalists are less than forthcoming about these plans, we also have paranoid-style conspiracy theorizing. Earlier writings by Cornwall Alliance leaders raised concerns that environmentalists were advocating unnecessary and harmful government regulations. This new argument took those concerns to extreme levels. Note that the fear of totalitarian global government has been a long-running theme in the evangelical right, one embraced by Tim LaHaye and Jerry B. Jenkins (authors of the *Left Behind* series of novels) and Pat Robertson, among others.[62] Once Cornwall Alliance leaders decided to depict environmentalists as principal enemies of Christianity and subject them to paranoid-style attacks, it was natural for these leaders to deploy this theme as well.

Cornwall Alliance leaders lay out this third claim in session 10 of the DVD series, which is titled "Threats to Liberty and the Move toward a Global Government." The introductory section includes Richard Land of the Southern Baptist Convention making an earnest plea to viewers:

> Through this lecture you will have the opportunity to see what leading environmentalists say about their own intentions for reducing your freedoms, eroding your national sovereignty, and ushering in global governance by elitists. I urge you to study this further and to act to preserve your freedom and the limited, constitutional, national government bequeathed to you by the Founding Fathers.

In other words, environmentalism is a threat to the United States as we know it.

Beisner's lecture provides the details of why this is the case. Beisner begins by noting that one of the most common phrases among environmentalists is, "Global problems demand global solutions." This, he claims, is a hint of one of the greatest dangers of the environmental movement. He moves on to the meaning of the word "environment," which comes from a French word meaning "surroundings." "Surroundings," he muses, includes everything:

> The environment is everything, so environmentalism becomes everythingism. Now, there's another word that we use for everything. It's the totality of things. If you are talking about everything that is, you mean the totality of what is. Total, right? And we have a political term that is related to that one, don't we? Totalitarianism. Environmentalism equals everythingism equals totalitarianism. And if environmentalists want to bring the whole of the environment under the care of the government, one way or another, then what they are really saying is: "We want to control everything about your life. We want total control."

Wanliss's book echoes Beisner's assertion that environmentalists seek world domination, but indulges in more heated rhetoric, as usual. Wanliss also adds the substantive point that Christian are being fooled into supporting this scheme:

> All the solutions to environmental collapse offered by politicians require tough government controls on individuals. The new slogan is planetary salvation, and Green leaders think Christians will wiggle and fawn like pleasure-drunk puppies because of the God-talk. Professing Christian environmentalists are the useful idiots of the Green Dragon. They affirm "love to neighbor" or "creation stewardship," which makes it sound as if they affirm the Bible, keeping dubious Christians constantly confused. Then, while the baffling slogans flash like machine guns in the minds of their hearers, Greens hustle in the fads of the political left as they progressively rob and enslave their brothers.[63]

To call the Resisting the Green Dragon campaign extreme would be an understatement. This is the paranoid style with remarkable attention to *style*. What could have motivated the Cornwall Alliance and its supporters to go down this route? On the one hand, this campaign can be seen as a well-crafted strategic move to stem the influence of centrist evangelical leaders on the evangelical rank and file regarding the issue of climate change.[64] After all, the paranoid style has a proven track record of effectiveness in the evangelical world. The Heritage Foundation, which assisted with the Resisting the Green Dragon campaign, has long been known for sophisticated marketing of conservative Christian ideas. Once Cornwall Alliance leaders decided to go down the paranoid route, the details of the campaign were obviously planned with great care. For example, the image of the Green Dragon's eye in the DVDs is a blatant copy of the Eye of Sauron from Peter Jackson's *Lord of the Rings* movies. This is one of many examples of evangelical leaders co-opting pop culture. On the other hand, given the angry rhetoric aimed at centrist evangelical leaders, one gets the sense that the campaign is personal as well as strategic. Why treat centrist leaders in this manner when they're allies on nearly everything except climate change? Perhaps this is an example of the infamous "sibling rivalry" dynamic. The closeness of the two parties may be exactly what makes the disagreement on climate change so bitter. Whatever is behind the Resisting the Green Dragon campaign, one thing is certain: having jumped headlong into the abyss of the paranoid style, there is no going back for the Cornwall Alliance.

Assessing the Evangelical Rank and File

How effective was the Resisting the Green Dragon campaign in swaying ordinary evangelicals? It's impossible to know for sure, since its launch coincides with other events affecting public views on climate change. The most significant of these events was the rise of the Tea Party movement, a backlash against the Obama presidency that drew deeply from the paranoid-style tradition. A 2013 survey found that 52 percent of those who identify with the Tea Party movement also identify with the Christian Right.[65] Clearly, Tea Party politics influences a sizeable chunk of the evangelical population. Since Obama made attempts to reduce carbon emissions an early priority in his presidency (a significant shift from the George W. Bush administration's assault on climate science), it wasn't surprising that the Tea Party made denial of anthropogenic climate change one of its core principles. Following the 2010 midterm elections, the Tea Party managed to drive out what little acceptance of anthropogenic climate change still existed among Republican elected officials, and denial of the problem became the "orthodox" position.[66]

Whether influenced by the Resisting the Green Dragon campaign, Republican politics, or both, evangelicals after 2010 are consistently less likely to believe in anthropogenic climate change than other religious groups, according to surveys. For example, a September 2011 survey by the Public Religion Research Institute in partnership with the Religious News Service found that strong majorities of all religious groups believed that the Earth was getting warmer. However, only 31 percent of white evangelicals believed that human activity was responsible for the trend, compared to 43 percent of white mainline Protestants, 50 percent of Catholics, and 52 percent of the unaffiliated.[67]

In November 2011 the *New Republic* ran an article titled "Whatever Happened to the Evangelical-Environmental Alliance?" The article contrasted the wave of optimism around the time of the Evangelical Climate Initiative in 2006 with the pessimism that reigned a few years later. The article featured Joel Hunter, a Florida megachurch pastor who was one of the early signers of the ECI statement and who had worked hard to spread the creation care message. "A glum Hunter told me that he holds out hope for the next generation, conceding that his generation probably won't be shaking up the climate change debate like they'd hoped. The old fault lines, which Cizik told *The New Republic* in 2006 were 'no more,' are still very much alive."[68]

The goal of centrist evangelical leaders to spread the creation care agenda to the rank and file has largely failed. Politics played a major role, but evangelical attitudes toward science were certainly another important factor. As we've seen in previous chapters, centrist evangelical leaders have encouraged skepticism of mainstream science in the areas of evolution and human sexuality. Why, then, should ordinary evangelicals heed their advice to accept mainstream climate science? By encouraging a paranoid-style mentality on other fronts, centrist leaders made ordinary evangelicals easier prey for the Cornwall Alliance's anti-environmentalism campaign.

The Impossible Defense of Dominion Theology

As I've noted, Cornwall Alliance leaders often cite Julian Simon and other cornucopians for empirical confirmation of beliefs associated with their dominion theology, particularly the idea that economic development and population growth are parts of God's plan for humans and will therefore have positive effects. This maneuver assumes that the claims of cornucopian economics are uncontestable truth. In fact, these claims are highly contested among social scientists.

Cornucopianism is part of a larger constellation of economic theory hailing the virtues of free markets. Much of this theory was developed at the University of Chicago Economics Department (the Chicago school). Chicago school icon Milton Friedman was a major advocate of Julian Simon's ideas and wrote "an appreciation" for the second edition of Simon's book *The Ultimate Resource*.[69] Although it's influential in the broader field of economics, free market economic theory has been largely dismissed by other social science fields. Psychologists have argued that its "rational choice" view of human decision making is inaccurate, while sociologists have criticized the lack of attention to the social structures in which economic activity takes place. These critics charge that free market economic theory is based on simplistic models that have little empirical support. Some have even suggested that the Chicago school has a quasi-religious quality about it.[70]

In addition, a number of critiques have been aimed specifically at cornucopian economics. The sociologist Michael Bell lists three common critiques of the work of Julian Simon. The first is that Simon's picture of human progress ignores social inequality. As Bell points out,

> Although the lives of many have improved, the percentage of the world's people who live in poverty, facing hunger and malnutrition throughout their lives, hasn't declined all that much in the last 50 years. The sheer number living in poverty has doubled. It is true that even the desperately poor are generally living longer, in part because of medical and other technological improvements, but life expectancy is still very uneven across the world.[71]

The second critique challenges Simon's claim that larger populations mean more brainpower to work out problems:

Innovativeness depends on social circumstances that encourage creative thinking, such as democratic discussion and a good educational system, not mere numbers of people. . . . Also, the kind of improvements that Simon looks to are mainly high-tech. But the bulk of population growth currently is taking place among those who do not have the educational backgrounds to contribute to high-tech solutions.[72]

Bell's third critique is that Simon is overly optimistic about the ability of technology to solve scarcity problems by creating substitutes: "But will technology always come to the rescue in time to prevent serious problems? This question is particularly germane as we encounter limits in resources that seem less substitutable, such as fresh water, clean air, land for agriculture, and habitat for biodiversity."[73]

The political scientist Leigh Raymond provides an empirical test and critique of the cornucopian view that economic growth will improve the environment in his article "Economic Growth as Environmental Policy? Reconsidering the Environmental Kuznets Curve." The Environmental Kuznets Curve (EKC) is the hypothesized relationship between economic growth and environmental damage/improvement. It is an inverted U-shaped curve that posits that while economic growth is initially damaging to the environment, further growth leads to superior environmental quality once per capita income rises beyond a specific threshold. Its name derives from the fact that it mirrors a similar relationship between income inequality and per capita income first hypothesized by the economist Simon Kuznets. To test the EKC model, Raymond made use of data collected for a project called the Environmental Sustainability Index (ESI). "As a comprehensive summary of environmental quality and conditions in over 140 nations, the ESI provides a number of useful new dependent variables for a detailed discussion of the relationship between economic growth and environmental impact."[74] Raymond's analysis suggests that the EKC model is mostly inaccurate:

Thus, the preceding analysis of the ESI data confirms many of the objections to using the EKC model as a basis for public policy. Besides being a reduced-form model with uncertain mechanisms for causality, it is also apparent from these results that the relationship indeed holds only for limited types of environmental impacts. The few true EKC curves that emerge from the data all have relatively high turning points where environmental quality begins to improve, indicating that many environmental benefits associated with economic growth may be too little, too late. . . . In short, there is little in this analysis that should make anyone confident that nations can indeed "grow" their way out of their national and international environmental dilemmas.[75]

Given its dubious nature, cornucopian economics can't provide empirical proof for the claims of dominion theology. This situation isn't surprising. As we've discussed in previous chapters, using science to verify any system of theology is a dicey affair. Moreover, the Cornwall Alliance's dominion theology, like other Christian Right projects, is based on a creationist worldview that is antithetical to real science. Attempts to authenticate this theology were doomed from the start. Of course, none of this matters to Cornwall Alliance leaders. In a pattern of selective skepticism reminiscent of the ex-gay movement, they pretend that cornucopian economics is uncontestable truth even as they dismiss the claims of mainstream climate science as unsubstantiated.

Still More Fair-Weather Postmodernists

We saw in chapter 1 that intelligent design proponents are committed to a typical evangelical style of modernism, one that combines Enlightenment thought with commitment to the Bible, resulting in the belief that the Bible and (good) science confirm each other and together lead to absolute truth. Yet the intelligent design movement also uses postmodernist rhetoric, which undermines the authority of science, when it's useful for attacking evolution. Complicating matters further, Phillip E. Johnson wrote at least one essay castigating postmodern theories of science. We find a similar love-hate relationship with postmodernism among Cornwall Alliance leaders.

Cornwall Alliance leaders' commitment to the evangelical style of modernism is clear in their early documents, which slide effortlessly between alleged scientific facts and biblical verses. E. Calvin Beisner makes this perspective explicit in a 2013 article posted on the Cornwall Alliance website titled "Can Faith and Science Cooperate? A Meteorologist Appeals to Scripture about Global Warming." In this article Beisner attempts to defend the meteorologist and Cornwall Alliance member Anthony J. Sadar's practice of citing the Bible as support for his understanding of anthropogenic global warming. Beisner claims that he'll do this by "explaining the real relationship between religious sources and scientific understanding."[76] Beisner begins by drawing on philosophical arguments to assert that religious beliefs aren't fundamentally different from assent to scientific propositions:

> Notice that believing a mathematical proposition, a chemical proposition, a historical proposition, or a religious/theological proposition differs not as different mental acts but solely in the sorts of propositions believed. Consequently, belief in God and belief in global warming are the same sort of act—assent to the proposition that God exists and that the earth is getting warmer.[77]

From there he cites the apologist Nancy Pearcey and the chemist Charles Thaxton, two figures from the intelligent design movement, to argue that "the biblical worldview and no other could and did give birth to science."[78]

Finally, Beisner uses these two points to assert that the Bible is a valid source of data for evaluating the state of the environment:

> Assent to the proposition that raising atmospheric carbon-dioxide concentration from 27 to 54 thousandths of a percent will warm the earth enough to cause grave harm to humanity and the rest of life on earth is belief, faith. Assent to the proposition that a wise, faithful, powerful God so designed the earth's climate system that it is not so fragile is also belief, faith. Neither is scientifically privileged. Neither is philosophically privileged. Each must seek its support from a variety of sources, whether divine propositional revelation (the Bible) or divine natural revelation (the creation). And no historically or philosophically informed understanding of the methods of science can exclude Biblical propositions from the evidence to be considered.[79]

Beisner's aim is not to lower science to the level of mere opinion but to raise the Bible (as interpreted by conservative evangelicals) to the level of scientific evidence. It's not surprising that he uses arguments from the intelligent design movement, as his project is reminiscent of Phillip E. Johnson's "theistic realism."

Yet, like Johnson, Beisner and other Cornwall Alliance leaders borrow from the postmodernist playbook in an effort to deconstruct their scientific opponents—in this case, mainstream climate science. As we've discussed, Cornwall Alliance leaders dismiss the scientific credibility of mainstream climate scientists, who supposedly are biased by a search for funding, a lack of courage to dissent from the majority, and pro-environmentalist politics. This mirrors the postmodern critique of the objectivity of science. They also rely on Thomas Kuhn's concept of "paradigm shift" to argue that the current pessimistic thinking about global warming will soon be replaced by the more optimistic perspective embraced by the Cornwall Alliance. Again, we see a parallel with intelligent design proponents, who see themselves as possessing the future dominant paradigm in biology.

The sociologist Laurel Kearns makes this same observation about the broad (religious and secular) climate change denial movement in her 2007 essay "Cooking the Truth: Faith, Science, the Market, and Global Warming":

> Advanced not just by scholars in various fields, but also by nuclear activists, environmentalists, feminists, and postcolonial critics, [the postmodern critique of science's objectivity] takes on the inherent subjectivity and belief systems or paradigms that shape scientific research and the interpretation of its results. Frequently, as Sandra Harding, and before her, Thomas Kuhn, have noted, scientists make assumptions that reflect the dominant cultural assumptions, such that research on only white men is taken to provide a definitive picture of universal, or "human," health. [*Wall Street Journal* writer James] Schlesinger draws upon this critique of science to undermine the authority of climate change science by citing the examples of Galileo and Copernicus to prove that the dominant scientific view is not always "right."[80]

There's more to the story. With the Resisting the Green Dragon campaign, the Cornwall Alliance has done something more audacious than anything attempted by intelligent design—it has accused its scientific opponents of abandoning traditional science and embracing postmodern deconstruction. To understand why this claim is not even remotely believable, we need to consider one of the basic insights of sociology: social groups of all kinds attempt to increase their status. Scientific fields are no exception. But the goal of postmodern deconstruction is to *decrease* the status of science. While an individual scientist may "go rogue" and embrace postmodernism, it's inconceivable that an entire scientific field would do so.

The University of Delaware climatologist David Legates presented the preliminary version of this claim about climate science in DVD session 6, which is titled "Putting Out the Dragon's Fire on Global Warming." After presenting alleged flaws in mainstream climate science, including the inaccuracy of computer models, he asks how the field got to this point.

> Well, we got here because science as you and I probably learned it is changing. It's no longer what we call "normal science." We didn't call it "normal science." We called it "science." But now it's called "post-normal science." And the idea of post-normal science is that things have changed. In the olden days science was looking for truth and order in the natural world. We looked for facts. Facts drove your assessment of risks. Risks drove what policy changes you were expected to apply. . . . Nowadays it's all different.

To substantiate this claim, Legates presents a slide quoting Mike Hulme, whom he identifies as a professor of climate change at the University of East Anglia (Norwich, England). The slide contains the heading "Post-Normal Science." Underneath this it reads, "'Normal' science assumes science can find truth and that truth-based policy will then follow." Following this is an italicized quote attributed to Hulme: "What matters about climate change is not whether we can predict the future with some desired level of certainty and accuracy . . . we need to see how we can use the idea of climate change to rethink how we take forward our political, social, economic and personal projects over the decades to come." The quote comes from Hulme's book *Why We Disagree about Climate Change: Understanding Controversy, Inaction and Opportunity*, which Legates never indicates. Legates implies but never states that Hulme embraces the concept of "post-normal science" for climate science.

Legates then offers a second quote from Hulme, again on a slide with the heading "Post-Normal Science": "Because the idea of climate change is so plastic, it can be deployed across many of our human projects and can even serve many of our psychological, ethical, and *spiritual* needs."[81] Legates then comments further. "Spiritual needs? Science? It wasn't supposed to be that way. Apparently now it is. That's the world of post-normal science. It is no longer simply advocacy science. You don't pick the facts to serve your needs. Science is there as a means to an end."

In sum, Legates uses quotes from Mike Hulme in an attempt to prove that climate science has shifted from "normal science" to "post-normal science" and in the process has abandoned the pursuit of facts for various other human goals. This is not fundamentally different from earlier Cornwall Alliance critiques of the alleged lack of objectivity of climate science. However, in January 2013 Beisner took Legates's arguments to the next level in a lecture titled "Public School Science Standards: Political or Pure?" delivered to the Annual Educational Policy Conference of the Constitutional Coalition.

Beisner devotes the first half of his lecture to critiques of Darwinism, drawing from arguments developed by the intelligent design movement. In the second half he turns to climate scientists who believe in catastrophic anthropogenic global warming (CAGW), whom he labels "those who intentionally politicize science—the proponents and practitioners of post-normal science."[82] He then offers his definition of post-normal science:

> Post-normal science is essentially postmodern deconstruction—a literary theory, developed in the humanities, that holds that language doesn't convey meaning or truth but only projects power.... Post-normal science is postmodern deconstruction applied to sciences. For post-normal science, scientific procedures—observations, hypothesis, experimentation, testing, computer modeling, even peer review for publication—are undertaken not to discover truth about the world but to project power, to further an agenda. Consequently, post-normal scientists go through the motions of what we all think of as science, but only for show.[83]

Beisner goes on to identify Mike Hulme as "one of the world's foremost proponents of post-normal science" and argues that he is central to the "climate alarmist movement."[84] Beisner then adds, "Much as we might disagree with Hulme's views on CAGW and reject his post-normal science, though, we should be thankful for his candor."[85] He then presents five quotes from Hulme's *Why We Disagree about Climate Change* that are meant to substantiate Beisner's claims.

To understand the flaws in Legates and Beisner's portrayal of climate science, we need to begin by examining what Hulme's book really says. Hulme affirms the value of traditional scientific research methodology, and he maintains that belief in anthropogenic climate change is based on empirical data. However, he also writes that in addition to the physical phenomenon of climate change, there is the "idea of climate change" that exists in the social realm:

> As we have slowly, and at times reluctantly, realised that humanity has become an active agent in the reshaping of physical climates around the world, so our cultural, social, political and ethical practices are reinterpreting what climate change means. Far from simply being a change in physical climates—a change in the sequences of weather experienced in given places—climate change has become an idea that now travels well beyond its origins in the natural sciences. And as this idea meets new cultures on its travels and encounters the worlds of politics, economics, popular culture, commerce and religion—often through the interposing role of the media—climate change takes on new meanings and serves new purposes.[86]

Legates and Beisner accuse Hulme of replacing the scientific with the social and religious, but in fact Hulme is advocating a both/and approach. Legates and Beisner also take Hulme's statements about the "idea of climate change" and falsely argue that these represent Hulme's views on the physical phenomenon of climate change.

Now let's turn to the real post-normal science. The term comes from Silvio O. Funtowicz and Jerome R. Ravetz's 1993 article "Science for the Post-Normal Age." The authors focus on the social role of science, particularly the ways it informs public policy. The authors write that the challenge of policy issues related to risk and the environment has led to a new type of science: "In this, uncertainty is not banished but is managed and values are not presupposed but made explicit. The model of scientific argument is not a formalized deduction but an interactive dialogue."[87] This new type of science exists alongside earlier models, rather than replacing them. "One way of distinguishing among the different sorts of research is by their goals: applied science is 'mission-oriented'; professional consultancy is 'client-serving'; and post-normal science is 'issue-driven'. These three can be contrasted with core science—the traditional 'pure' or 'basic' research—which is 'curiosity-motivated.'"[88] Significantly, the authors describe post-normal science as "an alternative to post-modernity" rather than a type of postmodern deconstruction of science.[89]

Hulme cites Funtowicz and Ravetz's essay and proposes that their concept of post-normal science is appropriate for climate change:

> In cases such as climate change, then, science must take on a different form. As well as seeking to observe, theorise and model in the quest to establish "facts"—to formulate what is known—science must pay much more attention to establishing and communicating what is unknown, or at best what is uncertain. In addition to striving to eliminate bias and prejudice from the practice of science—to adhere to Merton's norm of "disinterestedness"—scientists must also recognise and reflect upon their own values and upon the collective values of their colleagues. These values and world views continually seep into their activities as scientists and inflect the knowledge that is formed. The goal of "disinterestedness" can still be aspired to, whilst simultaneously and crucially recognising that, in failing to achieve it, scientific knowledge will inevitably take on a different character.[90]

Again, we should note the both/and character of Hulme's approach to science that involves retaining the traditional pursuit of facts. One may legitimately take issue with Hulme's arguments in *Why We Disagree about Climate Change*, but it's not accurate to accuse him of being a postmodern deconstructionist or of seeking to replace empirical research with politics. Legates and Beisner are resorting to the straw person fallacy, attacking an opponent that they themselves have created.

Even if Hulme were a raging postmodernist, Legates and Beisner's characterization of climate science would still not be valid, since Hulme is only one individual in a sizeable field. Legates and Beisner both claim that Hulme is representative of the larger field of climate science, but neither of them offers any compelling evidence for this. This closely resembles Phillip E. Johnson's attempt to make Richard Dawkins representative of evolutionary biology. Indeed, Beisner's comment that "we should be thankful for [Hulme's] candor" parallels Johnson's argument that Dawkins says publicly what other biologists say in private. Thus, in addition to the straw person fallacy, Legates and Beisner also rely on the hasty generalization fallacy, drawing conclusions about a population (climate scientists) based on a sample that's not large enough (one person).

To recap this section, the Cornwall Alliance's contradictory relationship to postmodernism initially paralleled that of the intelligent design movement. However, Legates and Beisner added a new twist by making the completely unbelievable claim that climate scientists have embraced postmodern deconstruction, offering "evidence" based on dual fallacies. Once again, Beisner and his colleagues have shown themselves to be virtuosi of the paranoid style.

Beisner's "Total" Fabrication

Beisner's straw person portrayal of climate scientists as postmodern deconstructionists is matched in absurdity only by his portrayal of environmentalists as totalitarians. Let's review the arguments behind the latter claim: (1) the word "environment" is derived from the French word for "surroundings"; (2) the surroundings include everything; (3) "everything" is a synonym for "total"; (4) totalitarianism is related to the word "total"; (5) therefore, environmentalists are totalitarians.

In any other context this would look more like an attempt at humor than a serious argument. Unfortunately, Beisner and his colleagues are serious. So let's analyze what specifically is wrong. The fundamental flaw in Beisner's reasoning is a gross oversimplification of the rules of etymology, the derivations of words. A word can relate to its source(s) in a variety of potential ways, including through the use of analogy. However, in Beisner's world a word must relate to its source through a literal equality of meaning. Environmentalists are concerned with literally everything. Being concerned with the total (in this case, the ecological whole) makes one literally a totalitarian. To illustrate the problem with this approach, consider the word "ghostwriter." This is a person who writes for another while their identity is hidden. The ghostwriter is invisible in a manner analogous to a ghost or spirit of a deceased person. Following Beisner's logic, however, a ghostwriter would have to be a literal ghost who writes. Fortunately for ghostwriters everywhere, being dead is not a requirement for the job. Neither is there any reason to believe that environmentalists are totalitarians.

Or consider what happens when you go through a checkout line and the cashier declares, "Your total comes to . . ." They just *totaled* your bill. Are cashiers totalitarians? In Beisner's world the answer would be yes. In the real world the answer would be no.

Beisner continues his wordplay-as-evidence routine later in the same DVD session while commenting on Al Gore's 1992 book *Earth in the Balance*. The final chapter of the book outlines a "Global Marshall Plan" so save the environment. One facet of the plan is a program to increase the amount of climate data, preferably in a way that facilitates public education: "Specifically, I propose a program involving as many countries as possible that will use schoolteachers and their students to monitor the entire earth daily, or at least those portions of the land area that can be covered by participating nations."[91] As Gore makes clear, the plan involves voluntary participation—notice the reference to "participating nations," which implies that some nations are not involved. However, in Beisner's paranoid imagination the plan is evidence of a totalitarian conspiracy:

> [Gore] said that we needed this Global Marshall Plan to prevent global warming. And he described how we would enlist all the teachers in all the schools around the world to assign their students projects to gather data that could be collected and used to help us monitor what was happening with the climate around the world. Enlist. Really? You know, those students are free people, are they? And yet, they've just been conscripted, haven't they? They have just been conscripted. Their liberty has been threatened. The teachers have been conscripted into a particular agenda.

Beisner uses the word "enlist" in a way that suggests that it appears in the text of the book. In fact, it doesn't. His purpose is to create a verbal steppingstone to get to the word "conscript." This is an even more problematic move, given that "enlist" and "conscript" are not synonyms but antonyms. "Enlist" means to secure voluntary service, while "conscript" means to secure service by force. He's not simply bending the rules of language, he's disregarding them altogether.

Beisner and his colleagues are clearly dedicated to the belief that environmentalists aim to bring about a totalitarian world government. So strong is this belief that even crude language tricks like Beisner's are treated as convincing evidence. Such is the power of the paranoid worldview.

Conclusion

Just as the intelligent design movement insists on a false choice between Christianity and evolution, so the evangelical right's Cornwall Alliance insists on a false choice between Christianity and environmentalism. Having lost the fight for centrist evangelical leaders, the Cornwall Alliance appealed directly to the evangelical rank and file through its Resisting the Green Dragon campaign. Alliance leaders made their case against environmentalism in the most effective way they know—by employing the paranoid style. If paranoid-style rhetoric were an Olympic sport, the Cornwall Alliance would score a 10 for creativity and a 10 for execution, handily beating its "competition" in the intelligent design, ex-gay, and conservative bioethics movements. Certainly the qualities of "heated exaggeration, suspiciousness, and conspiratorial fantasy" with which Hofstadter identified the paranoid style are here in abundance.[92] Unfortunately, these aren't games. They're serious attempts to influence public opinion and ultimately government policy.

The Cornwall Alliance's hypocrisy is staggering. Alliance members accuse climate scientists of chasing money and environmentalists of being wealthy elitists. Meanwhile, they fund their projects with money from the deep pockets of the fossil fuel industry. They accuse climate scientists of "politicized" science. Meanwhile, they enlist the evangelical right's political machine in their crusade against environmentalism. They accuse climate scientists of lacking the empirical data to support their claims. Meanwhile, they uncritically accept the dubious claims of cornucopian economists. They accuse the designers of climate computer models of being detached from reality. Meanwhile, they invent implausible stories of postmodernist climate scientists and totalitarian environmentalists. They accuse environmentalists of idolatrous worship of the Earth. Meanwhile, they worship at the altar of free market capitalism.

The Cornwall Alliance is a product of the evangelical right, but centrist evangelical leaders are largely responsible for its success and their own failure to convince rank-and-file evangelicals to accept the reality of anthropogenic global warming. As we saw in the previous chapters, centrist evangelical leaders have encouraged skepticism of real science, uncritical readings of the Bible, and the paranoid-style search for adversaries. Their decision to embrace the findings of climate science was too little, too late.

Conclusion

Hofstadter ended his famous essay on the paranoid style with a note of sympathy for those gripped by this mentality: "We are all sufferers from history, but the paranoid is a double sufferer, since he is afflicted not only by the real world, with the rest of us, but by his fantasies as well."[1] As a sociologist of religion, I can certainly understand how Christian Right leaders are behaving in ways that make perfect sense within a worldview that (falsely) depicts evangelical Christians as an embattled religious minority group. Yet I have to admit that I have trouble generating the same feelings of sympathy that Hofstadter did. I'm so much more concerned about those outside the Christian Right who suffer because of the agenda these leaders seek to impose on American society. I'm concerned about children being denied a comprehensive science education because intelligent design proponents and their political allies can't stand the thought of evolution being taught in public schools. I'm concerned about the gay and lesbian people who are pressured into attempting the impossible task of becoming heterosexual rather than accepting who they are. I'm concerned that states can't have honest debates about medical aid in dying because of religiously motivated obsessions with imaginary victims. Finally, I worry about what kind of Earth our descendants will inherit because of the corporate and religious forces enabling our addiction to fossil fuels. Besides, I'm not convinced that those in paranoid movements suffer all that much. There's obviously something attractive about portraying oneself as a righteous outsider, given how often we see those portrayals in American history.[2]

As I stated at the outset, this book doesn't argue that the Christian Right represents the single greatest threat to American society. Yet there's no doubt that this movement does a significant amount of harm despite whatever honorable intentions its leaders have. Why is this the case? When it comes to dealing with science, perhaps the key issue is the ease with which these individuals deny reality when they find it undesirable. To state the matter bluntly, conservative evangelicalism is to a large extent a subculture living in a fantasy world.[3]

The Purpose-Driven Life of Unreality

For a clear illustration of the Christian Right's aversion to reality, let's turn to the most popular book the movement has ever produced, Rick Warren's *The Purpose Driven Life: What on Earth Am I Here For?*[4] The book was first published in 2002 and was an instant *New York Times* number 1 bestseller; by 2013 an expanded version could proclaim on its cover "Over 32 Million Sold" and "Bestselling Non-Fiction Hardback in History."[5] When Rick Warren speaks, millions of evangelicals (and apparently even some non-evangelicals) listen.

One of the two principal claims in *The Purpose Driven Life* is the dominant evangelical view that the Bible is a flawless (inerrant) book that must be accepted without question as the primary authority in a person's life. How important is this belief to Warren? It's worth dispensing with reason, if necessary:

> Many of our troubles occur because we base our choices on unreliable authorities: culture ("everyone is doing it"), tradition ("we've always done it"), reason ("it seemed logical"), or emotion ("it just felt right"). All four of these are flawed by the Fall. What we need is a perfect standard that will never lead us in the wrong direction. Only God's Word meets this standard. . . .
>
> In the early years of his ministry, Billy Graham went through a time when he struggled with doubts about the accuracy and authority of the Bible. One moonlit night he dropped to his knees in tears and told God that, in spite of confusing passages he didn't understand, from that point on he would completely trust the Bible as the sole authority for his life and ministry. From that day forward, Billy's life was blessed with unusual power and effectiveness.[6]

Is Warren really portraying reason as the enemy of faith? Not quite. *The Purpose Driven Life* presents itself as a perfectly reasonable articulation of evangelical beliefs. No, the problem is with reason that leads people "in the wrong direction," such as toward the belief that the Bible does in fact contain errors and contradictions. In these instances, Warren considers reason to be among "unreliable authorities" that should be ignored for the sake of faith. Of course, rejecting reason is tantamount to turning one's back on reality. Warren considers it appropriate to do so when a core evangelical belief is at stake.

The second principal claim in *The Purpose Driven Life* is that God controls all that happens in the universe.[7] Again, Warren doesn't let reality get in the way of his belief. Chapter 2 of the book, titled "You Are Not an Accident," focuses on this second claim and its implications for an individual's life: "God prescribed every detail of your body. He deliberately chose your race, the color of your skin, your hair, and every other feature. He custom-made your body just the way he wanted it. He also determined the natural talents you would possess and the uniqueness of your personality."[8] At the beginning of the chapter is a quote from Albert Einstein to lend credibility to Warren's belief that the universe is planned: "God doesn't play dice."[9]

However, there's one very serious problem with this. Einstein was wrong.

The physicist Brian Greene gives the context for Einstein's quote in his book *The Elegant Universe: Superstrings, Hidden Dimensions, and the Quest for the Ultimate Theory*. Physics had long described a clockwork universe "whose individual constituents were set in motion at some moment in the past and obediently fulfilled their inescapable, uniquely determined destiny."[10] However, quantum mechanics radically changed this picture by describing electrons in atoms as having indeterminate futures that could only be described in terms of probability. In other words, science can only tell us the probability that any particular future will happen, not which future will actually arrive.

> Many find this conclusion troubling or even downright unacceptable. Einstein was one. In one of physics' most time-honored utterances, Einstein admonished the quantum stalwarts that "God does not play dice with the Universe." He felt that probability was turning up in fundamental physics because of a subtle version of the reason it turns up at the roulette wheel: some basic incompleteness in our understanding. . . . But experiment after experiment—some of the most convincing ones being carried out after his death—convincingly confirm that Einstein was wrong.[11]

What we have in *The Purpose Driven Life*, therefore, is Rick Warren pretending that a scientific falsehood is a scientific fact in order to support his religious belief. Unfortunately, this isn't an aberration. It's how Christian Right leaders deal with science. Whether the issue is evolution, the changeability of sexual orientation, the beginnings of human life, or the existence of anthropogenic climate change, the results are the same—if scientific reality is at odds with their religious beliefs, they choose their religious beliefs and invent a false reality.

The Scandal of the Evangelical Mind Revisited

The pattern evident in both *The Purpose Driven Life* and the four case studies in this book reveals a serious problem with critical thought in evangelical culture. This problem has not gone unnoticed by evangelical insiders. The evangelical historian Mark Noll's 1994 book *The Scandal of the Evangelical Mind* offered a bold critique of his co-religionists. The opening paragraph of the first chapter laid out the problem as Noll saw it:

> The scandal of the evangelical mind is that there is not much of an evangelical mind. An extraordinary range of virtues is found among the sprawling throngs of evangelical Protestants in North America, including great sacrifice in spreading the message of salvation in Jesus Christ, open-hearted generosity to the needy, heroic personal exertion on behalf of troubled individuals, and the unheralded sustenance of countless church and parachurch communities. Notwithstanding all their virtues, however, American evangelicals are not exemplary for their thinking, and they have not been so for several generations.[12]

We can admire Noll's courage in writing this book, but unfortunately it didn't go far enough in describing evangelicalism's intellectual shortcomings. For example, while Noll rightfully criticized the creation science movement, he foolishly praised the intelligent design leader Phillip E. Johnson for being among "careful Christian thinkers" and for his "attacks on the philosophical pretensions of grand-scale Darwinistic theories."[13] Noll extended this misplaced praise several years later when he described the intelligent design movement as a "sign of hope" in evangelical dealings with science: "A fourth sign of hope is the rising intellectual quality of specifically religious objections to the free ride of scientific naturalism. Here the work of a pugnacious legal scholar, Phillip Johnson, a conscientious biochemist, Michael Behe, and a number of careful philosophers, like J. P. Moreland and William Dembski, is especially important."[14] If the paranoid rants of Johnson and company qualify as a sign of hope, then the evangelical situation is dire indeed.[15]

In 2011 Noll offered further reflections on the state of evangelical intellectual life in *Jesus Christ and the Life of the Mind*. Though he stood by his previous critique, he offered a more optimistic picture of the future: "Were I to attempt another full-scale historical assessment like *The Scandal of the Evangelical Mind*, it would have a different tone—more hopeful than despairing, more attuned to possibilities than problems, more concerned with theological resources than with theological deficiencies."[16] Given this statement, it's not surprising that there were several major oversights in Noll's new work as well. For example, he praised the conservative Christian periodicals *Books & Culture* and *First Things* and claimed that they "provide meaningful engagement with significant issues of contemporary life."[17] Yet both periodicals have served as major platforms for paranoid science, featuring authors related to the intelligent design, ex-gay, and conservative bioethics movements.

This book is not intended as a comprehensive assessment of American evangelical intellectual life. Like Noll, I acknowledge that evangelical institutions of higher learning produce some serious scholarship (despite most of them requiring faculty members to sign intellectually troubling statements affirming biblical inerrancy). Moreover, the vast diversity of American evangelicalism, a religious subculture with no agreed-upon boundaries, means that there are always those challenging the ideas of mainstream leaders. The emerging church movement, which features authors such as Brian McLaren and Tony Jones, is a good example of this.[18] Still, the involvement of mainstream evangelical leaders and institutions in paranoid science movements is a clear sign that the evangelical mind is far from healthy.

Wheaton College, Noll's employer from 1979 to 2006, is an example of how serious this problem is. Wheaton has long been one of American evangelicalism's most prominent colleges, celebrated by its admirers as "the Harvard of Christian colleges." Noll had sufficient affection for his academic home to dedicate *The Scandal of the Evangelical Mind* to "the faculty and trustees of Wheaton College." However, two years prior to the publication of the book, the trustees had appointed a conservative pastor named Duane Litfin as president of the school. It soon became clear that one of Litfin's main priorities would be to enforce Wheaton's statement of faith more strictly. As with most evangelical schools, Wheaton's statement of faith affirms the inerrancy of the Bible. But the statement goes further, insisting on a literalistic reading of Genesis: "We believe that God directly created Adam and Eve, the historical parents of the entire human race; and that they were created in His own image, distinct from all other living creatures, and in a state of original righteousness."[19] Then in 1996 Wheaton created a new provost position to serve as the school's chief academic officer. Wheaton's provost was chosen from among the faculty. The finalist was none other than Stanton L. Jones, who, as we've seen, is one of the top leaders of the ex-gay movement.

A sympathetic yet frank look at Wheaton under the leadership of Litfin and Jones is provided by Andrew Chignell's 2010 essay "Whither Wheaton? The Evangelical Flagship College Charts a New Course." Chignell is a philosophy professor at Cornell University and one of several Wheaton alumni in his family. His essay was invited by the editor of *Books & Culture* as Wheaton was searching for a new president to take office in 2010. (Jones served as provost until the spring of 2016.) "The goal here," Chignell writes, "is to view Wheaton the way it views itself: as the preeminent religious college in the country and the training ground for generations of Christian leaders. To lay claim to such responsibility, there has to be a willingness . . . to honestly evaluate past administrations in the process of appointing new ones."[20]

Chignell noted that at least some among the faculty and students expressed "deep concern about the unusually pro-active roles that Litfin and his provost, Stanton Jones, have assumed as the definers and defenders of orthodoxy across the college."[21] Chignell describes three major episodes of heavy-handed doctrinal enforcement from Litfin and Jones. The first two involved questions of human origins, specifically God's special creation of Adam and Eve and the incompatibility of an evolutionary perspective with the Christian faith. The third episode involved a candidate for a professorial position named Christina Van Dyke who failed to affirm Jones's position on the Bible and homosexuality. Specifically, when she signed Wheaton's Statement of Faith, she inserted a clarification saying that it was not clear to her that the Bible unambiguously condemns monogamous same-sex relationships. "That did not entail, Van Dyke notes, 'either that I was in favor of them, or that I thought God was.' Rather, it was meant as a hermeneutical point about the precise content of Scripture."[22] Chignell describes what happened next:

> The department chair asked Van Dyke whether she would be willing to remove the clarification, since Christianity and homosexuality is the provost's area of expertise and her reservation was "certain to raise red flags." But Van Dyke opted to keep the reservation as it was. Sure enough:
>
>> I got a call from Stan Jones, asking me a number of questions about my reservations. I kept saying that I was not claiming to have figured this out, but that it was not at all clear to me from my own research and study that the Bible's position on homosexual behavior was unambiguous. We talked about how I would handle students who came to me to talk about questioning their own sexuality, and I said I would be willing to send them elsewhere. He sent me a whole stack of reading material (much of which he'd written) arguing that the Bible's position on homosexual behavior was, in fact, clear. I read it all. . . . I didn't change my mind.[23]

It's not surprising that Jones wouldn't allow such dissent. He informed the department chair that Van Dyke was no longer a candidate for the position, demonstrating that ex-gay movement orthodoxy was the law at Wheaton.

Perhaps equally as disturbing as Chignell's story about Wheaton is the author's account of the "story behind the story" of the article he wrote and its path to publication.[24] "The article made it all the way to the proofs stage. . . . But a day or so before the issue went to the press, Harold Smith, the CEO of Christianity Today International (which owns *Books & Culture*) unexpectedly stepped in and told Wilson that he would not let it run."[25] Smith demanded two rounds of revisions before ultimately killing the piece for good. "In a note to me, Smith expressed sympathy but gave no explanation, except to say that 'new hurdles' had arisen. He did promise that no one from Wheaton College had directly intervened."[26] The *SoMA Review*, a non-evangelical religious blog, ultimately agreed to run the piece. Apparently, criticism of the intellectual integrity of American evangelicalism's flagship college, even as mild as Chignell's, would not be tolerated by the American evangelical elite.

In sum, Noll was correct to call attention to the intellectual deficiencies of American evangelicalism. But those deficiencies are far more serious than Noll has ever been willing or able to admit. How ironic it was that his own school took a giant step backwards following the publication of *The Scandal of the Evangelical Mind*. Having a provost who was a leading advocate of paranoid science was definitely not a recipe for intellectual progress.

Looking Forward

Many readers of this book who consider themselves part of the "reality-based community" supporting science will want to know what can be done to counter the paranoid science movements described here. Unfortunately, it's not likely that American evangelicalism will change its dominant approach to science anytime soon. A fabricated sense of embattlement, marginalization, and danger from external threats is part of the American evangelical "cultural DNA." This encourages manifestations of the paranoid style, including paranoid battles against modern science. Confronting paranoid movement leaders with facts or logic only confirms in their mind that wicked enemies are determined to stop them, and that they must fight even harder for their cause.

The main bright spot in this book is that leaders from the evangelical left have steered clear of the four paranoid science movements. However, the evangelical left has always been a marginal part of the American evangelical subculture. Ironically, it's the relative reasonableness of evangelical left leaders, who avoid portraying evangelicals as an embattled religious minority, that makes them less appealing to the evangelical rank and file.[27] There are no indications that the evangelical left will be moving off the sidelines anytime soon.

If the Christian Right's campaign of paranoid science can't be deescalated, then it has to be contained. This will involve the hard work of monitoring local attempts to bring creationism and climate change denial into public schools, work that the National Center for Science Education has done valiantly for many years. It will also involve moderate and liberal Christian congregations educating members about alternative ways of understanding faith and science, especially the long history of Christian theologies that affirm evolution. Finally, it will involve greater public awareness of the tactics employed by the Christian Right to undermine legitimate scientific research. We can begin by publicly calling intelligent design, the ex-gay movement, conservative bioethics, and climate change denial what they really are: paranoid science.

NOTES

PREFACE

1 I generally stay away from scientific critiques of these movements, which are best left to scientists in relevant fields such as evolutionary biology and climatology. The exception to this is in the chapter on the ex-gay movement. Because that movement is based in psychiatry, and because sociology is a related field, I offer some critiques of movement leaders' (mis)use of statistical data.

2 Just as the evangelical world contains tremendous diversity, so there is tremendous diversity among those claiming to be progressive Christians. The most popular writers in the latter category are those associated with the Jesus Seminar, including John Shelby Spong, Marcus Borg, and John Dominic Crossan. I see these writers as more "retro-liberal" (that is, recycling older liberal ideas) than actually moving forward in a manner suggested by the word "progressive." I hope to delve into a more detailed discussion of this in a future book.

3 Of course, supporters of the Christian Right are free to read the book, but I'm not naïve enough to think that I'll change the minds of true believers.

4 One of the basic insights from psychology is that human beings aren't rational creatures. What people believe isn't usually the result of logical analysis of factual data. Rather, beliefs tend to signal identification with particular social groups.

5 See Alumkal 2012 on the shortcomings of liberal social justice efforts. There are groups other than the Christian Right that undermine science, but they are beyond the scope of this book.

INTRODUCTION

1 Gagnon 2002:42.

2 Gagnon 2002:42.

3 Hofstadter 2008 [1965]:3.

4 Hofstadter 2008 [1965]:4.

5 Hofstadter 2008 [1965]:29.

6 Hofstadter 2008 [1965]:29.

7 Hofstadter 2008 [1965]:32.

8 Wilentz 2008:xxvii.

9 Hofstadter 2008 [1965]:23.

10 Hofstadter 2008 [1965]:24.

11 On the effects of media segregation on beliefs about global warming, see Feldman at al. 2014.

12 On the spread of misinformation, including conspiracy theories, through social media, see Del Vicario et al. 2016.

13 Hofstadter 2008 [1965]:37.

14 Hofstadter 2008 [1965]:30.

15 Hofstadter 2008 [1965]:31.

16 Martin 1996.

17 Noll 2001:13

18 Wuthnow 1988; C. Smith 1998.

19 See LaHaye and Jenkins 1995.

20 Balmer 1993.

21 C. Smith 1998:121.

22 C. Smith 1998:131.

23 C. Smith 1998:137.

24 C. Smith 1998:142.

25 There are obvious parallels with movements that support conservative racial ideologies in the post–civil rights era. These have tended to portray white Americans as unfairly marginalized by "racial quotas" engineered by liberals, or as threatened by nonwhite immigrants who'll "take over" the country. These movements ignore the many ways white Americans continue to exercise dominance in American society.

26 Greeley and Hout 2006:67.

27 Gushee 2008.

28 Gushee 2008:41–42.

29 Gushee 2008:59, italics in original.

30 Gushee 2008:88.

31 Gushee 2008:89.

32 Gushee 2008:89.

33 Gushee (2014) eventually announced his break with the evangelical center on the issue of homosexuality and endorsed same-sex marriage.

34 For a liberationist critique of the evangelical left, see De La Torre 2010.

35 Christian Right leaders are willing to work with allies, such as conservative Catholics, but they clearly see themselves as responsible for leading the efforts to advance their moral agenda. In contrast, evangelical left leaders tend to treat their allies (mainline Christians, the black church, and so forth) as equal partners as they advance their moral agenda.

36 Contrary to popular belief, evangelicals don't claim to take the entire Bible literally. They admit that at least some passages contain poetic language (for example, the personification of nature in the Psalms). Also, critics correctly point out that many evangelicals engage in a selective literalism that allows them to disavow slavery and permit divorce while condemning homosexuality (see Balmer 2006). However, it's correct to say that literalism is the default mode of biblical interpretation for most evangelicals.

37 Danner 2007:23.

38 Suskind 2004:51.

CHAPTER 1. FEAR OF A DARWINIST CULTURE

1 "The Republican Debate at the Reagan Library," *New York Times*, September 7, 2011, www.nytimes.com, accessed May 15, 2014.

2 Santorum 2006.

3 Given the social significance of the intelligent design movement, it has received surprisingly little attention from sociologists. Jenkins (2007) uses Christian Smith's (1998) theory of evangelical embattlement to argue that intelligent design proponents seek out "disputatious engagements," or fights with opponents, to increase the vitality of the movement. This chapter will detail some of these fights, but it's not clear to me whether they're the result of rational calculation, as Jenkins implies, or whether they naturally emerge as the consequence of a paranoid worldview. Foster, Clark, and York (2008) critique the movement from a Marxist perspective, but they don't engage the scholarly literature on evangelicalism and seem to have little grasp of their subject matter.

4 Most biblical scholars argue that Genesis contains two separate creation accounts written by different authors and not reconcilable when read literally. Creationists insist that Genesis was written by Moses and argue that chapters 1 and 2 of Genesis are fully reconcilable even when read literally.

5 Of course, Newtonian physics was eventually superseded by other paradigms. Many liberal Protestant theologians continued to argue that belief in miracles was not scientifically credible, despite no longer having a convincing scientific case.

6 Bozeman 1977.

7 Bozeman 1977:3.

8 See also Marsden 1991 and Noll 1994.

9 Numbers 2006; Marsden 1991.

10 Numbers 2006; Thaxton, Bradley, and Olson 1984; Denton 1986; Davis and Kenyon 1989.

11 Goode 1999.

12 Goode 1999.

13 Johnson 1991.

14 In a search of *Sojourners*, the leading evangelical left magazine, I found very few mentions of intelligent design and nothing that implied an endorsement of the movement.

15 I retain the terms "Darwinism" and "Darwinist" when paraphrasing intelligent design arguments.

16 Johnson 1991:66.

17 Johnson 1991:83.

18 Johnson 1991:114–15.

19 Johnson 1991:124.

20 Johnson 1991:125.

21 Johnson 1991:128.

22 Johnson 1991:140.

23 Johnson 1991:141.
24 Johnson 1993:165.
25 Johnson 1993:159.
26 Johnson 1995.
27 Johnson 1995:7–8.
28 Johnson 1995:8.
29 Johnson 1995:21, italics in original.
30 Johnson 1995:22.
31 Johnson 1995:25.
32 Johnson 1995:35.
33 Johnson 1995:37.
34 Johnson 1995:37.
35 Johnson 1995:49.
36 Johnson 1995:96.
37 Johnson 1995:107–8.
38 Johnson 1995:202.
39 Johnson 1997.
40 Johnson 1997:10.
41 Johnson 1997:88.
42 Johnson 1998.
43 Johnson 2000.
44 Johnson 2000:14–15.
45 Johnson 2002.
46 Johnson 2002:116.
47 Johnson 2002:162.
48 Solzhenitsyn 1973.
49 Johnson 2002:130.
50 Like other Christian Right leaders, Johnson ignores the existence of intersex people. See chapter 2.
51 Johnson 2002:140.
52 Johnson and Reynolds 2010. The tagline for this division is "Think Deep. Live Smart."
53 Johnson and Reynolds 2010:8.
54 Johnson and Reynolds 2010:7.
55 Dembski 2006:11.
56 Tolkien's work draws a wide range of fans. Not all of them are aware of the extensive Christian symbolism embedded in *The Lord of the Rings*. Gandalf's descent into the Earth, resurrection, and transfiguration (grey to white) clearly parallel New Testament depictions of Christ.
57 Bradley 2006:308.
58 Behe 1996.
59 Dembski 1998.
60 Dembski 1999.

61 Dembski 1999:153.
62 Gonzalez and Richards 2004.
63 Gonzalez and Richards 2004:xii.
64 Gonzalez and Richards 2004:xiii.
65 Gonzalez and Richards 2004:19.
66 Gonzalez and Richards 2004:xv.
67 Gonzalez and Richards 2004:248.
68 Gonzalez and Richards 2004:248.
69 Gonzalez and Richards 2004:248–49.
70 Pennock 1999.
71 Miller 1999; Collins 2006.
72 Johnson 2000:126.
73 Johnson 2000:126, italics in original.
74 Johnson 2000:139.
75 Johnson 2000:139.
76 Dembski 1999:237.
77 Pennock 1996.
78 Pennock 1996:84.
79 Johnson 1996:99–100.
80 Dembski 1999:119.
81 Johnson 1993:165, brackets in original.
82 Johnson and Reynolds 2010:8.
83 Johnson and Reynolds 2010:24.
84 Johnson and Reynolds 2010:11–12.
85 The National Center for Science Education provides information on the Dover case, including links to Judge Jones's decision, in "Kitzmiller v. Dover: Intelligent Design on Trial," n.d., https://ncse.com, accessed November 8, 2015. See also "Judgment Day: Intelligent Design on Trial," *NOVA*, 2007, www.pbs.org, accessed September 27, 2016.
86 Dembski 2006:21.
87 Dembski 2006:21.
88 Catsoulis 2008.
89 Byassee 2008.
90 Louisiana Science Education Act, RS 17:285.1, http://legis.la.gov, accessed September 23, 2016.
91 Louisiana Science Education Act, RS 17:285.1, http://legis.la.gov, accessed September 23, 2016.
92 Act to Amend Tennessee Code Annotated, Title 49, Chapter 6, Part 10, Relative to Teaching Scientific Subjects in Elementary Schools, www.capitol.tn.gov, accessed September 23, 2016.
93 Benford and Snow 2000:614.
94 According to Benford and Snow, an inconsistency in framing may be the result of infighting within a movement, with different factions advancing different frames,

or movement leaders consciously adjusting their frames to appeal to different audiences, with the assumption that these audiences are segregated and will be unaware of the inconsistency. Their model needs to be expanded to account for the type of framing I discuss here, where the frames are not only blatantly contradictory but can appear together *in the same document*, and where the movement doesn't contain competing factions.

95 The sociologist Thomas Gieryn (1999) refers to this as maintaining the "cultural boundary" of science.

96 As I stated earlier, Phillip E. Johnson has always included young-earth creationists in the intelligent design movement. However, many individuals who hold this view find Johnson's "agree to disagree" approach with old-earth creationists to be unacceptable.

97 Strobel 2004.

98 Behe 1996:197.

99 Behe 1996:248.

100 Behe 2007. However, Behe testified during *Kitzmiller v. Dover* that he personally believes that the designer is God, but that the identification is not underwritten by science. See Talk Origins Archives, "Kitzmiller v. Dover Area School District," www.talkorigins.org, accessed September 27, 2016.

101 Witt 2007.

102 Bartkowski 2004.

103 Bartkowski 2004:53.

104 Dembski 2006:14.

105 Dembski 2006:17.

106 Dembski 2006:19.

107 Dembski 2006:20.

108 Forrest and Gross 2004.

109 Discovery Institute n.d.:14.

110 Discovery Institute n.d.:14.

111 Discovery Institute n.d.:8–9, italics in original.

112 Forrest and Gross 2004.

113 Watson (1997:177) rejects a similar interpretation of the Christian Coalition that holds, "Its use of the rhetoric of recognition and affirmations of the pluralist ethos have been deceptions, a 'Trojan horse' to gain access to the political power it needs to 'take over.'" According to Watson, the Trojan horse interpretation ignores the complexity and ambiguity of human motivation. It also fails to account for the fact that Christian Coalition leaders' more "theocratic" rhetoric was hardly hidden from the public. "One must wonder, if [Pat] Robertson has been clever enough to gain power through stealth and deception, why has he not been clever enough to stop talking about his true goals? If he has a 'stealth agenda,' why should he provide his critics with such a huge quantity of publicly available evidence?" (177).

114 The haphazardness of this strategy is obvious in the edited volume *Intelligent Design 101: Leading Experts Explain the Key Issues* (House 2008). All of the authors

carefully stick to the "pure science" frame, with the exception of Phillip E. Johnson, who mostly uses the "religious crusade" frame with occasional tacking to the "pure science" frame. The contrast is jarring and greatly undermines the book's effectiveness.

115 Johnson 1993:165.

116 Johnson 1995:7–8.

117 Johnson 1995:8.

118 Cherry, DeBerg, and Porterfield 2001; C. Smith 2003.

119 Cherry, DeBerg, and Porterfield 2001.

120 Cherry, DeBerg, and Porterfield 2001:292–93.

121 For a similar take on campus religious life, see Schmalzbauer 2013. Those like Johnson who favor evangelical Christian dominance wouldn't be pleased to see religious pluralism being fostered.

122 Gross and Simmons 2009.

123 Gross and Simmons 2009:103. The survey results for the entire sample are as follows:

    I don't believe in God: 9.8 percent.

    I don't know whether there is a God: 13.1 percent.

    I do believe in a higher power: 19.2 percent.

    I find myself believing in God some of the time: 4.3 percent.

    While I have doubts, I feel that I do believe in God: 16.6 percent.

    I know that God really exists and I have no doubts about it: 34.9 percent.

    No answer: 2.2 percent.

124 Gross and Simmons 2009:124, italics in original.

125 The survey results for biology professors are as follows:

    I don't believe in God: 27.5 percent.

    I don't know whether there is a God: 33.3 percent.

    I do believe in a higher power: 2.0 percent.

    I find myself believing in God some of the time: 2.0 percent.

    While I have doubts, I feel that I do believe in God: 13.7 percent.

    I know that God really exists and I have no doubts about it: 21.6 percent.

126 Ecklund (2010) also found considerable religious diversity among university scientists, contradicting Johnson's early assertions.

127 In *The Wedge of Truth* Johnson admits that many professors at less prestigious schools accept "supernatural theism"—belief in a God who communicates with humans and can answer prayers. But he claims that very few elite scientists, such as those elected to the National Academy of Sciences, hold this belief: "Disbelief in supernatural theism among Academy members was over 90 percent, and for biologists it was 95 percent. Remember, these responses were anonymous. If biologists had to stand up publicly in front of their scornful peers to answer, the percentage of avowed supernatural theists would probably be even smaller" (Johnson 2000:86). There are multiple problems with this. First, to say that atheism only dominates among the most elite scientists contradicts his earlier as-

sertions that colleges and universities in general are places of nonbelief. Second, if elite scientists can't successfully transmit atheism to non-elite scientists, then they have little chance of transmitting atheism to the broad public. Third, like many Christian Right leaders, Johnson too quickly dismisses those who don't share his beliefs as not having "real" religion. Finally, he incorrectly equates lack of a belief with hostility toward those holding the belief. Consequently, his imagined scenario of "scornful peers" is based in paranoid thinking rather than empirical data.

128 Newport 2010.

129 See Johnson 2008:28.

130 See Olson 1995.

131 See McLaren 2010, who writes that we should treat the Bible as a library rather than as a constitution.

132 The most common critique of liberal Protestantism by evangelicals is that liberal Protestants abandon historic Christian beliefs as they accommodate to contemporary culture. The reality is that all forms of Christianity are shaped by their cultural contexts.

133 As Balmer (2006:122) observes, "But faith alone has never been sufficient for the advocates of intelligent design. They want to 'prove' their claims, to cloak their presuppositions with academic and scholarly legitimacy, and, thereby, to win legitimacy in scientific circles."

134 See, for example, Foucault 1970 [1966] and Feyerabend 1978.

135 Pennock 1999:211.

136 Pennock 2010.

137 Johnson 1998:152.

138 Fuller 1996.

139 Meyer et al. 2007; Meyer 2009.

140 In his book *Science v. Religion? Intelligent Design and the Problem of Evolution*, Fuller (2007:91) claims, "I am not an advocate of—or expert in—either [intelligent design theory] or, for that matter, neo-Darwinism." His secular leanings may prevent him from becoming a "card-carrying member" of the movement, but arguing for the legitimacy of intelligent design is a type of advocacy. However, having read a number of his works, I have no problem accepting his claim that he lacks expertise.

141 Hofstadter 2008 [1965]:35.

142 Numbers 2006:398.

CHAPTER 2. SEX, SIN, AND SCIENCE

1 Alan Chambers, "Exodus Int'l President to the Gay Community: 'We're Sorry,'" June 19, 2013, alanchambers.org.

2 Chambers, "Exodus Int'l President to the Gay Community: 'We're Sorry.'"

3 S. Jones 2013.

4 Steffan 2013.

5 John M. Becker, "Dr. Robert Spitzer Apologizes to Gay Community for Infamous 'Ex-Gay' Study," Truth Wins Out, April 25, 2012, www.truthwinsout.org, accessed October 30, 2013.

6 Evan Hurst, "John Paulk Releases a More Complete Apology," Truth Wins Out, April 24, 2013, www.truthwinsout.org, accessed January 23, 2014. This was an expanded version of the apology that he had released the previous week.

7 "Welcome to Restored Hope Network," www.restoredhopenetwork.com, accessed October 30, 2013.

8 Dresher 2001.

9 Dresher 2001:9.

10 Rado 1969:x.

11 Rado 1969:212–13. This publication was based on course lectures given between 1945 and 1955.

12 Rado 1969:213.

13 Bieber 1962:303.

14 Bieber 1962:310.

15 Bieber 1962:313.

16 Socarides 1968:43.

17 Socarides 1968:44.

18 Socarides 1968:54.

19 Bayer 1981:38–39.

20 Bayer 1981:40.

21 Bayer 1981.

22 Bayer 1981:102.

23 Bayer 1981:102–3.

24 Bayer 1981:104.

25 Bayer 1981:112.

26 Bayer 1981:123.

27 Bayer 1981:137.

28 Bayer 1981:138.

29 Bayer 1981:148.

30 Bayer 1981:151.

31 Bayer 1981:194.

32 As many social scientists have discovered, predicting the future is risky business. Bayer failed to foresee the increasing social acceptance of homosexuality in American society that would follow soon after his book was published. He also failed to understand that both the pro-gay and the anti-gay factions in the APA were making some truth claims that could be tested against empirical data, and that the empirical data would increasingly make the anti-gay case problematic.

33 American Psychiatric Association 1999.

34 See the home page of Nicolosi's website: http://josephnicolosi.com, accessed November 13, 2013.

35 NARTH, "NARTH and the APA—A Brief History," n.d., www.narth.com, accessed November 12, 2013.

36 Alliance for Therapeutic Choice and Scientific Integrity, "Alliance Formation Announcement," n.d., www.therapeuticchoice.com, accessed December 5, 2015.

37 Alliance for Therapeutic Choice and Scientific Integrity, "Alliance Formation Announcement."

38 Erzen 2006.

39 Spring 1984.

40 Spring 1984:58.

41 Stafford 1989:21.

42 Cook 1989.

43 White 1977.

44 Nancy 1980.

45 Davies and Rentzel 1993.

46 Erzen 2006:188.

47 Erzen 2006:18.

48 Courage is not to be confused with DignityUSA, a pro-gay Catholic group that operates independently of and in opposition to the Roman Catholic hierarchy.

49 Courage, "FAQs," www.couragerc.net, accessed November 22, 2013.

50 Courage, "FAQs."

51 See Gerber 2009.

52 This doesn't mean that the older message completely disappeared. Ideological transformations are rarely complete.

53 See Emerson and Smith 2001.

54 Gerber (2011) finds the theme of free will to be prominent both in Exodus International and in evangelical weight-loss groups.

55 Moberly 1983:2.

56 Moberly 1983:40.

57 Moberly 1983:43.

58 Nicolosi and Nicolosi 2002:14.

59 Erzen 2006:145.

60 Here we see significant overlap with the Roman Catholic hierarchy in the United States, which also claims that gay rights movements, especially those supporting same-sex marriage, threaten both "traditional" families and religious freedom. The Roman Catholic approach to homosexuality clearly leaves room for elements of the paranoid style.

61 As Erzen (2006) discusses extensively, the experience of participants in ex-gay ministries don't necessarily conform to the narrative crafted by ex-gay leaders.

62 Hofstadter 2008 [1965]:34.

63 These books include Comiskey 1989, 2003, and 2010; Dallas 1996 and 2003; Davies 2001; Davies and Rentzel 1993; Gagnon 2001; Jones and Yarhouse 2000 and 2007; Konrad 1987; Moberly 1983; Nicolosi and Nicolosi 2002; Paulk 2003; Paulk and Paulk 1999; Payne 1981; Satinover 1996; Schmidt 1995; Yarhouse 2010.

64 Satinover 1996:26. Satinover was also featured as a physics expert in the New Age–inspired film *What the Bleep Do We Know!?*, which was widely criticized for its inaccurate presentation of science. This is further evidence of Satinover's religious eclecticism as well as his attraction to religiously motivated pseudoscience.

65 See Cadge 2002.

66 Jones and Yarhouse 2000:28–29.

67 Dallas 1996:98–99.

68 Comiskey 1989:43.

69 Davies and Rentzel 1993:22.

70 Dallas 1996; Gagnon 2001; Jones and Yarhouse 2000; Konrad 1987; Paulk 2003.

71 Comiskey 2010; Davies 2001; Davies and Rentzel 1993; Konrad 1987; Paulk 2003; Paulk and Paulk 1999; Payne 1981; Satinover 1996.

72 Konrad 1987:11, italics and ellipses in original.

73 Yarhouse 2010.

74 Satinover 1996:48, italics in original.

75 Satinover 1996:59–60.

76 Satinover 1996:58, brackets in original.

77 Schmidt 1995:122.

78 Gagnon 2001.

79 Jones and Yarhouse 2000:112–13.

80 Konrad 1987:265–66.

81 Gagnon 2001:453.

82 Gagnon 2001:459, italics in original. Note that Gagnon maligns all families with adopted children, regardless of the sexuality of the parents, when he suggests that "one's own biological children" stabilize relationships more than other types of children. This probably wasn't his intent, but these families became "collateral damage" in his war on same-sex couples.

83 Gagnon 2001:481.

84 Konrad 1987:114.

85 Comiskey 1989.

86 Moberly 1983:37.

87 Schmidt 1995:45–46.

88 Gagnon 2001:41.

89 Comiskey 2010; Gagnon 2001; Konrad 1987; Satinover 1996; Schmidt 1995.

90 Gagnon 2001; Jones and Yarhouse 2000; Satinover 1996; Schmidt 1995.

91 Comiskey 2003; Dallas 1996; Gagnon 2001; Jones and Yarhouse 2000; Satinover 1996; Schmidt 1995.

92 Satinover 1996:31.

93 Satinover 1996:32.

94 NARTH, "Our Track Record," n.d., www.narth.com, accessed February 1, 2006.

95 National Association for Research and Therapy of Homosexuality 2003.

96 NARTH, "FAQs," www.narth.com, accessed December 4, 2013.

97 Exodus International, "Who We Are," n.d., www.exodus.to, accessed July 31, 2009. Italics in original.

98 Restored Hope Network, "Mission Statement," n.d., www.restoredhopenetwork. com, accessed December 4, 2013.

99 NARTH, www.narth.com, accessed February 1, 2006.

100 NARTH, "Same-Sex 'Marriage' and the Fate of Religious Liberty," n.d., www. narth.com, accessed July 30, 2009.

101 R. Albert Mohler Jr., "The Homosexual Agenda: Religious Liberty under Fire," NARTH, n.d., www.narth.com, accessed December 5, 2013.

102 NARTH, "FAQs," www.narth.com, accessed December 9, 2015.

103 NARTH, "FAQs," www.narth.com, accessed December 4, 2013.

104 NARTH, "FAQs," accessed December 4, 2013.

105 Erzen 2006:34.

106 Erzen 2006:213.

107 For the classic study of failed prophecy in a UFO-based new religious movement, see Festinger, Riecken, and Schachter 1956. A substantial difference between the two cases is that the ex-gay movement isn't a self-contained sect; it exists within the wider world of American evangelicalism. Institutions like *Christianity Today* and InterVarsity Press that support the ex-gay movement are presumably staffed primarily by straight people who have no experience of trying (and failing) to overcome homosexuality.

108 Erzen 2006:34.

109 Comiskey 2003:12.

110 Comiskey 2003:12–13.

111 Jones and Yarhouse 2000:138.

112 Spitzer 2003.

113 Jones and Yarhouse 2007:13–14.

114 Stafford 2007a.

115 Stafford 2007b.

116 One of the few such references is Jones and Yarhouse's (2000:15) claim that they reject postmodernism in favor of critical realism. For critical realists, a real world does exist and can be known, but perceptions of that world are influenced by individuals' social locations. Jones and Yarhouse argue that the critical realist view "establishes the possibility of true dialogue between science and religion, a risky dialogue that actually could and does involve science influencing what we believe about religion (as when Galileo changed our view of the physical universe and hence how we understand certain passages of scripture)." However, the authors never deviate from mainstream evangelical beliefs, despite the fact that many of these beliefs are scientifically problematic. In other words, there's no evidence that they're genuinely open to changing their minds in response to science. Their claim to be critical realists can best be understood as an attempt to present themselves as more sophisticated than they really are.

117 Dallas 2003:93–94.

118 Bayer 1981:5.

119 Moon (2004) examines two United Methodist congregations with opposing views on homosexuality. Members of both congregations used the label "politics" to delegitimize certain types of arguments: "For many of the congregation members, even political activists, the category of 'politics' serves as a code for self-interest, cynicism, and worldliness in contrast to the love, community, and timelessness of godly truth" (15). This closely parallels the use of "politics" in the ex-gay literature.

120 Dresher 2003.

121 Spitzer 2003.

122 Spitzer 2003:410.

123 Nicolosi 2003.

124 Yarhouse 2003. Yarhouse did admit that a longitudinal study would be more compelling, an issue that he addressed in Jones and Yarhouse 2007.

125 Pruden 2012.

126 See, for example, S. Hook 1959; Grünbaum 1984.

127 Buhle 1998.

128 Perhaps the most convincing critique of penis envy is one that I spotted on a t-shirt selling in a novelty shop: "What? Envious of *that?*"

129 Satinover 1996.

130 www.satinover.com, accessed July 5, 2006.

131 Gagnon (2001:460) is the only one of these writers who relies on evolutionary theory. He claims that evolution has produced human men who are so driven by sexual stimulation that male-male monogamy is impossible. Only when paired with women, who are more sexually subdued, can men be coaxed into accepting monogamy. To say that the fundamental nature of human sexuality was determined by evolution contradicts the Creation/Fall framework for sexuality that Gagnon shares with other ex-gay writers. He seems to be more concerned with finding rhetorical "ammunition" than with maintaining logical consistency.

132 See, for example, Reis 2009.

133 Liberal Christian theologians generally argue that evil and tragedy are the necessary by-products of the freedom that God has granted the universe. See Polkinghorne 1998.

134 See Lewis 2015 [1940].

135 "Critical" biblical scholars employ the historical critical method, which uses the tools of the social sciences to analyze biblical texts. The historical critical method has received only limited acceptance in the evangelical world since it inevitably reveals that the Bible contains numerous historical errors and contradictions, violating the core evangelical belief in an infallible (or inerrant) Bible.

136 Poiani 2010; Sommer and Vasey 2006. Note that anti-gay psychoanalytic theorists such as Bieber and Socarides were explicit about their assumption that only heterosexuality can be "natural." This belief is no longer credible in light of modern zoology.

137 See Wilson and Rahman 2005. Ex-gay leaders often discount the genetic basis for homosexuality because no scientist has found the "gay gene." This phrase assumes

a one-to-one correspondence between a trait (homosexuality) and a gene. This is not even close to current understandings of human genetics.

138 In a representative sample study, every member of the population under study has an equal chance of being surveyed. Few studies actually reach this ideal, but polling techniques like those used by the Gallup organization come much closer than a nonrepresentative or "convenience" sample, such as one generated by placing an ad in a newspaper asking for volunteers. Statisticians agree that we can't make statistical estimates of the characteristics of a population based on a nonrepresentative sample.

139 All samples contain some element of random flux that will usually prevent them from perfectly matching the statistical characteristics of the population that was sampled. The difference between two statistics (for example, the mean number of sexual partners for straight men versus gay men) will be deemed "statistically significant" only if there is a high degree of certainty or "confidence" that the difference actually exists in the population and is not merely due to random flux.

140 Moon (2004) found that members of the "liberal" United Methodist church that she studies also tended to downplay bisexuality in favor of a sharp distinction between homosexuality and heterosexuality.

141 See Bogle 2008.

142 Ellison (2004) noted the divide in the LGBT community between "marriage advocates" and "marriage critics," and raised concerns that the advocates weren't adequately addressing the patriarchal norms in traditional marriage. The ranks of "marriage advocates" have probably grown since Ellison's book was published.

143 CIA, "Country Comparison: Life Expectancy at Birth," World Factbook, n.d., www.cia.gov, accessed January 23, 2014.

144 Shirley K. Chan et al., "Likely Female-to-Female Transmission of HIV—Texas, 2012," *Morbidity and Mortality Weekly Report*, March 14, 2014, www.cdc.gov, accessed December 2, 2015.

145 Looking at the New Testament as a whole, one is hard pressed to find any portion that presents disease or physical infirmity as a direct consequence of an individual's sin. Chapter 9 of the Gospel of John, which concerns Jesus's encounter with a man born blind, appears to make the opposite argument. Jesus is reported as saying that neither the man's sins nor those of his parents are responsible for the man's blindness.

146 C. Smith 1998.

147 Thomas and Olson 2012:269.

148 See Jones, Cox, and Navarro-Rivera 2014.

CHAPTER 3. "OUR WAY OR A BRAVE NEW WORLD"

1 Per the Center on Human Exceptionalism section of the website, www.discovery. org, accessed July 24, 2014.

2 Christian Right leaders consistently use "euthanasia" as a broad term to describe any effort to end a patient's life, whether by "active" means (supplying or

administering lethal medication) or "passive" means (withdrawing life support). "Euthanasia" is sometimes used more narrowly to refer to a physician directly administering the means of ending a patient's life, in contrast to medical aid in dying (physician-assisted suicide), in which a physician provides a prescription for lethal medication that must be self-administered by the patient.

3 See, for example, C. Hook 2004:93; W. Smith 2004:84 and 2006:xvii; Tada 1992:78.

4 Neuhaus 1988.

5 W. Smith 2004:21.

6 National Institutes of Health 2006:28.

7 National Institutes of Health 2006:28.

8 National Institutes of Health 2006:31.

9 National Institutes of Health 2006:29.

10 See Knoepfler 2013.

11 Shannon 2003:172. This is a revised version of an essay first published in 1997.

12 At least one major evangelical school, Biola University, included this view in its official doctrinal statement. "The Bible is clear in its teaching on the sanctity of life. Life begins at conception." Biola University, "Doctrinal Statement," n.d., www.biola.edu, accessed August 16, 2014.

13 Balmer 2006.

14 Balmer 2006:13–14.

15 Balmer 2006:16.

16 As Greeley and Hout (2006:123) argue, it's important not to overstate evangelicals' opposition to abortion, since most of them support legal access to abortion in cases such as danger to a mother's health, risk of birth defects, and pregnancy by rape. Still, opposition to legal abortion remains a significant part of the contemporary American evangelical culture.

17 See Gallagher 2004.

18 The cost for evangelicals of making the anti-abortion cause their own is that Catholics had to be transformed from enemies to moral allies. Not that this was done completely or smoothly. Plenty of anti-Catholicism remains in the evangelical world, especially among the rank and file. But it's safe to say that by the 1980s Catholics were no longer seen as a primary threat to establishing a society based on Christian (that is to say, evangelical) morality.

19 Evans 2010:49.

20 Luker 1984.

21 For recent statistics on contraceptive use among evangelicals, Catholics, and others in the United States, see Jones and Dreweke 2011. For a description of lay opposition to the Roman Catholic encyclical on birth control, see Greeley 1978.

22 Focus on the Family, "Use of Contraceptives in Marriage," n.d., http://family.custhelp.com, accessed June 10, 2015.

23 Focus on the Family, "Use of Contraceptives in Marriage."

24 Focus on the Family, "Use of Contraceptives in Marriage," italics in original.

25 Focus on the Family, "Use of Contraceptives in Marriage."

26 For example, consider the Christian Medical and Dental Association's 1998 statement on birth control pills: "But, while additional investigation is needed, current knowledge does not confirm or refute conclusions that routine use of hormonal birth control causes abortion. CMDA will continue to monitor new developments" (Cutrer and Glahn 2005:194).

27 See Cameron 2004:35.

28 Pew Research Center, "Declining Majority of Americans Favor Embryonic Stem Cell Research," July 17, 2008, www.pewforum.org, retrieved June 10, 2015.

29 Pew Research Center 2013:6.

30 Center for Bioethics and Human Dignity, "Human Cloning: The Need for a Comprehensive Ban," n.d., https://cbhd.org, accessed July 10, 2014.

31 See, for example, Carlson 1994 and Moore and Persaud 1998, two of the books cited by the Center for Bioethics and Human Dignity.

32 This contrasts with the dominant Christian Right strategy of condemning mainstream scientists for practicing flawed science and peddling falsehoods. In this instance, Christian Right leaders appeal to mainstream science for validation by giving the false impression that mainstream scientists share their view. Perhaps there are parallels with ex-gay leaders' use of Ronald Bayer's *Homosexuality and American Psychiatry*. As discussed in the previous chapter, these leaders grossly distort Bayer's thesis in order to substantiate their claim that pro-gay psychologists are "political," while they themselves are "scientific."

33 Tada and Cameron 2006:160, italics in original.

34 Saunders 2004:128–29, italics in original.

35 Saunders 2004:135, italics in original.

36 Cameron 2004:24.

37 New Revised Standard Version.

38 Tada and Cameron 2006:52.

39 Colson 2004:16.

40 Saunders 2004:123, italics in original.

41 W. Smith 2004:126, italics in original.

42 See in particular W. Smith 2004 and Prentice 2004.

43 W. Smith 2004; Prentice 2004.

44 Prentice and Macrito 2013:6.

45 Colson and Cameron 2004:8.

46 See Evans 2010 on the differing views of religious Americans on reproductive genetic technologies.

47 W. Smith (2004:162) mentions gene therapy among "biotechnology that does not threaten human dignity." Of course, using Christian Right leaders' logic, one could easily argue that gene therapy is the beginning of a slippery slope toward genetic engineering, which ends with a Brave New World. This illustrates the fact that the beginning (or threshold) of an alleged slippery slope is entirely arbitrary.

48 Jenkins (2007:1697) argues that evangelical leaders have increasingly treated DNA as a sacred icon. "As blood has symbolized the sacred power of life and death in

various ritual practices, so now cell life has become a powerfully sacred religious symbol."

49 Tada and Cameron 2006:59.

50 Cameron 2004:32.

51 W. Smith 2004:147.

52 Mitchell 2004:71.

53 Tada and Cameron 2006:161, italics in original.

54 W. Smith 2004:134.

55 C. Hook 2004:94.

56 While "physician-assisted suicide" was once the dominant terminology, the medical and ethical literature increasingly refers to "medical aid in dying" or "assisted dying." Proponents of the practice object to the implications of the word "suicide," while opponents argue that it is accurate. I use "physician-assisted suicide" or "PAS" when paraphrasing the arguments of Christian Right leaders, as this is the terminology they invariably use.

57 Tada 1992:180.

58 Tada 1992:97.

59 Tada 1992:98, 103, 104.

60 Tada 1992:112–13, italics in original.

61 Tada 1992:113.

62 Tada 1992:113.

63 Tada 1992:150–51, brackets in original. Note that this fits with evangelicals' understanding of themselves as a marginalized group in the contemporary United States.

64 Tada 1992:75, italics in original.

65 Tada 1992:75–77.

66 Tada 1992:76.

67 Tada 1992:77.

68 Tada 1992:77.

69 Tada 1992:77–78.

70 Tada 1992:78–79. Note that the Pandora's Box metaphor is a variation on the slippery slope. A closed box is the equivalent of the safe area in front of the slope. Opening the box just a little is equivalent to stepping onto the slope, which quickly leads to a disastrous situation equivalent to the bottom of the slope.

71 Tada and Cameron 2006:81.

72 W. Smith 2006:ix.

73 W. Smith 2006:xii.

74 W. Smith 2006:xiii.

75 W. Smith 2006:xvii.

76 W. Smith 2006:23. Note the parallels with intelligent design proponents' arguments concerning Richard Dawkins—Singer is "candid" enough to reveal the hidden agenda of the Christian Right's opponents.

77 W. Smith 2006:7–8, italics in original.

78 W. Smith 2006:103.

79 W. Smith 2006:141–42.

80 W. Smith 2006:148.

81 W. Smith 2006:150.

82 W. Smith 2006:43.

83 W. Smith 2006:44.

84 In a 2007 editorial the *Christian Century*, long considered the flagship magazine of the mainline Protestant world, took issue with a Vatican declaration that it is morally wrong to remove feeding tubes from patients who are in permanent vegetative states:

> Responding in part to perplexity over the Terri Schiavo case, the Congregation for the Doctrine of the Faith stated that delivery of food and water, even by artificial means and even to someone who is permanently unresponsive, is "ordinary" care—care that caregivers are morally obligated to provide in virtually all cases in order to preserve the patient's human dignity. (*Christian Century* 2007:5)

The editorial listed several objections to this ruling. First, the Vatican was applying its tradition in an absolutist way that was a departure from past practices of practical reasoning about what is "ordinary" and "extraordinary" care. Second, given that delivery of food and water through a feeding tube constitutes a medical intervention, it is beyond (or at least at the edges of) ordinary care. Third, the question of whether a medical intervention is ordinary or extraordinary has traditionally focused not on the kind of intervention used but on whether the intervention is burdensome to the patient. The editorial concluded by challenging the Vatican's assumption that its stance represents the only means of preserving human dignity.

85 W. Smith 2006:220.

86 W. Smith 2006:224.

87 When I discuss problems with slippery slope arguments in my classes, students often try to defend the concept by referring to individual-level change. "What about a person smoking crack? Aren't they on a slippery slope?" I respond that social change is a much more complex phenomenon than individual change. It doesn't take much to ruin an individual life, and crack addiction is likely to do it. Ruining an entire society, assuming that there are clear criteria of what a "ruined" society looks like, is much more difficult to accomplish and is unlikely to be triggered by a single, internal cause.

88 Callahan, who is Catholic, is not considered part of the Christian Right. She partially agrees with the Christian Right on the issue of abortion, but many of her other stances are similar to those of the evangelical left.

89 Callahan 1986:232.

90 That Callahan never uses the term "slippery slope" in her article doesn't change the fact that she quite obviously employs a slippery slope argument. Most users of logical fallacies don't inform their audience about their tactics ("Let me present

you with a false choice . . ."). The slippery slope is often the exception, since the declaration "It's a slippery slope!" can be effective in frightening people.

91 Callahan 1986:236.

92 Callahan 1986:236.

93 Callahan 1986:236, italics in original.

94 Guttmacher Institute, "U.S. Abortion Rate Hits Lowest Level since 1973," February 3, 2014, www.guttmacher.org, retrieved December 16, 2014.

95 Luker 1984:14.

96 Luker 1984:27.

97 The First Amendment gives religious organizations wide leeway in practice; only extreme behavior (such as abusing children) brings legal sanction. This is why conservative Christian denominations can refuse to ordain women and not face gender discrimination suits. It's also why the claim that churches could be forced to perform same-sex marriages was never credible. Same-sex marriage involves an expansion, not a refutation, of monogamy. The argument that it leads to polygamy therefore has no logical basis. Finally, animals are not persons under U.S. law and therefore aren't authorized to enter into any legal agreements, including but not limited to marriage.

98 This raises the question of why social movements rely on slippery slope arguments. A rational choice approach might suggest that the short-term benefits could outweigh the long-term costs. But a better answer is that some movement leaders, especially those operating in the paranoid style, genuinely believe in the slippery slope. From this perspective, employing a slippery slope argument is not so much an attempt to mislead others as an invitation for them to share the movement leaders' paranoid worldview.

99 I haven't conducted research on the political campaigns related to the Death with Dignity Act and can't determine the accuracy of Smith's portrayal. His larger argument fails regardless.

100 W. Smith 2006:116.

101 W. Smith 2006:124.

102 Van Delden, Visser, and Borst-Eilers 2004:209.

103 Van Delden, Visser, and Borst-Eilers 2004:208, italics in original.

104 Again, Christian Right leaders use "euthanasia" as a broad term including any means of hastening death.

105 Van der Heide et al. 2003:2.

106 Battin et al. 2007:591.

107 Battin et al. 2007:594.

108 See Foley and Hendin 2002.

109 See Quill and Battin 2004; Dieterle 2007; and Lindsay 2009.

110 The hospice industry throughout the United States has faced challenges in recent years as the federal government has cut funding and restricted eligibility. Any judgment of Oregon's hospice industry must take this context into account.

111 Oregon Hospice Association, "Hospice and Oregon's Death with Dignity Act," n.d., https://oregonhospice.org, accessed January 7, 2015.

112 Ganzini 2004:169.

113 Tada and Cameron 2006:9.

114 Tada and Cameron 2006:16.

115 Colson 2004; W. Smith 2004.

116 W. Smith 2004:109.

117 Colson 2004:17.

118 There is a clear parallel between this misuse of *Brave New World* and ex-gay movement leaders' misuse of Ronald Bayer's *Homosexuality and American Psychiatry*. In both cases, Christian Right leaders are more concerned with how the book can advance their agenda than with what the book actually says.

CHAPTER 4. SEEING RED OVER GREEN EVANGELICALS

1 Beisner's more aggressive side, and a hint of things to come, was publicly revealed in 2006. Bill Moyers had interviewed Beisner for the *Is God Green?* PBS documentary, which discussed the intra-evangelical debate on the environment. Beisner later commented in the newsletter for his organization, the Interfaith Stewardship Alliance, "When Moyers interviewed me for the documentary last spring, he very candidly told me that he is a liberal Democrat and intended for the documentary to influence the November elections to bring control of Congress back to the Democrats. Don't expect good science, economics, or ethics—or even journalistic balance." Moyers characterized the statement as "a lie" and demanded an apology and a retraction. Moyers posted the full exchange on his *Moyers on America* website. See "Is God Green?," www.pbs.org.

2 Beisner 1997:86.

3 The terms "climate change" and "global warming" are used nearly interchangeably by both environmentalists and their critics. Some scientists prefer "climate change" because of its more inclusive scope.

4 Hoggan 2009; Mooney 2005; Oreskes and Conway 2010; Mann 2012.

5 Sirico 2007:viii.

6 Sirico 2007:viii.

7 Wilkinson 2012:9.

8 Gushee 2008:176.

9 See Sirico 2007:viii ; and Cornwall Alliance, "Our History in Highlights," n.d., www.cornwallalliance.org, accessed December 11, 2015.

10 Beisner 2013a.

11 Cornwall Alliance, "About," n.d., www.cornwallalliance.org, accessed December 11, 2015.

12 The Evangelical Climate Initiative posted the text of its statement at www.christiansandclimate.org.

13 The letter was initially posted on Focus on the Family's Citizen Link website, www.citizenlink.com, accessed March 3, 2010.

14 That Alan Chambers was positioning himself within the evangelical right shows just how far his political ideology moved between 2007 and 2013.

15 Gushee 2008:97.

16 Pulliam 2009.

17 For more about this division, see Danielsen 2013.

18 Gushee 2008:178.

19 Kearns 2007:114.

20 Fang 2010. Ties between the Cornwall Alliance and CFACT were reported earlier in Kearns 2007.

21 People for the American Way 2010:3.

22 Beisner et al. 2007:70.

23 Cornwall Alliance 2009:8.

24 Beisner 1997:20.

25 Beisner 1997:25.

26 Beisner 1997:102.

27 Beisner 1997:112.

28 Cornwall Alliance 2009:6.

29 Cornwall Alliance 2009:14–15.

30 Cornwall Alliance 2009:15.

31 Cornwall Alliance 2009:17.

32 Cornwall Alliance 2009:19.

33 Cornwall Alliance 2009:19. Anyone familiar with environmental movements knows that they don't support the use of biofuels. Ethanol, the most prominent biofuel, is mostly supported by the corn lobby. The fact that the Cornwall Alliance inserts biofuels into the discussion likely reflects the interests of its backers in the fossil fuel industry.

34 Cornwall Alliance 2008:14.

35 Cornwall Alliance 2009:20.

36 Beisner 1997:59.

37 Beisner 1997:59.

38 Beisner 1997:66.

39 Kuhn was not a postmodernist or a deconstructionist. However, as Pennock (1999:208) has argued, "it was the superficial relativist interpretation of Kuhn's work that spread" to these philosophical camps.

40 Beisner 1997:91.

41 Beisner 1997:91.

42 Beisner 1997:91.

43 Beisner 1997:91.

44 Cornwall Alliance 2009:31.

45 Cornwall Alliance 2009:27.

46 See Kearns 2007.

47 The petition can be found at http://petitionproject.org.

48 Cornwall Alliance 2009:39.

49 The intelligent design petition, titled "A Scientific Dissent from Darwinism," can be found on the Discovery Institute's website at www.discovery.org. The National Center for Science Education responded with Project Steve, "a tongue-in-cheek parody of a long-standing creationist tradition of amassing lists of 'scientists who doubt evolution' or 'scientists who dissent from Darwinism.'" The latter petition included scientists named Steve who support the teaching of evolution and can be found at http://ncse.com.

50 Sunderlin 2003:121.

51 Simon 1981.

52 Beisner 1997:70.

53 Wilkinson 2012:70

54 Hofstadter 2008 [1965]:29.

55 Wanliss 2013:36.

56 Wanliss 2013:42.

57 Wanliss 2013:43.

58 Wanliss 2013:52.

59 Wanliss 2013:65.

60 Wanliss 2013:41.

61 Wanliss 2013:70. Note that Wanliss borrows the phrase "Darwin's dangerous idea" from the new atheist writer Daniel Dennett's book of the same name.

62 See LaHaye and Jenkins 1995 and Robertson 1991.

63 Wanliss 2013:257.

64 When I describe the campaign as "strategic," I'm not implying that the individuals involved don't believe what they're saying. Evangelical right leaders have probably convinced each other of the truth of their arguments; for a discussion of "subculture evolution" in some new religious movements, see Bainbridge and Stark 1979.

65 Jones, Cox, and Navarro-Rivera 2013.

66 See Breslow 2012.

67 Markoe 2011. Note that this survey sorts people into the evangelical or mainline category using denominational affiliation.

68 Redden 2011.

69 Simon 1996.

70 See Wolfe 1991.

71 Bell 2012:111.

72 Bell 2012:111.

73 Bell 2012:111.

74 Raymond 2004:329.

75 Raymond 2004:344.

76 Beisner 2013b.

77 Beisner 2013b.

78 Beisner 2013b.

79 Beisner 2013b.

80 Kearns 2007:113.

81 The italicized word was underlined in the slide, but not in the original book.
82 Beisner 2013a.
83 Beisner 2013a.
84 Beisner 2013a.
85 Beisner 2013a.
86 Hulme 2009:xxv-xxvi.
87 Funtowicz and Ravetz 1993:740.
88 Funtowicz and Ravetz 1993:740.
89 Funtowicz and Ravetz 1993:740.
90 Hulme 2009:78–79.
91 Gore 1992:356.
92 Hofstadter 2008 [1965]:3.

CONCLUSION
1 Hofstadter 2008 [1965]:40.
2 See Moore 1987.
3 Balmer (1993:282) makes a similar observation about the various manifestations of American evangelicalism that he observed, as well as about the subculture as a whole:

> All of these socially constructed realities, then, offer an alternate, idealized view of the world, a place of retreat and escape, no less than the utopian communities that dotted the American landscape in the nineteenth century. Indeed, the entire evangelical subculture itself is a socially constructed reality, a place of retreat built primarily after the Scopes Trial of 1925, when fundamentalists became convinced that the larger American culture had abandoned them.

4 As I mentioned in chapters 1 and 4, Warren is part of the "evangelical center." He promotes intelligent design but doesn't support the climate change denial of the Cornwall Alliance.
5 Warren 2013.
6 Warren 2002:187.
7 Warren never discusses the historical origins of this belief, but he's clearly drawing on the Calvinist doctrine of predestination. The main theological objection to belief in an all-controlling God has been its inability to account for the immense amount of evil, suffering, and tragedy in the world. Other theological approaches address this issue by positing a God who gives the universe freedom rather than micromanaging it. See Polkinghorne 1998.
8 Warren 2002:22–23.
9 Warren 2002:22.
10 Greene 1999:107.
11 Greene 1999:107-8.
12 Noll 1994:3.
13 Noll 1994:197.

14 Noll 2001:149.
15 Noll appears to be driven by his contempt for "scientific naturalism," which he fails to adequately define. In any case, he overlooks that Johnson and Dembski falsely equate methodological naturalism and ontological naturalism (see chapter 1), and thus are incapable of producing a reasonable critique of naturalism among scientists.
16 Noll 2011:153.
17 Noll 2011:162. *Books & Culture* is published by *Christianity Today*, the flagship magazine of the evangelical center. *First Things* features both conservative Catholic and evangelical writers.
18 See Marti and Ganiel 2014.
19 Wheaton College, "Statement of Faith and Educational Purpose," n.d., www.wheaton.edu, accessed August 26, 2015.
20 Andrew Chignell, "Whither Wheaton? The Evangelical Flagship College Charts a New Course," *SoMA Review*, January 13, 2010, www.somareview.com, accessed August 26, 2015.
21 Chignell, "Whither Wheaton?"
22 Chignell, "Whither Wheaton?"
23 Chignell, "Whither Wheaton?"
24 Andrew Chignell, "The Story behind the Story," n.d., www.whitherwheaton.org, accessed August 26, 2015.
25 Chignell, "The Story behind the Story."
26 Chignell, "The Story behind the Story."
27 See Gallagher 2004 on the marginalization of "evangelical feminists," who overlap with the evangelical left.

REFERENCES

Alumkal, Antony W. 2012. "Racial Justice in the Protestant Mainline: Liberalism and Its Limits." In *Faith and Race in American Political Life*, edited by Robin Jacobson and Nancy Wadsworth, 275–98. Charlottesville: University of Virginia Press.

American Psychiatric Association. 1999. "Position Statement on Psychiatric Treatment and Sexual Orientation." *American Journal of Psychiatry* 156:1131.

Bainbridge, William Sims, and Rodney Stark. 1979. "Cult Formation: Three Compatible Models." *Sociological Analysis* 40:283–95.

Balmer, Randall. 1993. *Mine Eyes Have Seen the Glory: A Journey into the Evangelical Subculture in America*. New York: Oxford University Press.

———. 2006. *Thy Kingdom Come: How the Religious Right Distorts the Faith and Threatens America*. New York: Basic Books.

Bartkowski, John P. 2004. *The Promise Keepers: Servant, Soldiers, and Godly Men*. New Brunswick: Rutgers University Press.

Battin, Margaret P., Agnes Van der Heide, Linda Ganzini, Gerrit Van der Wal, and Bregje D. Onwuteaka-Philipsen. 2007. "Legal Physician-Assisted Dying in Oregon and the Netherlands: Evidence concerning the Impact on Patients in 'Vulnerable' Groups." *Journal of Medical Ethics* 33:591–97.

Bayer, Ronald. 1981. *Homosexuality and American Psychiatry: The Politics of Diagnosis*. New York: Basic Books.

Behe, Michael J. 1996. *Darwin's Black Box: The Biochemical Challenge to Evolution*. New York: Free Press.

———. 2007. *The Edge of Evolution: The Search for the Limits of Darwinism*. New York: Free Press.

Beisner, E. Calvin. 1997. *Where Garden Meets Wilderness: Evangelical Entry into the Environmental Debate*. Grand Rapids, MI: Eerdmans.

———. 2013a. "Public School Science Standards: Political or Pure?" Cornwall Alliance, January 30. www.cornwallalliance.org. Accessed March 24, 2014.

———. 2013b. "Can Faith and Science Cooperate? A Meteorologist Appeals to Scripture about Global Warming." Cornwall Alliance, October 9. www.cornwallalliance.org. Accessed March 24, 2014.

Beisner, E. Calvin, Michael Cromartie, Thomas Sieger Derr, Peter J. Hill, Diane Knippers, and Timothy Terrell. 2007. "A Biblical Perspective on Environmental Stewardship." In *Environmental Stewardship in the Judeo-Christian Tradition*, edited by Acton Institute for the Study of Religion and Liberty, 67–119. Grand Rapids, MI: Acton Institute.

Bell, Michael Mayerfeld. 2012. *An Invitation to Environmental Sociology*. 4th ed. Thousand Oaks, CA: Pine Forge.

Benford, Robert D., and David A. Snow. 2000. "Framing Processes and Social Movements: An Overview and Assessment." *Annual Review of Sociology* 26:611–39.

Bieber, Irving. 1962. *Homosexuality: A Psychoanalytic Study*. New York: Basic Books.

Bogle, Kathleen A. 2008. *Hooking Up: Sex, Dating and Relationships on Campus*. New York: New York University Press.

Bozeman, Theodore Dwight. 1977. *Protestants in an Age of Science: The Baconian Ideal and Antebellum American Religious Thought*. Chapel Hill: University of North Carolina Press.

Bradley, Walter L. 2006. "Phillip Johnson and the Intelligent Design Movement: Looking Back and Looking Forward." In *Darwin's Nemesis: Phillip Johnson and the Intelligent Design Movement*, edited by William A. Dembski, 305–14. Downers Grove, IL: InterVarsity.

Breslow, Jason M. 2012. "Bob Inglis: Climate Change and the Republican Party." *Frontline*, PBS, October 23. www.pbs.org. Accessed January 30, 2016.

Buhle, Mari Jo. 1998. *Feminism and Its Discontents: A Century of Struggle with Psychoanalysis*. Cambridge: Harvard University Press.

Byassee, Jason. 2008. "Expelled: No Intelligence Allowed." *Christian Century*, May 20, 42–43.

Cadge, Wendy. 2002. "Vital Conflicts: The Mainline Denominations Debate Homosexuality." In *The Quiet Hand of God: Faith-Based Activism and the Public Role of Mainline Protestantism*, edited by Robert Wuthnow and John H. Evans, 265–86. Berkeley: University of California Press.

Callahan, Sidney. 1986. "Abortion and the Sexual Agenda: A Case for Pro-Life Feminism." *Commonweal* 113:232–38.

Cameron, Nigel M. de S. 2004. "Christian Vision for the Biotech Century." In *Human Dignity in the Biotech Century*, edited by Charles W. Colson and Nigel M. de S. Cameron, 21–39. Downers Grove, IL: InterVarsity.

Carlson, Bruce M. 1994. *Human Embryology and Developmental Biology*. St. Louis: Mosby.

Catsoulis, Jeannette. 2008. "Resentment over Darwin Evolves into a Documentary." *New York Times*, April 18, E13.

Cherry, Conrad, Betty A. DeBerg, and Amanda Porterfield. 2001. *Religion on Campus*. Chapel Hill: University of North Carolina Press.

Christian Century. 2007. "Extraordinary Measures." 124 (October 16): 5.

Collins, Francis S. 2006. *The Language of God: A Scientist Presents Evidence for Belief*. New York: Free Press.

Colson, Charles W. 2004. "Introduction: Can We Prevent the 'Abolition of Man'? C. S. Lewis's Challenge to the Twenty-first Century." In *Human Dignity in the Biotech Century*, edited by Charles W. Colson and Nigel M. de S. Cameron, 11–20. Downers Grove, IL: InterVarsity.

Colson, Charles W., and Nigel M. de S. Cameron. 2004. Preface to *Human Dignity in the Biotech Century*, edited by Charles W. Colson and Nigel M. de S. Cameron, 7–9. Downers Grove, IL: InterVarsity.

Comiskey, Andrew. 1989. *Pursuing Sexual Wholeness: How Jesus Heals the Homosexual*. Lake Mary, FL: Creation House.

———. 2003. *Strength in Weakness: Healing Sexual and Relational Brokenness*. Downers Grove, IL: InterVarsity.

———. 2010. *Naked Surrender: Coming Home to Our True Sexuality*. Downers Grove, IL: IVP Books.

Cook, Colin. 1989. "I Found Freedom." *Christianity Today* 33 (August 18): 22–25.

Cornwall Alliance. 2008. "The Cornwall Stewardship Agenda." www.cornwallalliance. org. Accessed February 1, 2014.

———. 2009. "A Renewed Call to Truth, Prudence, and Protection of the Poor: An Evangelical Examination of the Theology, Science, and Economics of Global Warming." May 1. www.cornwallalliance.org. Accessed February 1, 2014.

Cutrer, William R., and Sandra L. Glahn. 2005. *The Contraception Guidebook: Options, Risks, and Answers for Christian Couples*. Grand Rapids, MI: Zondervan.

Dallas, Joe. 1996. *A Strong Delusion: Confronting the "Gay Christian" Movement*. Eugene: Harvest House.

———. 2003. *Desires in Conflict: Hope for Men Who Struggle with Sexual Identity*. Updated ed. Eugene: Harvest House.

Danielsen, Sabrina. 2013. "Fracturing over Creation Care? Shifting Environmental Beliefs among Evangelicals, 1984–2010." *Journal for the Scientific Study of Religion* 52:198–215.

Danner, Mark. 2007. "Words in a Time of War: On Rhetoric, Truth, and Power." In *What Orwell Didn't Know: Propaganda and the New Face of American Politics*, edited by András Szántó, 16–36. New York: Public Affairs.

Davies, Bob. 2001. *Portraits of Freedom: Fourteen People Who Came Out of Homosexuality*. Downers Grove, IL: InterVarsity.

Davies, Bob, and Lori Rentzel. 1993. *Coming Out of Homosexuality: New Freedom for Men and Women*. Downers Grove, IL: InterVarsity.

Davis, Percival, and Dean H. Kenyon. 1989. *Of Pandas and People: The Central Question of Biological Origins*. Dallas: Haughton.

De La Torre, Miguel A. 2010. *Latina/o Social Ethics: Moving beyond Eurocentric Moral Thinking*. Waco: Baylor University Press.

Del Vicario, Michela, Alessandro Bessi, Fabiana Zollo, Fabio Petroni, Antonio Scala, Guido Caldarelli, H. Eugene Stanley, and Walter Quattrociocchi. 2016. "The Spread of Misinformation Online." *Proceedings of the National Academy of Sciences* 113:554–59.

Dembski, William A. 1998. *The Design Inference: Eliminating Chance through Small Probabilities*. Cambridge: Cambridge University Press.

———. 1999. *Intelligent Design: The Bridge between Science and Theology*. Downers Grove, IL: InterVarsity.

———. 2006. Preface to *Darwin's Nemesis: Phillip Johnson and the Intelligent Design Movement*, edited by William A. Dembski, 11–24. Downers Grove, IL: InterVarsity.

Denton, Michael. 1986. *Evolution: A Theory in Crisis*. Bethesda, MD: Adler and Adler.

Dieterle, J. M. 2007. "Physician Assisted Suicide: A New Look at the Arguments." *Bioethics* 21:127–39.

Discovery Institute. N.d. "The 'Wedge Document': 'So What?'" www.discovery.org. Accessed July 27, 2013.

Dresher, Jack. 2001. "I'm Your Handyman: A History of Reparative Therapies." In *Sexual Conversion Therapy: Ethical, Clinical and Research Perspectives*, edited by Ariel Shidlo, Michael Schroeder, and Jack Dresher, 5–24. New York: Haworth Medical Press.

———. 2003. "An Interview with Robert L. Spitzer, MD." *Journal of Gay and Lesbian Psychotherapy* 7:97–111.

Ecklund, Elaine Howard. 2010. *Science vs. Religion: What Scientists Really Think*. New York: Oxford University Press.

Ellison, Marvin. 2004. *Same-Sex Marriage? A Christian Analysis*. Cleveland: Pilgrim Press.

Emerson, Michael O., and Christian Smith. 2001. *Divided by Faith: Evangelical Religion and the Problem of Race in America*. New York: Oxford University Press.

Erzen, Tanya. 2006. *Straight to Jesus: Sexual and Christian Conversions in the Ex-Gay Movement*. Berkeley: University of California Press.

Evans, John H. 2010. *Contested Reproduction: Genetic Technologies, Religion, and Public Debate*. Chicago: University of Chicago Press.

Fang, Lee. 2010. "Exclusive: The Oily Operators behind the Religious Climate Change Denial Front Group, Cornwall Alliance." ThinkProgress, June 15. http://thinkprogress.org. Accessed March 30, 2014.

Feldman, Lauren, Teresa A. Myers, J. D. Hmielowski, and Anthony Leiserowitz. 2014. "The Mutual Reinforcement of Media Selectivity and Effects: Testing the Reinforcing Spirals Framework in the Context of Global Warming." *Journal of Communication* 64:590–611.

Festinger, Leon, Henry W. Riecken, and Stanley Schachter. 1956. *When Prophecy Fails: A Social and Psychological Study of a Modern Group That Predicted the Destruction of the World*. New York: Harper-Torchbooks.

Feyerabend, Paul. 1978. *Science in a Free Society*. New York: NLB.

Foley, Kathleen, and Herbert Hendin. 2002. *The Case against Assisted Suicide: For the Right to End-of-Life Care*. Baltimore: Johns Hopkins University Press.

Forrest, Barbara, and Paul R. Gross. 2004. *Creationism's Trojan Horse: The Wedge of Intelligent Design*. New York: Oxford University Press.

Foster, John Bellamy, Brett Clark, and Richard York. 2008. *Critique of Intelligent Design: Materialism versus Creationism from Antiquity to Present*. New York: Monthly Review Press.

Foucault, Michel. 1970 [1966]. *The Order of Things: An Archaeology of the Human Sciences*. New York: Random House.

Fuller, Steve. 1996. "Does Science Put an End to History, or History to Science?" *Social Text* 46/47:27–42.

———. 2007. *Science v. Religion? Intelligent Design and the Problem of Evolution.* Cambridge: Polity.

Funtowicz, Silvio O., and Jerome R. Ravetz. 1993. "Science for the Post-Normal Age." *Futures* 25:739–55.

Gagnon, Robert A. J. 2001. *The Bible and Homosexual Practice: Texts and Hermeneutics.* Nashville: Abingdon.

———. 2002. "Gays and the Bible." *Christian Century* 119 (August 14–27): 40–43.

Gallagher, Sally. 2004. "The Marginalization of Evangelical Feminism." *Sociology of Religion* 65:215–37.

Ganzini, Linda. 2004. "The Oregon Experience." In *Physician-Assisted Dying: The Case for Palliative Care and Patient Choice,* edited by Timothy E. Quill and Margaret P. Battin, 165–83. Baltimore: Johns Hopkins University Press.

Gerber, Lynne. 2009. "From Gays to Men: Ex-Gay Ministries and the Re-Configuration of Evangelical Masculinity." Paper presented at annual meeting of the Association for the Sociology of Religion, San Francisco, CA.

———. 2011. *Seeking the Straight and Narrow: Weight Loss and Sexual Reorientation in Evangelical America.* Chicago: University of Chicago Press.

Gieryn, Thomas F. 1999. *Cultural Boundaries of Science: Credibility on the Line.* Chicago: University of Chicago Press.

Gonzalez, Guillermo, and Jay W. Richards. 2004. *The Privileged Planet: How Our Place in the Cosmos Is Designed for Discovery.* Washington, D.C.: Regnery.

Goode, Stephen. 1999. "Johnson Challenges Advocates of Evolution." *Insight,* October 25. www.arn.org. Accessed September 23, 2010.

Gore, Al. 1992. *Earth in the Balance: Ecology and the Human Spirit.* Boston: Houghton Mifflin.

Greeley, Andrew. 1978. *The American Catholic: A Social Portrait.* New York: Basic Books.

Greeley, Andrew, and Michael Hout. 2006. *The Truth about Conservative Christians: What They Think and What They Believe.* Chicago: University of Chicago Press.

Greene, Brian. 1999. *The Elegant Universe: Superstrings, Hidden Dimensions, and the Quest for the Ultimate Theory.* New York: Norton.

Gross, Neil, and Solon Simmons. 2009. "The Religiosity of American College and University Professors." *Sociology of Religion* 70:101–29.

Grünbaum, Adolf. 1984. *The Foundations of Psychoanalysis: A Philosophical Critique.* Berkeley: University of California Press.

Gushee, David P. 2008. *The Future of Faith in American Politics: The Public Witness of the Evangelical Center.* Waco: Baylor University Press.

———. 2014. *Changing Our Mind.* Canton, MI: Read the Spirit Books.

Hofstadter, Richard. 2008 [1965]. *The Paranoid Style in American Politics and Other Essays.* New York: Vintage.

Hoggan, James. 2009. *Climate Cover-Up: The Crusade to Deny Global Warming.* Vancouver: Greystone.

Hook, C. Christopher. 2004. "Techno Sapiens: Nanotechnology, Cybernetics, Transhumanism and the Remaking of Humankind." In *Human Dignity in the Biotech Century: A Christian Vision for Public Policy*, edited by Charles W. Colson and Nigel M. de S. Cameron, 65–97. Downers Grove, IL: InterVarsity.

Hook, Sidney, ed. 1959. *Psychoanalysis: Scientific Method and Philosophy*. New York: New York University Press.

House, H. Wayne, ed. 2008. *Intelligent Design 101: Leading Experts Explain the Key Issues*. Grand Rapids, MI: Kregel.

Hulme, Mike. 2009. *Why We Disagree about Climate Change: Understanding Controversy, Inaction and Opportunity*. Cambridge: Cambridge University Press.

Jenkins, Kathleen E. 2007. "Genetics and Faith: Religious Enchantment through Creative Engagement with Molecular Biology." *Social Forces* 85:1693–711.

Johnson, Phillip E. 1991. *Darwin on Trial*. Downers Grove, IL: InterVarsity.

———. 1993. *Darwin on Trial*. 2nd ed. Downers Grove, IL: InterVarsity.

———. 1995. *Reason in the Balance: The Case against Naturalism in Science, Law, and Education*. Downers Grove, IL: InterVarsity.

———. 1996. "Response to Pennock." *Biology and Philosophy* 11:561–63.

———. 1997. *Defeating Darwinism by Opening Minds*. Downers Grove, IL: InterVarsity.

———. 1998. *Objections Sustained: Subversive Essays on Evolution, Law and Culture*. Downers Grove, IL: InterVarsity.

———. 2000. *The Wedge of Truth: Splitting the Foundations of Naturalism*. Downers Grove, IL: InterVarsity.

———. 2002. *The Right Questions: Truth, Meaning and Public Debate*. Downers Grove, IL: InterVarsity.

———. 2008. "Bringing Balance to a Fiery Debate." In *Intelligent Design 101: Leading Experts Explain the Key Issues*, edited by H. Wayne House, 21–40. Grand Rapids, MI: Kregel.

Johnson, Phillip E., and John Mark Reynolds. 2010. *Against All Gods: What's Right and Wrong about the New Atheism*. Downers Grove, IL: IVP Books.

Jones, Rachel K., and Joerg Dreweke. 2011. *Countering Conventional Wisdom: New Evidence on Religion and Contraceptive Use*. New York: Guttmacher Institute.

Jones, Robert P., Daniel Cox, and Juhem Navarro-Rivera. 2013. *The 2013 American Values Survey: In Search of Libertarians in America*. Washington, D.C.: Public Religion Research Institute.

———. 2014. *A Shifting Landscape: A Decade of Change in American Attitudes about Same-Sex Marriage and LGBT Issues*. Washington, D.C.: Public Religion Research Institute.

Jones, Stanton L. 1989. "Homosexuality according to Science." *Christianity Today* 33 (August 18): 26–29.

———. 2013. "Exodus in the Wilderness." *Christianity Today*, June 24. www.christianitytoday.com. Accessed October 30, 2013.

Jones, Stanton L., and Mark A. Yarhouse. 2000. *Homosexuality: The Use of Scientific Research in the Church's Moral Debate*. Downers Grove, IL: InterVarsity.

————. 2007. *Ex-Gays? A Longitudinal Study of Religiously Mediated Change in Sexual Orientation*. Downers Grove, IL: InterVarsity Academic.

Kearns, Laurel. 2007. "Cooking the Truth: Faith, Science, the Market, and Global Warming." In *Ecospirit: Religions and Philosophies for the Earth*, edited by Laurel Kearns and Catherine Keller, 97–124. New York: Fordham University Press.

Knoepfler, Paul. 2013. *Stem Cells: An Insider's Guide*. Singapore: World Scientific Publishing.

Konrad, Jeff. 1987. *You Don't Have to Be Gay: Hope and Freedom for Males Struggling with Homosexuality or for Those Who Know of Someone Who Is*. Hilo, HI: Pacific Publishing House.

LaHaye, Tim, and Jerry B. Jenkins. 1995. *Left Behind: A Novel of the Earth's Last Days*. Wheaton, IL: Tyndale House.

Lewis, C. S. 2015 [1940]. *The Problem of Pain*. New York: HarperOne.

Lindsay, Ronald A. 2009. "Oregon's Experience: Evaluating the Record." *American Journal of Bioethics* 9 (3): 19–27.

Luker, Kristin. 1984. *Abortion and the Politics of Motherhood*. Berkeley: University of California Press.

Mann, Michael E. 2012. *The Hockey Stick and the Climate Wars: Dispatches from the Front Lines*. New York: Columbia University Press.

Markoe, Lauren. 2011. "Poll Finds Evangelicals Stand Apart on Evolution, Climate Change." PRRI, September 22. http://publicreligion.org. Accessed April 24, 2014.

Marsden, George M. 1991. *Understanding Fundamentalism and Evangelicalism*. Grand Rapids, MI: Eerdmans.

Marti, Gerardo, and Gladys Ganiel. 2014. *The Deconstructed Church: Understanding Emerging Christianity*. New York: Oxford University Press.

Martin, William. 1996. *With God on Our Side*. New York: Broadway Books.

McLaren, Brian D. 2010. *A New Kind of Christianity: Ten Questions That Are Transforming the Faith*. San Francisco: HarperOne.

Meyer, Stephen C. 2009. *Signature in the Cell: DNA and the Evidence for Intelligent Design*. New York: HarperOne.

Meyer, Stephen C., Scott Minnich, Jonathan Moneymaker, Paul A. Nelson, and Ralph Seelke. 2007. *Explore Evolution: The Arguments for and against Neo-Darwinism*. London: Hill House.

Miller, Kenneth R. 1999. *Finding Darwin's God: A Scientist's Search for Common Ground between God and Evolution*. New York: HarperCollins.

Mitchell, C. Ben. 2004. "The New Genetics and the Dignity of Humankind." In *Human Dignity in the Biotech Century*, edited by Charles W. Colson and Nigel M. de S. Cameron, 60–74. Downers Grove, IL: InterVarsity.

Moberly, Elizabeth R. 1983. *Homosexuality: A New Christian Ethic*. Cambridge, England: James Clark.

Moon, Dawne. 2004. *God, Sex, and Politics: Homosexuality and Everyday Theologies*. Chicago: University of Chicago Press.

Mooney, Chris. 2005. *The Republican War on Science*. New York: Basic Books.

Moore, Keith L., and T. V. N. Persaud. 1998. *The Developing Human: Clinically Oriented Embryology*. 6th ed. Philadelphia: Saunders.

Moore, R. Laurence. 1987. *Religious Outsiders and the Making of Americans*. New York: Oxford University Press.

Nancy. 1980. *Homosexual Struggle*. Downers Grove, IL: InterVarsity.

National Association for Research and Therapy of Homosexuality. 2003. "NARTH and Civil Rights." www.narth.com. Accessed February 1, 2006.

National Institutes of Health. 2006. "Stem Cells: A Primer." In *The Stem Cells Controversy: Debating the Issue*, 2nd ed., edited by Michael Ruse and Christopher A. Pynes, 27–35. Amherst, NY: Prometheus.

Neuhaus, Richard J. 1988. "The Return of Eugenics." *Commentary* 85 (April 1): 15–26.

Newport, Frank. 2010. "Four in 10 Americans Believe in Strict Creationism." Gallup, December 17. www.gallup.com. Accessed October 1, 2013.

Nicolosi, Joseph. 2003. "Finally, Recognition of a Long-Neglected Population." *Archives of Sexual Behavior* 32:445–47.

Nicolosi, Joseph, and Linda Ames Nicolosi. 2002. *A Parent's Guide to Preventing Homosexuality*. Downers Grove, IL: InterVarsity.

Noll, Mark A. 1994. *The Scandal of the Evangelical Mind*. Grand Rapids, MI: Eerdmans.

———. 2001. *American Evangelical Christianity: An Introduction*. Malden, MA: Blackwell.

———. 2011. *Jesus Christ and the Life of the Mind*. Grand Rapids, MI: Eerdmans.

Numbers, Ronald. 2006. *The Creationists: From Scientific Creationism to Intelligent Design*. Expanded ed. Cambridge: Harvard University Press.

Olson, Roger E. 1995. "Postconservative Evangelicals Greet the Postmodern Age." *Christian Century*, May 3, 480–83.

Oreskes, Naomi, and Erik M. Conway. 2010. *Merchants of Doubt: How a Handful of Scientists Obscured the Truth on Issues from Tobacco Smoke to Global Warming*. New York: Bloomsbury.

Paulk, Anne. 2003. *Restoring Sexual Identity: Hope for Women Who Struggle with Same-Sex Attraction*. Eugene: Harvest House.

Paulk, John, and Anne Paulk. 1999. *Love Won Out*. Wheaton, IL: Tyndale.

Payne, Leanne. 1981. *The Broken Image: Restoring Personal Wholeness through Healing Prayer*. Wheaton, IL: Crossway Books.

Pennock, Robert T. 1996. "Naturalism, Evidence, and Creationism: The Case of Phillip Johnson." *Biology and Philosophy* 11:543–49.

———. 1999. *Tower of Babel: The Evidence against the New Creationism*. Cambridge: MIT Press.

———. 2010. "The Postmodern Sin of Intelligent Design Creationism." *Science and Education* 19:757–58.

People for the American Way. 2010. "The 'Green Dragon' Slayers: How the Religious Right and the Corporate Right Are Joining Forces to Fight Environmental Protection." www.pfaw.org. Accessed April 10, 2014.

Pew Research Center. 2013. *Abortion Viewed in Moral Terms*. Washington, D.C.: Pew Research Center.

Poiani, Aldo. 2010. *Animal Homosexuality: A Biosocial Perspective*. Cambridge: Cambridge University Press.

Polkinghorne, John. 1998. *Belief in God in an Age of Science*. New Haven: Yale University Press.

Prentice, David A. 2004. "The Biotech Revolution: Major Issues in the Biosciences." In *Human Dignity in the Biotech Century*, edited by Charles W. Colson and Nigel M. de S. Cameron, 60–74. Downers Grove, IL: InterVarsity.

Prentice, David, and Rosa Macrito. 2013. *Stem Cells, Cloning, and Human Embryos: Understanding the Ethics and Opportunity of Scientific Research*. Washington, D.C.: Family Research Council.

Pruden, David. 2012. "All the Talk about the Spitzer Study." NARTH. http://narth.com. Accessed May 18, 2012.

Pulliam, Sarah. 2009. "A Costly Shift." *Christianity Today* 53 (February): 11.

Quill, Timothy E., and Margaret P. Battin. 2004. *Physician-Assisted Dying: The Case for Palliative Care and Patient Choice*. Baltimore: Johns Hopkins University Press.

Rado, Sandor. 1969. *Adaptational Psychodynamics: Motivation and Control*. New York: Science House.

Raymond, Leigh. 2004. "Economic Growth as Environmental Policy? Reconsidering the Environmental Kuznets Curve." *Journal of Public Policy* 24:327–48.

Redden, Molly. 2011. "Whatever Happened to the Evangelical-Environmental Alliance?" *New Republic*, November 3. www.newrepublic.com. Accessed April 24, 2014.

Reis, Elizabeth. 2009. *Bodies in Doubt: An American History of Intersex*. Baltimore: Johns Hopkins University Press.

Robertson, Pat. 1991. *The New World Order*. Nashville: W Publishing.

Santorum, Rick. 2006. Foreword to *Darwin's Nemesis: Phillip Johnson and the Intelligent Design Movement*, edited by William A. Dembski, 9–10. Downers Grove, IL: InterVarsity.

Satinover, Jeffrey. 1996. *Homosexuality and the Politics of Truth*. Grand Rapids, MI: Baker Books.

Saunders, William L. 2004. "The Human Embryo in Debate." In *Human Dignity in the Biotech Century*, edited by Charles W. Colson and Nigel M. de S. Cameron, 115–35. Downers Grove, IL: InterVarsity.

Schmalzbauer, John. 2013. "Campus Religious Life in America: Revitalization and Renewal." *Society* 50 (2): 115–31.

Schmidt, Thomas E. 1995. *Straight and Narrow? Compassion and Clarity in the Homosexual Debate*. Downers Grove, IL: InterVarsity.

Shannon, Thomas. 2003. "Fetal Status: Sources and Implications." In *Moral Issues and Christian Responses*, edited by Patricia Beattie Jung and Shannon Jung, 172–77. 7th ed. Belmont, CA: Wadsworth/Thompson.

Simon, Julian L. 1981. *The Ultimate Resource*. Princeton: Princeton University Press.

———. 1996. *The Ultimate Resource 2*. Princeton: Princeton University Press.

Sirico, Robert A. 2007. Foreword to *Environmental Stewardship in the Judeo-Christian Tradition*, edited by Acton Institute for the Study of Religion and Liberty, vii-viii. Grand Rapids, MI: Acton Institute.

Smith, Christian. 1998. *American Evangelicalism: Embattled and Thriving*. Chicago: University of Chicago Press.

———, ed. 2003. *The Secular Revolution: Power, Interests, and Conflict in the Secularization of American Public Life*. Berkeley: University of California Press.

Smith, Wesley J. 2004. *Consumer's Guide to a Brave New World*. San Francisco: Encounter Books.

———. 2006. *Forced Exit: Euthanasia, Assisted Suicide, and the New Duty to Die*. New York: Encounter Books.

Socarides, Charles W. 1968. *The Overt Homosexual*. New York: Grune and Stratton.

Solzhenitsyn, Aleksandr. 1973. *The Gulag Archipelago*. New York: Harper and Row.

Sommer, Volker, and Paul L. Vasey, eds. 2006. *Homosexual Behaviour in Animals: An Evolutionary Perspective*. Cambridge: Cambridge University Press.

Spitzer, Robert L. 2003. "Can Some Gay Men and Lesbians Change Their Sexual Orientation? 200 Participants Reporting a Change from Homosexual to Heterosexual Orientation." *Archives of Sexual Behavior* 32:403–17.

Spring, Beth. 1984. "These Christians Are Helping Gays Escape from Homosexual Lifestyles." *Christianity Today* 28 (September 21): 56–58.

Stafford, Tim. 1989. "Coming Out." *Christianity Today* 33 (August 18): 16–21.

———. 2007a. "An Older, Wiser Ex-Gay Movement." *Christianity Today* 51 (October): 48–51.

———. 2007b. "The Best Research Yet." *Christianity Today* 51 (October): 52–54.

Steffan, Melissa. 2013. "After Exodus: Evangelicals React as Ex-Gay Ministry Starts Over." *Christianity Today*, June 21. www.christianitytoday.com. Accessed January 28, 2014.

Strobel, Lee. 2004. *The Case for a Creator: A Journalist Investigates Scientific Evidence That Points toward God*. Grand Rapids, MI: Zondervan.

Sunderlin, William D. 2003. *Ideology, Social Theory, and the Environment*. Lanham, MD: Rowman and Littlefield.

Suskind, Ron. 2004. "Without a Doubt." *New York Times Magazine* 154 (October 17): 44–106.

Tada, Joni Eareckson. 1992. *When Is It Right to Die? Suicide, Euthanasia, Suffering, Mercy*. Grand Rapids, MI: Zondervan.

Tada, Joni Eareckson, and Nigel M. de S. Cameron. 2006. *How to Be a Christian in a Brave New World*. Grand Rapids, MI: Zondervan.

Thaxton, Charles B., Walter L. Bradley, and Roger L. Olson. 1984. *The Mystery of Life's Origin: Reassessing Current Theories*. New York: Philosophical Library.

Thomas, Jeremy N., and Daniel V. A. Olson. 2012. "Evangelical Elites' Changing Responses to Homosexuality, 1960–2009." *Sociology of Religion* 73:239–72.

Van Delden, Johannes J. M., Jaap J. F. Visser, and Els Borst-Eilers. 2004. "Thirty Years' Experience with Euthanasia in the Netherlands: Focusing on the Patient as a Person." In *Physician-Assisted Dying: The Case for Palliative Care and Patient Choice*, edited by Timothy E. Quill and Margaret P. Battin, 202–16. Baltimore: Johns Hopkins University Press.

Van der Heide, Agnes, Luc Deliens, Karin Faisst, Tore Nilstun, Michael Norup, Eugenio Paci, Gerrit Van der Wal, and Paul J. Van der Maas. 2003. "End-of-Life Decision-Making in Six European Countries: Descriptive Study." *Lancet*, June 17. http://image.thelancet.com. Accessed January 22, 2015.

Via, Dan O., and Robert A. J. Gagnon. 2003. *Homosexuality and the Bible: Two Views*. Minneapolis: Augsburg Fortress.

Wanliss, James. 2013. *Resisting the Green Dragon: Dominion, Not Death*. 2nd ed. Burke, VA: Cornwall Alliance for the Stewardship of Creation.

Warren, Rick. 2002. *The Purpose Driven Life: What on Earth Am I Here For?* Grand Rapids, MI: Zondervan.

———. 2013. *The Purpose Driven Life: What on Earth Am I Here For?* Expanded ed. Nashville: Thomas Nelson.

Watson, Justin. 1997. *The Christian Coalition: Dreams of Restoration, Demands for Recognition*. New York: St. Martin's Griffin.

White, John. 1977. *Eros Defiled: The Christian and Sexual Sin*. Downers Grove, IL: InterVarsity.

Wilentz, Sean. 2008. Foreword to *The Paranoid Style in American Politics and Other Essays*, by Richard Hofstadter, xi-xxx. New York: Vintage.

Wilkinson, Katharine K. 2012. *Between God and Green: How Evangelicals Are Cultivating a Middle Ground on Climate Change*. New York: Oxford University Press.

Wilson, Glenn, and Qazi Rahman. 2005. *Born Gay: The Psychobiology of Sex Orientation*. London: Peter Owens.

Winant, Howard. 2004. *The New Politics of Race: Globalism, Difference, Justice*. Minneapolis: University of Minnesota Press.

Witt, Jonathan. 2007. "The Origin of Intelligent Design: A Brief History of the Scientific Theory of Intelligent Design." Discovery Institute, October 30. www.discovery. org. Accessed July 25, 2016.

Wolfe, Alan. 1991. *Whose Keeper? Social Science and Moral Obligation*. Berkeley: University of California Press.

Wuthnow, Robert. 1988. *The Restructuring of American Religion: Society and Faith since World War II*. Princeton: Princeton University Press.

Yarhouse, Mark A. 2003. "How Spitzer's Study Gives a Voice to the Disenfranchised within a Minority Group." *Archives of Sexual Behavior* 32:462–63.

———. 2010. *Homosexuality and the Christian: A Guide for Parents, Pastors, and Friends*. Minneapolis: Bethany House.

INDEX

ABOUT THE AUTHOR

Antony Alumkal is Associate Professor of Sociology of Religion at the Iliff School of Theology in Denver, Colorado. He is the author of *Asian American Evangelical Churches: Race, Ethnicity, and Assimilation in the Second Generation.*